DRAWING DOWN THE SUN

ABOUT THE AUTHOR

Stephanie Woodfield has been a practicing Witch and Priestess of the Morrigan for over sixteen years. Her lifelong love of Irish mythology led to a close study of Celtic Witchcraft. Her articles have appeared in *SageWoman* magazine and *The Portal*. She is one of the founding members of Morrigu's Daughters, an online sisterhood dedicated to the Morrigan. She lives in Connecticut.

Please visit her online at www.stephanie-woodfield.com.

DRAWING
DOWN
THE
SUN

REKINDLE THE MAGICK
OF THE
SOLAR GODDESSES

STEPHANIE WOODFIELD

Llewellyn Publications
Woodbury, Minnesota

FIRST EDITION
First Printing, 2014

Cover design by Lisa Novak
Cover illustration: Mia Bosna

Llewellyn Publications is a registered trademark of Llewellyn Worldwide Ltd.

Library of Congress Cataloging-in-Publication Data
Woodfield, Stephanie, 1983–
  Drawing down the sun : rekindle the magick of the solar goddesses / Stephanie Woodfield. — 1st ed.
     pages cm
  Includes bibliographical references and index.
  ISBN 978-0-7387-4037-9
  1. Goddesses. 2. Goddess religion. 3. Sun—Mythology. I. Title.
  BL473.5.W66 2014
  299'.94—dc23
                              2013046323

Llewellyn Worldwide Ltd. does not participate in, endorse, or have any authority or responsibility concerning private business transactions between our authors and the public.
  All mail addressed to the author is forwarded, but the publisher cannot, unless specifically instructed by the author, give out an address or phone number.
  Any Internet references contained in this work are current at publication time, but the publisher cannot guarantee that a specific location will continue to be maintained. Please refer to the publisher's website for links to authors' websites and other sources.

Llewellyn Publications
A Division of Llewellyn Worldwide Ltd.
2143 Wooddale Drive
Woodbury, MN 55125-2989
www.llewellyn.com

Printed in the United States of America

OTHER BOOKS BY THIS AUTHOR

Celtic Lore & Spellcraft of the Dark Goddess

DEDICATION
To all the forgotten goddesses,
may your light shine forth again.

And for Nick, for always being proud of me.

CONTENTS

CHARGE OF THE
SUN GODDESS

Be still and listen to the words of Sekhmet, Sunna, Saule, Amaterasu, Sulis, Brighid, and Yhi, the queens of heaven and bringers of light, who long ago were hailed Mother Sun!

I am the spark that engulfs. I am the light of a new day, the traveler of shadowed lands, and the sun in her glory. I am the mother of all things, the light that calls the seed from beneath the soil, and the cleansing fire that burns away the old. I am the warrior who does not waver, unapologetic in my victory. I am the bringer of swift justice and the bright flame of inspiration. I am with you through each day and every season. And when my light passes into darkness, my warm caress comforts the dead. I burn brighter for the darkness. I bring order where there is chaos, and succor where there is pain.

I ask only that you see the radiance that burns within you. That you sing, feast, and dance in my exultation, knowing that like myself you shall rise and rise again from the ashes of the old. My mystery is this, that light has no definition without the dark. That we must walk boldly through our darkest moments to burn ever brighter.

Introduction
Reclaiming the Goddess of the Sun

The moon has become one of the central images of Goddess spirituality. However ... we need to examine its contra-imaginal potency—the Sun. If the Goddess is to be fully represented in our society, she must also be the guiding light and warmth of our conscious lives. The Sun is not to be regarded solely as an unreclaimable patriarchal symbol, but one that presents the life and joyous delight of the Goddess.

—Caitlin Matthews,
Voices of the Goddess: A Chorus of Sibyls

To our ancestors, the sky was the window to the universe. They watched the heavens with awe and reverence, using the heavenly bodies they observed to calculate time, mark the seasons, and foretell the future. It is no surprise that the sun and the moon, the two most visible celestial bodies in the sky, would hold a special fascination for them. Every culture on the planet has some sort of myth revolving around these two luminaries. Often they are brother and sister or husband and wife, with the stars and the earth their cosmic children. In the majority of their myths, the sun and moon are seen as complementary opposites.

The sun is an active force, ruling over healing, light, and abundance via its ability to make crops grow. The moon is seen as passive, ruling over night, the psyche, and the seas through its ability to create the tides. But if I were to ask you for the genders of these luminaries, what would you say? Almost always the answer would be that the sun is male and the moon female. After all, the moon is perhaps the most well-known symbol of the divine feminine in modern Goddess spirituality. But if you had asked a Pagan of the past the same question, you probably would have gotten a very different answer. While the Greeks and Romans revered the moon as Artemis and Diana and hailed the sun as Helios and Apollo, the concept of a masculine sun and a feminine moon was not a universal idea shared by all mythological systems. From the tribes of the Celts to the Inuits of North America, the sun was seen more often as a goddess than a god.

So why do we see the sun as exclusively male today? When we compare the roles and genders of the luminaries between cultures, it becomes clear that our Pagan ancestors couldn't reach a universal agreement on whether or not the sun was male or female. We find pantheons that worshiped solar gods and lunar goddesses, and others that saw the sun as feminine and the moon as masculine. The Celts, it seemed, couldn't make up their minds either way, having moon goddesses as well as numerous sun goddesses who coexisted alongside sun gods. Similarly, the Egyptians also had both sun gods and goddesses. So if some cultures worshiped the sun as a goddess and others as a god, and yet others as both a goddess and a god, why are we today so unfamiliar with the concept of a feminine sun? Ultimately, the concept of the sun being an exclusively masculine force is a fairly recent one, and has its roots in the Victorian era.

The Victorian era brought with it a renewed interest in ancient mythology, particularly solar mythology. Archeology and the study of folklore were brand-new fields of study, and books on classical mythology were extremely popular. The myths of the Greeks and Romans became the universal norms that all other mythological systems were measured against, and with them the concept of sun/god and moon/goddess became accepted as the "correct" way to view the luminaries. If myths from other cultures differed, they were deemed a reflection of a culture's inferiority or an "accidental" deviation from the mythological norm. The work of Friedrich Max Müller, one of the founders in the field of comparative mythology, further popularized the concept of the solar masculine, connecting every deity and hero to the sun and claiming that all religions stemmed from one original solar monotheism that viewed the sun as a male creator. Müller's theories were later ridiculed, but their influences were lasting.

Although the sun goddess may seem like a foreign concept to most of us, she is more present in modern Paganism than one would think; we just don't always call her by her proper name. Brighid, one of the most popular goddesses of the Celtic pantheon and whose festival modern Pagans honor each Imbolc, has numerous solar attributes. Despite this, Brighid is usually referred to as a goddess of fire and inspiration, never as a sun goddess. Her solar connections remained even in the stories of Saint Brigit, the Christianized version of the goddess. Saint Brigit was born at sunrise. She shone with such brilliance that her neighbors thought her house was on fire, when really the light they saw was emanating from the saint. She was also said to have hung her cloak on a sunbeam. The saint was also known for her ability to heal blindness, a common ability attributed to sun goddesses, since the sun was a kind of heavenly "eye" in the sky. It is also interesting to note that both the Irish and Old English noun for *sun* is feminine, indicating the people who worshiped her saw the sun as a feminine force. Brighid's cross, with its many rays, is itself a symbolic representation of the sun.

Although I had worked with Brighid for many years, it never once occurred to me that she might be a sun goddess, simply because the concept of a female sun was something I had never heard of before.

When I finally made the connection between Brighid and the sun, I initially thought she was an anomaly. But the more I learned about Celtic mythology, the more apparent it became that Brighid was just one of many Celtic sun goddesses. To the Celts, the sun goddess could be a healer, a warrior, or a source of endless inspiration. In their collective pantheons, the Celts had more sun goddesses than any other culture. To the Irish she was Brighid, Áine, and Gráinne; to the Welsh she was Olwen and Rhiannon; and in England she was Sulis and Brigantia.

As I learned about other sun goddesses, I began incorporating them into my seasonal rituals and my magickal practices. At midday I might invoke Áine, then at night work with the moon goddess Arianrhod, under the light of a full moon. In some of my rituals, Brighid represented the sun's energies, and in others I saw the sun as the god Lugh or Belenos. For me the most intriguing aspect of the Celtic mindset was that they saw the Goddess in both the sun and the moon. To me this dual nature fit perfectly with the ever-changing image of the Goddess. If she could transform from youthful maiden to wise crone, why couldn't she transform from the luminous sun goddess to the mysterious lady of the moon as well? Eventually I would learn the Celts were not unique in viewing the sun as feminine. But although I had begun working with several sun goddesses, I had never once encountered the concept of the feminine sun in modern Witchcraft. For many Pagans, even acknowledging that sun goddesses existed was a rather taboo subject.

Why haven't modern Goddess worshipers acknowledged the sun goddess? I think perhaps our reluctance to accept the sun goddess is because we automatically assume that to accept the Goddess as an active, radiant force, we must in doing so give up the goddess of the moon. The moon has become the most recognizable symbol of the Goddess in modern Paganism. For many, myself included, reclaiming the moon as a symbol of the divine feminine was an empowering experience on the journey into Witchcraft and Paganism. I very distinctly remember looking up at the full moon one night and think-ing, "That's not the *man* in the moon—I'm looking at the face of the Goddess." Some have even gone as far as to call Witchcraft, rather unfairly, a "moon religion."

While the moon is an important part of Paganism, we must re-member that the sun is also just as important. We honor both the cy-cles of the moon from full to dark and mark the cycles of the seasons through the movements of the sun through the sky. Both are intricately important to the Craft. It is clear that the Pagans of the past saw the Goddess as both a passive and active force. At times she was the mys-terious moon, watery keeper of intuition; other times she personified the active, fiery powers of the sun, fertilizing the crops, avenging the gods, and healing the sick. Like all women, she was many-faceted, her face changing given the circumstances. The Greek and Roman model of sun/masculine and moon/feminine is not incorrect; it is simply one way of viewing things.

What I have learned from the traditions of the Celts is that there is no wrong way to see the Goddess. To the ancient Celts she could be an earth goddess, a goddess of sacred wells and the sea, a goddess of death and battle, a goddess of the moon, and a goddess of the sun. She was in everything—the earth, the sea, the sky, the plants and ani-mals—because she created everything. She was the divine creatrix, and there was nothing in the world that was not part of her. That is what embracing the sun goddess entails, to see the Goddess in all things, to not see limits to the ways she can manifest. Our ancestors saw both the Goddess and God in the sun, and now it is time for us to recognize a more complete image of the Great Goddess, to once again reclaim an active, radiant aspect of the divine feminine. It is time to draw down the sun goddess!

HOW TO USE THIS BOOK

You hold in your hands a guide to the hidden mysteries of the sun goddess, and most importantly a guide to seeing the Goddess in a new light. This book is divided into three parts, the first of which will give you an insight into the background of the solar feminine. In part one, we will be exploring both how we have come to view the sun as purely masculine today and the common themes and patterns found in the mythology of the solar feminine. We will also explore the common symbols and totems associated with this side of solar divinity. From the myths of the Inuits to the British Isles, the themes surrounding the solar feminine repeat themselves and shed insight into the mysteries of the feminine sun.

In part two, we will look at the individual myths and mysteries of solar goddesses from around the world. The sheer number of solar goddesses makes it impossible to talk about each and every one in great detail, so not every goddess mentioned in part one will have her own chapter. Instead, the solar goddesses we will be working with are those whose stories and myths are the most intact. I encourage you to use the resources in the bibliography to learn more about any of the goddesses who are only briefly mentioned.

The goddesses we will be connecting with are divided by the regions of the world from which they originate. You will find information about how each region worshiped and viewed the sun in general prior to the chapters concerning the goddesses of that area or culture. Spells, rituals, correspondences, and guided mediations are given for each goddess, giving you a framework to incorporate the goddesses' energy into your practices.

In part three, you will find practical ways to connect and work with the energies of the sun in a modern spiritual system, including how to harness the sun in your magickal practices. Just as we plan our magick in accordance with the moon's waning and waxing phases, so too can we enhance our magick by the sun's cycle through the sky. You will also find information here about herbs, oils, stones, and gems associated with the sun.

Although I do suggest you first read the information in part one regarding the sun goddess's symbols and myths, the rest of the book does not have to be read in any particular order. If you feel drawn to working with Sekhmet or Brighid, then read through the section for that goddess before moving on to another aspect of the solar feminine.

Journaling

As you work with each goddess, I suggest you keep a journal to document your experiences. While most people think of a journal as a detailed account of one's day or experiences, this does not have to be the case. Everyone's journaling style is different. Your entries can be as simple as writing down a date and a few quick impressions, or they can be a full journal entry. What is important is that you are documenting your experiences. Months down the road, you may not be able to remember the date or outcome of a ritual, the meaning of a divination, or a piece of advice received in a guided meditation.

It is also important to pick the style of journal that works best for you. If you are like me and have horrible handwriting, you might prefer typing your journal entries and keeping them on your computer. They could even take the form of blog posts if you wish to share your experiences with others. If you prefer having a traditional journal, a three-ring binder will work just as well as a decorative journal.

When working with solar deities, it is also very helpful to know exactly when sunrise and sunset occur, as you may wish to meditate on a specific sun goddess or invoke her energies for magick during these times. You can find this information in your local newspaper or in an almanac. There are also several applications you can download directly to your cell phone that will give you the times for sunrise and sunset, as well as the dates for solar eclipses. This is also information you may want to keep or document in your journal.

Pathworking

Prior to the information about each goddess in this book, you will find a guided meditation or pathworking. Pathworking is an excellent way to connect and explore the energies of a deity. As with any meditation, you should find a quiet place to sit or lie down to begin your pathworking. A comfortable chair will work just as well as your sacred space. Begin by taking several deep, cleansing breaths. Ground and center, then imagine white, iridescent energy surrounding and filling you. If you are working in a group, you may wish to choose one person to read the guided meditation to the rest of the participants; or if you are working alone, you might wish to record the meditation for yourself.

Each pathworking is based on my own pathworking experiences with these goddesses. They are a starting point for you to build a connection to these goddesses. If you begin a pathworking and it suddenly takes on a life of its own, don't worry. That goddess may have something different to say to you than what I experienced. During your pathworking, you may wish to light incense or a candle, or use a symbol that corresponds to the particular goddess you will be working with. A list of correspondences for each goddess can be found at the end of each goddess's section.

Spells and Rituals

Throughout this book you will find spells and rituals for each of the goddesses we will be working with. These spells and rituals are not traditional to the cultures of these goddesses, although I try to draw inspiration from how these cultures would approach ritual work. The same goes for recipes for things like incense: while I use herbs and ingredients connected to each goddess, they are my own creations, drawn from my experiences working with each goddess. My own practices are rooted in Witchcraft, so most of the rituals and spellwork you will find follow this framework. Feel free to use them as they appear or to change and adapt them to your own tradition or ritual style. Or use them as inspiration for creating your own rituals and spellwork.

PART ONE
THE SUN AND THE DIVINE FEMININE

We must shift ground in this philosophic dispute, disengage from the false dichotomies that our culture offers, and claim the light as well as the darkness, the sky as well as the earth, as part of the Goddess.

—Patricia Monaghan, *O Mother Sun!*

In all of human history, there has never been a time when the sun, in one form or another, has not been worshiped or held sacred. The frequent depiction of circular discs, rayed wheels, and other sun symbols in primitive paintings and Neolithic graffiti attests to the importance and reverence our distant ancestors gave to the sun. The sun's importance in the life of our forbearers is also evident in the plethora of monuments humanity has erected that align to the sun. Stonehenge is perhaps the most well-known of these monuments, with the summer-solstice sun rising over the henge's heel stone each year. Predating Stonehenge by roughly a thousand years, the Nabta Playa, a megalithic stone circle in the Sahara desert, also aligned to the summer-solstice sun. In Wyoming the stones of the Bighorn Medicine Wheel align to the rising and setting sun on the solstice. The Goseck circle in Germany, possibly the earliest sun observatory in Europe, marked both the summer and winter solstices. In Polynesia the Ha'amonga Maui megalithic arch was also built to align to the sun on the solstices.

To the early peoples in these regions, the sun's ability to give light and warmth must have seemed magickal. The warmth and light of the sun drew animals out of hibernation and made crops grow. Without the heat of the summer sun, these people could not feed themselves or their herds. Snow fell when the hours of sunlight waned, plants withered, the ground turned hard, and leaves fell dead from the trees. Animals disappeared, going into hibernation or migrating elsewhere.

When the sun was at its peak, these early people honored the fertility it brought, and during the darkest half of the year they held rituals to entice the sun's return. The sun's power was monumental. It brought life as well as light, and it is no wonder many of their yearly celebrations honored the sun's celestial dance across the sky, or that they envisioned the sun as a divine being. In all the varied pantheons across the globe, there is not one that does not have a sun deity or that does not envision the sun as a divine entity of some sort. Even in Christianity the sun has been equated with the divine. St. Patrick in his *Confessio* says of the sun: "Woe to its unhappy worshipers, for punishment awaits them. But we believe in and adore the true Sun, Christ!"[1]

Today the sun plays just as integral a role in the spiritual practices of modern Pagans as it did to our ancestors. While images of full moon rituals and drawing down the moon may come to mind when we think of modern Goddess spirituality, the sun plays just as much of a role in our spiritual practices as the moon. The seasonal changes we honor along the year wheel are the direct result of our planet's yearly revolution around this luminous body. Four of the eight major Sabbats are based on the astronomical position of the sun. At the equinoxes we honor the balance between day and night. At midsummer we celebrate the height of the sun's power, and on the winter solstice we honor the sun's rebirth. These are some of the most important sacred days within modern Paganism, and they all revolve around the sun.

Given the sun's ability to bring fertility and new life, one would have to wonder why our ancestors wouldn't have made the connection between the sun and the Goddess. The sun was a vital force of creation, not unlike the Great Goddess who brought fertility and creation as well. Yet the sun as a symbol of the Goddess is an alien concept to us today. While there certainly were cultures that saw the

---

1. Skinner, *Confession of Saint Patrick and Letter to Coroticus*, 60.

sun as a masculine force, there were just as many who saw the radiant power of the sun as belonging to the feminine. The solar feminine has just as rich a history as the solar masculine.

For us to truly rediscover the solar feminine, we must first understand what role she played in the mystical traditions of the past. We must learn her symbols and her roles in mythology. The sun goddess is not a sun god in a skirt. While she shares some of the same symbols and attributes as sun gods, many of the roles she plays in mythology are unique to the female sun. Most importantly, we must endeavor to understand why this aspect of the Goddess has become so obscure.

The Hidden Sun

The idea that the moon goddess is the norm, and the sun goddess the exception, is partly due to the way in which earlier writers did their research ... from the view that whatever was Greek was good. As a result, the moon and sun had to fit the mold of Helios and Selene.

—Sheena McGrath,
The Sun Goddess: Myth, Legend and History

Wherever we find the sun goddess, we find the myth of the hidden sun. The sun departs from the world, often hiding in a cave, plunging the world into the cold and darkness of winter. Like the sun goddess hiding in her cave, the concept of the feminine sun has become hidden from us. The goddess of the sun waits for us to lure her out of the shadows; she waits for us to rediscover her light. But before we learn who exactly this radiant figure is, it is important to understand why she has been hidden from us in the first place.

Our first hint to how our ancestors viewed the sun can be found in the language we use to describe this celestial orb. Humans have the tendency to assign male or female traits to things that are inherently genderless. For example, how many times have you heard a car enthusiast refer to their car as a "she"? This kind of gender assignment can be found in the very roots of a language and sheds light on the attributes we assign to certain objects. While today we are used to referring to the sun in the masculine, in many cases the language used to describe the sun was originally feminine in gender, attesting to the onetime prominence of the solar feminine. According to Alan Weber, paraphrasing Friedrich Max Müller, "The sun is feminine in all Teutonic languages; and it is only through the influence of classical models that in English moon has been changed into a feminine, and sun into a masculine."[2]

The concept that the sun was a woman is firmly ingrained in the language we use to describe the sun. Our own English language emerged from the invasion of England by Germanic tribes, the Angles and the Saxons. These tribes brought with them their sun goddess Sunna, whose name is reflected in the Old English word for sun, *sunne*, which is also feminine. As late as the 1500s, the sun still had feminine connotations in the English language. In his sermon on St. Stephen's Day in 1552, English bishop Hugh Latimer referred to the sun as a "she": "Not that the sun itself of her substance shall be darkened; no, not so; for she shall give her light."[3]

In German, the word for sun, *Sonne*, is also feminine, while the word for moon, *Mond*, is masculine. The German saying "The sun in her glory; the moon in his wane" emphasizes the way in which they viewed the sun and moon.[4] Similarly, the Welsh word for sun, *haul*, and the Irish, *ghrian*, are both feminine, as was the Gothic word for sun, *sunno*. In Swedish, *månen*, the moon, is masculine, while *solen*, the sun, is feminine. In Lithuanian, the word for sun, *saule*, was also given a feminine gender. The Arabic word for sun, transliterated as *shams*, is feminine, while moon, *qamar*, is masculine.[5] Conversely, in Latin the word for sun is *sol*, which is masculine, and the world for moon, *luna*, is feminine.

The gender assigned to the sun and moon, and the role the sun played in each culture's mythology, is reflected in the culture's language. In German mythology the sun is female, which is reflected in the femi-

---

2. Weber, *Nineteenth Century Science*, 268.
3. Latimer, *Sermons: Volume 2*, 98.
4. Latham, *The English Language*, 514.
5. Natan, *Moon-o-theism*, 391.

nine gender assigned to the word for *sun*, while the Latin gender assignment for *sun* reflects the fact that the Roman sun divinity was male.

It is unlikely that so many languages would assign a feminine gender to the sun without also viewing it as a goddess. Why then are we today used to viewing the sun, light, and illumination as belonging exclusively to the masculine? Did cultures that recognized the solar feminine transition over time to masculine sun deities? Or has the sun goddess become hidden from us for other reasons?

A few attempts were made to change the gender of the sun; the Shinto goddess Amaterasu is the best example. In 750 CE a monk attempting to merge aspects of Buddhism with Shinto beliefs claimed to have received a divine revelation in which it was revealed to him that although the sun goddess Amaterasu appeared female, she was in fact male, and an aspect of the Buddha. In the thirteenth century another attempt was also made to masculinize Amaterasu. Her name was changed to *Ameno-minaku-nushi*, the Heavenly Central Lord, a male deity of creation rather than a female one. Both these attempts failed, but the simple fact that they were made in the first place shows the resignation felt toward the sun as a female source of creativity and power.

Similarly, the Hattic sun goddess Estan was masculinized, becoming the sun god Hittite Istanu.[6] Many of the major deities in the Hittite pantheon underwent a similar sex change. Linguistics scholar Carol F. Justus suggests these changes reflect a major shift in the social and political status of women in the Hittite culture. As the social status of women declined, it no longer became acceptable for divine females to hold significant power. Thus the sun goddess, along with other regional goddesses, became gods, retaining their powers but not their gender.[7] Surprisingly, these attempts to alter the gender of the solar feminine were few and far between. While some cultures did attempt to replace their sun goddesses with male deities, our unfamiliarity with

---

6. Lerner, *The Creation of Patriarchy*, 157.
7. Ibid.

the goddess of the sun comes instead from how early folklorists perceived the beliefs of the Pagan cultures of the past.

Take a moment to think back to your middle school or high school history classes. Which cultures did you learn about? Other than the history of your own country, chances are that the cultures you spent the most time studying were the ancient Greeks and Romans. After all, the Greeks gave us democracy and the Roman Empire conquered most of the then-known world. If your classes were anything like mine, you might have even spent some time analyzing Greek myths. But why didn't you spend an extensive amount of time learning about other cultures? Or read the myths of, let's say, the Norse instead of the ancient Greeks? Classical gods and their mythology are undeniably the most recognizable to us today. If you asked a seventh-grader who Zeus is, she would most likely give you the correct answer, whether due to schoolwork or reading the Percy Jackson novels.

To the Greeks, the sun was Apollo drawing the sun across the sky in his golden chariot, and the moon was his twin sister, Artemis. The Romans followed a similar model of male = sun and female = moon; and being that we are the most familiar with classical myths, it is no wonder we follow a similar line of thought today. But classical mythology simply didn't become so well-known because we liked it more than, say, Latvian mythology. When interest in folklore and mythology began to take root in the Victorian era, these were the two cultures that received the most attention. Books concerning Greek and Roman myths and philosophy were immensely popular, especially in Britain. New fields of scholarship and learning concerning Greek antiquity found their way into European universities. It would be difficult *not* to find references to figures or themes of classical mythology within the works of Shelley, Tennyson, Keats, or Byron. As intellectual historian Frank M. Turner put it, "The classical world stood at the heart of major areas of Victorian thought, political philosophy, theology, and formal education. Moreover, except perhaps for work in the physical sciences, no other field of Victorian intellectual endeavor was so thoroughly European."[8]

The myths of other cultures were compared to those of the Greeks and Romans. Those that deviated from these models were deemed barbaric or the inventions of a backward culture. In his 1914 book *Sun Lore of All Ages*, William Tyler Olcott claimed that the sun goddess resulted from a "confusion in the sex, ascribed to the Sun and Moon." When her existence was acknowledged, it was done so in a derogatory way. She was an anomaly, a result of certain cultures' "confusion" as to the proper sex of the sun.

The studies of mythology and comparative religion were new fields, but the Victorians' interest in studying these stories was not the same as that of modern folklorists and mythographers. While today we endeavor to learn what these myths would have meant to the ancient Greeks and Romans themselves—and how they evolved within their given culture—the Victorians were more interested in finding a universal religious language. They compared the myths and philosophies of Greece and Rome to Christianity, attempting to find parallels. They viewed myths as fables, stories that described the human experience, rather than aspects of an ancient religion. Themes within Homer's poems were seen as teaching lessons similar to those in the Bible. The English historian and novelist James Anthony Froude compared the *Iliad* to Psalms.

Other writers of the time, in Turner's words, "claimed to have discovered evidences of distinctly Christian truth in Greek literature and particularly in Homer. The *Iliad* and the *Odyssey* as secular documents contained or bore witness to the doctrines or providential historical vision present in the Bible."[9] Early church fathers such as Eusebius of Caesarea and Justin Martyr theorized that the themes and moralities

---

8. Turner, *The Greek Heritage in Victorian Britain*, xii.
9. Ibid., xii.

expressed by ancient Greek philosophers were God's way of "preparing" humanity for the Gospel in Pagan times.[10]

Friedrich Max Müller was one the most influential figures in the study of Victorian-era solar mythology. Müller theorized that all myths had their origins in poetic descriptions within a once-shared language. This now-forgotten language had expressed the earliest thoughts of humanity, and eventually over time what had initially been poetic descriptions took on a life and personality of their own, becoming deities. In a speech to the Royal Institution in London, Müller described mythology as "a disease of language. A myth means a word, but a word which, from being a name or an attribute, has been allowed to assume a more substantial existence. Most of the Greek, the Roman, the Indian, and other heathen gods are nothing but poetical names, which were gradually allowed to assume a divine personality."[11]

As the sun was of particular interest to our ancestors, Müller proposed that the many poetic descriptions attributed to the sun explained the abundance of sun worship and sun lore through the ages. In the case of Apollo and Daphne, he traced the origins of their names to the Sanskrit words for *dawn*, arguing that their myths had their origins in ancient people observing that the sun overcame the dawn. Following this train of thought, Müller related practically all myths to every conceivable function of the sun. He went as far as to relate the labors of the Greek demigod Heracles to the tireless sun and its never-ending journey across the sky, despite the fact that the hero had no real connection to the sun.[12] The mere mention of dawn, sunset, or the sun in any context, in Müller's mind, made it a solar myth.

Like his contemporaries, Müller wished to relate the myths he studied to his own religious views: "Like an old precious medal, the

---

10. Chadwick, *Early Christian Thought and the Classical Tradition*, 64.
11. Müller, *Lectures on the Science of Language*, 11.
12. Feldman, *The Rise of Modern Mythology 1680–1860*, 480.

ancient religion, after the rust of ages has been removed, will come out in all its purity and brightness; and the image which it discloses will be the image of the Father ... the Word of God revealed." [13] Müller's theories, although later criticized, were very influential. The idea of the solar god or hero being a universal myth within all cultures helped reaffirm the belief that the sun was always male. As for the solar feminine, Müller simply disregarded or refused to recognize her despite her prevalence within world mythology.

Ultimately, an active female sun would not have agreed with the morals and social taboos of the Victorians. Their interest in a universal language and making ancient myths fit into the mold of Christianity made it impossible for the solar feminine to be recognized. A woman playing such a vital role in a religion didn't fit into their worldview. The passive, gentle moon reflected the ideal woman of the time far better than the vibrant, sometimes warlike sun. The popularity of classical myths further ingrained as the norm the idea of male/sun, female/moon.

The dismissal of the feminine sun continued into the twentieth century. The writings of Carl Jung, the father of modern analytical psychology, furthered the rigid belief that the sun was inherently male and the moon always female. The idea of the solar masculine and lunar feminine can clearly be seen in Jung's theories of the *animus* and *anima*. Jung theorized that we all have both male and female aspects to our psyche. In women there is the animus, which contains a woman's masculine side, while men have an anima that embodies the feminine. The animus Jung relates to light, logic, and the sun, and he relates emotion, the moon, and the feminine with the anima: "In a man it is the lunar anima, in a woman the solar animus, that influences consciousness in the highest degree." [14]

---

13. Müller, *Introduction to the Science of Religion*, 50.
14. Jung, *Mysterium Coniunctionis*, 225.

Jung's idea was revolutionary, but assigning the animus solar attributes followed the same prejudices of his Victorian predecessors. Recognizing the male and female aspects within each individual does not require us to label them solar or lunar energies. Jung related the sun and the moon to the male and female psyche because he saw them as unequivocal symbols of masculinity and femininity.

The only problem with this is that not all cultures connected male gods with the sun. Author Patrick Harpur writes, "[Jung] tended to assign fixed values to the gods and goddesses, and did not always appreciate that their value can change according to context. Thus, when his symbolism did not work, when some mythologies—Norse, for instance— seemed to assign a feminine value to the sun, Jung was forced to conclude that every archetype 'contains its own opposite.' But it is not a question of opposition. Norse mythology simply uses a system of analogy in which the terms are reversed."[15] Depending on the culture in question, we could just as easily make a connection between the moon and the divine masculine. Assigning the animus and anima solar and lunar attributes only works when we keep the Victorian bias in mind.

Today we fall into similar pitfalls. Through the writings and biased thinking of the nineteenth century, we have inherited the assumption that all solar deities are male. The classical model is only one way of viewing the sun's energies. Unfortunately, the attempts made by early mythographers to shape the mythology of the past to fit with their own world and religious views have left us with little knowledge of the feminine sun. We believe the lie that she is a rare anomaly, an entity that goes against the norm. With an understanding of why the sun goddess has become such an obscure figure, we must now fill the gaps in our understanding of solar lore. If we are to understand the sun goddess, we must first learn her symbols and the themes and roles she embodies.

---

15. Harpur, *The Philosophers' Secret Fire*, 98.

Themes and Patterns in Sun Goddess Mythology

It is necessary to our development as whole women and men,
living from the full spectrum of our female and male potentials,
that we recognize, reinstate, and honor the solar feminine in women
and the lunar masculine in men.

—Ruth-Inge Heinze,
Proceedings of the Tenth International Conference
on the Study of Shamanism and Alternate Modes of Healing

We are familiar with the myths of the masculine sun. He can be a god of healing like Apollo, or a god of enlightenment like Vishnu. At times he battles the forces of darkness, such as the Mesopotamian god Marduk, who yearly battled the forces of chaos. In modern Paganism he is the sun king who is born each year on the winter solstice. But what about the sun goddess? What are her myths, her symbols and attributes? Before we explore the myths of each individual goddess more fully, we must first understand the common themes that play an integral part in the mythology of the solar feminine.

No matter the culture we find her in, there are certain elements that are universal to the myths of all sun goddesses. She is usually a weaver of some sort, either inventing the art of weaving or passing her time weaving sunbeams. At times she departs from the world, usually after quarreling with another deity, and either hides in a cave, travels to another land, or stays on the other side of the world, leaving the earth in darkness. This theme represents the shorter, colder days of winter when the sun seems to depart from the earth.

She is then coaxed out of hiding, bringing longer days and the warmth of summer. She usually has an aspect that is connected to the underworld, often caring for the dead or offering them food. This theme is connected to the belief that the sun nightly traveled through the land of the dead before rising and bringing with her the new day. Mirrors and dance played a prominent role in both her myths and worship. Sometimes the mirror is a literal one; other times it is a sacred well that reflects the sun's light. At times she appears as a dual-faced goddess, one ruling the bright half of the year and her sister the dark half. Other times she is taken prisoner by a hag, who represents the winter sun. All of these themes give us insight into the role the sun goddess played in the past and how we can call upon her sacred light in today's world.

THE WOMAN WHO HIDES THE SUN

The retreating or hidden sun can be found in the mythology of almost all sun goddesses. The goddess retreats from the world. At times the catalyst for her departure is a disagreement with another god, usually her moon brother or husband, or she is frightened into hiding. Sometimes she is held captive by a crone who represents the winter sun. Her retreat has dire consequences, leaving the world in darkness and bringing winter to the earth and heavens. Almost always the sun retreats to a cave or some kind of subterraneal place within the earth, be it the heart of a mountain or the cavernous underworld believed to dwell within the earth.

While the sun's retreat to her cave is symbolic of winter and its shorter days, her emergence represents the coming of spring and longer hours of sunlight. In some stories the sun is coaxed out of her cave either through offerings, or her wrath is defused through trickery. On other occasions she escapes her prison, or is rescued from her prison by another solar deity. (See Amaterasu, Hathor, Brighid, Unelanuhi.)

THE MIRROR AND THE EYE

Both the sun and moon are often described as the "eyes" of certain deities, and eye motifs play a large role in the myths of the feminine sun. Sometimes she is described as an actual eye, as with Bast, Sekhmet, and Hathor, who were all given the title "Eye of Ra" or "Eye of the Sun." The Celtic goddess Sul's name also meant "eye."

Many of the sun goddess's myths revolve around her either plucking out her own eyes or being born from a supreme god washing his eyes. In the Celtic tradition, the solar goddesses usually have the ability to cure blindness or have sacred wells dedicated to them that were attributed with the ability to cure eye ailments.

As the celestial eye, the sun goddess was all-seeing. She saw all that happened in the world below, making the sun goddess the perfect deity to be invoked to uncover those responsible for wrongdoing and for finding lost objects, cattle, or even lovers for those who were lonely.[16] From her position in the sky, it was presumed she would be able to see who committed any wrongdoing. The sun performed these tasks not only for her earthly petitioners but for the other gods as well, usually being sent to punish those who had offended the gods.

The sun's ability to see all was usually enhanced with a magickal mirror. In Christianized Slavic folklore, the sun was a mirror into which God gazed each day to see the sins committed on the earth below. The reflection of his glory made the sun too bright to gaze upon. Originally in Slavic mythology the sun was female and the moon her husband. Despite later folklore disregarding the female sun, the connection between sun and mirror remained. Similarly, the Altai sun goddess Kun

---

16. Monaghan, *O Mother Sun!*, 91.

saw everything that occurred on the world below, which was reflected in the "Mirror of the Sun."[17]

Both mirrors and sacred wells were used to represent the sun's eye. Mirrors reflected the sun's light, as did the waters of sacred wells. Their circular shapes resembled the shape of the sun, and when the sun's light shown on them, they became in a sense sacred "eyes" themselves, reflecting the sun's radiant light and becoming vessels of the sun's healing power. In Ireland it was traditional to go to the top of a hill on Easter Sunday when the sun was said to dance in the sky. A mirror or a bucket of water was used to see her dance, to observe the sun's reflection. This is obviously a carryover from an older Pagan tradition, linking the sun and the mirror. Pools of water were arguably the first mirrors, reflecting both the sun and our own reflections, which may be why both have become so ingrained with the solar feminine mythos.

In Egypt, mirrors were especially sacred to the solar feminine. Ritual mirrors were used to reflect the light of the morning sun into the temple where Hathor's statue stood. In the Shinto religion, mirrors are used to represent the sun goddess instead of a statue. In central Asia, mirrors were connected to the sun goddess Kun and were used to decorate the costumes worn by shamans in healing rituals. Sickness was considered to be caused by pieces of a person's soul being stolen or lost in the Otherworlds, and the shaman was believed to be able to retrieve these missing parts of the soul using a mirror, just as the mirror captures the light of the sun. (See Hathor, Saule, Sulis, Amaterasu.)

THE SUN AS A PSYCHOPOMP

At first glance, it may seem odd that goddesses connected to light and life should be so closely connected with the underworld. When we think of the sun, light, warmth, and heat come to mind. We think of

---

17. Harva, *Finno-Ugric and Siberian Mythology*, 310.

the sun in its glory on a cloudless summer day. When she sinks below the horizon, we know she is shedding light on the lives of those on the other side of our planet. But to our ancestors, the sun's nightly journey beyond the horizon and eventual return was a sacred mystery. Where did the sun go? What did it do when it was not shining its light and warmth on the world? From these questions arose an almost universal myth found across all cultures. Whether she died, traveled underground, or went willingly to bring her light to the dead, the sun nightly journeyed to the underworld or to the land of spirits. This theme is also repeated in the sun goddess's habit of retreating to a cave. Caves were considered entrances to the underworld in several cultures, as the realm of spirits was often envisioned as a land below the earth. (See Amaterasu, Rhiannon, Hathor, Shapash.)

LADY OF THE VULVA, LADY OF THE DANCE

When exploring the myths of sun goddesses, one tends to run into a number of references to ecstatic dancing, in which the goddess or women imitating her during ritual processions lift their skirts to reveal their vulvas. This rather odd behavior can be found in the myths of sun goddesses around the world. When Amaterasu departs from the world and hides herself in a cave, it is not until the shaman Uzume dances ecstatically, revealing her vulva to the other gods, subsequently making them laugh, that the sun goddess leaves her cave to discover the source of their raucous laughter. Similarly, when Ra the Egyptian sun god was in a bad mood and departed from the world, Hathor (the feminine embodiment of the sun and his "eye") convinced him to return by dancing for him and lifting her skirts to reveal her vulva. This apparently put Ra in a good mood again, and he returned, subsequently bringing the sun's warmth and vibrance back into the world.

In Baltic lore, the sun goddess is described as lifting her skirts in farmers' fields. When she dropped her skirts, it was time to harvest the grain, suggesting that exposing her vulva to the earth brought it fertility; and when she withdrew her fertile nature (dropping her skirts), it brought about the harvest and with it winter.[18] The act of revealing the vulva and dancing are symbolic of renewed fertility. Life comes from the womb, which is often symbolized by caves or burial mounds. In the case of the sun goddesses, it becomes synonymous with the cave that the sun retreats to.

It is clear that the sun returns to the world through the womb of the goddess. By revealing the life-bearing womb, she brings its fertility to the world. Her dance is the dance of life; it is her dance across the sky and through the wheel of the year as the solar orb. Her dancing changes the seasons, transforming the bareness of winter into the promise of spring. (See Uzume, Hathor, Bast, Saule.)

GODDESS OF ORDER AND RULERSHIP AND DIVIDER OF TIME

Humans have always marked the seasons and divided time by the sun. The sun is a natural measurer of time. It divides day and night, and the time it takes the earth to make a full rotation around the sun divides time into measurable units, forming the solar year. Ancient monuments and burial mounds were aligned to the position of the sun on the solstices and equinoxes, providing our ancestors with an ancient sun calendar to mark the passage of time.

This natural ability to mark and measure time has connected the sun to order, divine law, and rulership. Sun goddesses are usually celestial queens or connected to rulership in some way. As a divine queen, her earthly priestesses also had a hand in rulership. Egyptian queens often served as the high priestesses of Hathor, one of the embodiments of the sun. Hittite queens served as the high priestess, or *tawananna*, of the sun goddess Arinniti. The tawananna not only served as a religious leader, being the living embodiment of the solar goddess, but also ruled when the king was ill or was away in battle.

---

18. McGrath, *The Sun Goddess*, 37.

As a symbol of order, the sun goddess often battles forces representing chaos or darkness, maintaining the celestial balance by keeping these forces at bay. Another aspect to the sun's connection to order was her role as a divine bringer of justice. As an all-seeing heavenly eye, no crime or wrongdoing could escape her gaze. (See Saule, Sulis, Unelanuhi.)

DUAL GODDESS AND SUN MAIDENS

Sun goddesses often appear in pairs, as sisters, as mother/daughter groupings, or as a young maiden paired with a crone. The most common pairing is the sun goddess and the sun maiden. Sometimes she has several daughters; other times she has a single daughter who usually ruled over the dawn (her connection to the new day symbolizing her youth) or with the morning star. The connection between goddesses of the dawn and the sun are often overlooked. It is easier to relegate these goddesses to a function of the sun, in this case dawn and its light, rather than recognizing them as the actual sun. Folk songs also describe Saule as a maid when the sun is not shining as brightly, suggesting she and her daughter share rulership over the sky during certain times: "Yesterday Saule was brilliant, but today she is so vague. Yesterday's sun was Saule herself—today she is just the Maid."[19]

The sun's relationship with her daughter is often troubled. The trouble usually begins when the daughter comes of age to be married or catches the attention of male deities. At times the daughter dies, and the sun leaves the world to mourn, bringing winter. In other myths, the sun's husband has an incestuous relationship with the sun maiden, at times willingly or through force, inspiring the wrath of the mother sun.

Like most love triangles in mythology, this most likely suggests a shift in power, in this case a seasonal shift. The mother sun who rules

---

19. Monaghan, *O Mother Sun!*, 93.

over summer is replaced by the younger sun maiden whose untested light represents the weaker sun of winter. In the end, mother and daughter are really two faces of the same goddess, both sharing the same moon or sky-god husband. Similarly, the Celts often viewed the sun as a pair of sisters, one ruling over the winter sun and the other the summer sun. At times the Celtic sun was a hag during the winter months who either held the maiden sun captive or transformed into a maiden during the summer months. Similarly, the Finnish sun goddess was held captive by a hag, causing the earth to be dark and cold until her release.

Instead of being seen as two separate goddesses in South America, the sun goddess Akewa alternately aged then grew younger at different point in the year. (See Saule, Cailleach, Päivätär.)

Destructive Aspect

At times the sun can be as destructive as she is beneficial. Like the element of fire, which she is closely connected to, her rays can just as easily scorch the land as they can cause the crops to grow. The sun goddesses' destructive side usually manifests in a warrior aspect, either battling her moon or storm brother or being called upon to protect a king, whether it be the king of the gods or a mortal ruler. In some Native American myths, the earth is made devastatingly hot when she feels slighted by her human grandchildren. In Canaanite stories, it is the absence of a storm deity that causes the sun's rays to burn the earth, making her seek out her polar opposite to restore balance. In Mesopotamia, the sun goddess was called upon for military victories. The Hittite goddess Arinniti was called upon to protect the king in battle. The Hittite king Mursili II described her as "the sun-goddess, my lady smote those hostile countries for me."[20] Similarly, in Japan, Amaterasu carried a sword and bow in her warrior aspect.

---

20. Gurney, *The Hittites*, 176.

The sun goddess's sacred fire is seen as both a creative and a destructive force. This destruction is necessary in order for life to continue and is a reflection of her connection to the underworld and the realm of death. When necessary, the sun goddess is a warrioress, protecting the gods and those she favors. (See Unelanuhi, Amaterasu, Shapash, Bast, Brighid, Sekhmet.)

Moon Brother, Moon Lover

The relationship between the sun and moon is perhaps one of the most common themes in celestial mythology. Sometimes they are brother and sister; other times they appear as husband and wife. Artemis and Apollo are perhaps the most famous brother-sister pair, but they are not the only celestial siblings. The Norse Sunna was paired with her brother, the moon god Mani. The Inuits saw these divine siblings as Malina and her brother Aningak. In Baltic mythology, the sun goddess Saule's husband was the moon god Menesis. In Egypt, the sun goddess Hathor was sometimes paired with the god Thoth, who was at times associated with the moon.

Sometimes the two themes are merged, and the sun enters into an incestuous relationship with her sibling. In some cases this is a willing union, as many pantheons paired brother and sister deities as husband and wife. In other myths the sun is raped or pursued by the lustful moon, either leading to the sun and moon's apparent chase across the skies or explaining why the sun rules over the day and the moon the night.

Connection to Storms, Weather, or Sky Gods

Although we tend to assume the sun and the moon should be paired together, either as brother and sister or husband and wife, this is not always the case. The solar goddess is just as often paired with sky gods—usually ones who represent storms or thunder, or ones who could control the weather. Since the sun "lived" in the sky and in many cultures had some sort of house or castle on a mystical "sky-hill" that she went up and down each day, it seems reasonable to believe she would have some sort of relationship with the deity who ruled over the sky. In some cases, her sky-god consort brings fertility to match her own with the life-giving rain. In other myths the storm god is an adversary casing chaos or mischief that usually results in the sun retreating from the heavens. (See Brighid, Shapash, Hathor, Saule, Amaterasu.)

GODDESS OF FERTILITY AND CREATION

The sun has always been a very potent symbol of fertility. From Neolithic times, humanity has observed the sun's role in germination and agriculture. In her myths she is either responsible for the creation of the world or responsible for the fertility of crops and livestock.

Sun goddesses were also considered mother goddesses in many cultures. In Japan, the sun was believed to be not only the ancestress of the Imperial family but of all Japan.[21] In Australia, the sun goddess Yhi brought all of life into creation. The Hurrians' solar goddess Hebat was called the "Mother of All Living," and Saule was called *Saule Mate*, or "Mother Sun." (See Saule, Bast, Hathor, Yhi.)

TENDER OR BRINGER OF FIRE

It would be impossible to delve into the lore of the sun goddess without discussing her connection to fire. In fact, more often than not, sun goddesses are mislabeled as fire goddesses. The Celtic solar feminine often had a sacred flame that would be tended by her worshipers and never allowed to be extinguished. Hearths were also particularly sacred to the sun goddess, who at times visited hearth fires or sent her solar children to tend them. Sometimes, rather than tending the sacred fire, she is envisioned as literally being made of fire, sometimes accidently burning through her sky home to fall to the earth.

---

21. Kinsley, *The Goddesses' Mirror*, 82.

At times the sun goddess is celebrated with torches or carries a torch (the sun) through the sky. (See Brighid, Sulis, Päivätär.)

WELLS AND THERMAL WATERS

As the sun is connected to the element of fire, it may seem odd that many solar goddesses are associated with holy wells and thermal waters. Water and fire seem like opposites, but the two are often mythologically connected. Patricia Monaghan suggests that the watery surfaces of wells were in fact the first mirrors. After all, some of the very first mirrors created were hammered copper whose surfaces were wetted in order to make them reflective, indicating a connection between water and mirrors. The surfaces of these wells may have been used to capture the healing properties of the sun within the well's waters. The practice of using the reflective surface of water as a "sun-mirror" seemed to be a prevalent practice among the Celts. In the Celtic mind, the sun was believed to travel beneath the earth, heating underground waters and bestowing them with healing properties. Thus the sun became linked with thermal waters, which rose from the ground heated as if by the sun. "[The] curative powers the sun instilled in the waters when it descended beneath the earth at night. In Celtic thought, the sun made nighttime stops in underground waters when it fell below the horizon," as Tamra Andrews puts it. [22] (See Brighid, Sulis.)

WEAVING AND SPINNING

The connection between sun goddesses and weaving most likely comes from their ability to divide and measure time. They weave order into the fabric of our lives and, like the Greek Fates, measure and cut the thread of life. The constantly moving spinning wheel was connected to the sun's circular movement through the sky. The process of making thread is in itself an act of creation. Several sun goddesses are either

---

22. Andrews, *Dictionary of Nature Myths*, 83.

credited with inventing the art of spinning or were thought to spin sunbeams in their heavenly homes. In some cases, their attendants carry spindles, such as the Hittite sun goddess Arinniti, who acted as a goddess of fate. The length of the thread she spun dictated the allotted time of the king's reign. (See Päivätär, Amaterasu, Unelanuhi, Shapash.)

THE SUN'S PURSUERS

In many myths, the sun is constantly pursued across the sky by a monstrous animal or demon. In some cultures, the rays of the sun goddess were thought to be the goddess's weapons, used to fight off the demons who pursued her. When a solar eclipse occurred, it was believed that the sun goddess had become lax in her vigilance and her monstrous pursuer had snuck up behind her, swallowing her whole. Fortunately, she would either be too hot and the monster was forced to spit her out, or she had a daughter who would take up her role in the heavens.

The Lithuanians believed a demon named Tiknis or Tiklis attacked the sun's chariot each day. At night the sun cannot shine, either because she is occupied with fighting off Tiknis or recovering from her battle with the demon.[23] When she is well again, she rises with the dawning day. Similarly, in Egypt the solar goddess Bast nightly fought the serpent Apep. While Apep did not pursue the sun through the sky, it could not rise from the underworld without defeating him.

In Korea, the luminaries were originally two children chased up a ladder from the sky, where they were put to work as the sun and moon. (See Sunna, Akycha.)

---

23. Grimm, *Teutonic Mythology: Volume 2*, 707.

THE SUN AND MOON SWITCH PLACES

In Asia and among some Native American tribes, the sun and moon often switch places. In Korea, the sun and moon were once a brother and sister who climbed to the heavens to escape a hungry tiger. Once in the heavens, the boy, Haesik, became the sun, and his sister, Dalsun, the moon. After a while, Dalsun complained that she was afraid of the dark. To accommodate his sister, Haesik switched places with her and became the moon instead.

The Maidu people, who live in present-day California, tell a similar story. The sun and moon were brother and sister who were chased into the sky by Angle Worm and Gopher to light the world.[24] Realizing their combined heat would be harmful to the earth, they traveled across the sky separately. At first the girl traveled the night sky as the moon, but because of her beauty, the stars fell in love with her and constantly harassed her for sex. Annoyed with the star's lewd behavior, she switched places with her brother.

The Ainu of Japan tell an almost identical story. The goddess Chup-Kamui was originally the moon, but being modest she was horrified at the adultery and illicit behavior humanity participated in at night. Her brother didn't mind human transgressions so much, so he switched places with her and became the moon.

SOLAR SYMBOLS AND TOTEMS

The symbols and animals that accompany a deity help to give us a clearer perspective of that god or goddess's attributes and personality. Many gods appear in the shape of their totem animals, and by doing so add that animal's power to their own. The symbols used to represent a given god or goddess—or the items they often appear surrounded by in ancient art or within their mythology—also give us vital clues to their functions.

---

24. Dixon, *Maidu Myths*, 113.

In our search for the goddess of the sun, these symbols and totems help validate the connection between the feminine and the sun, and draw parallels between the myths of the solar feminine across several cultures. Whether we are discussing the feminine sun of the Celtic tribes, the sun women of Australia, or the fierce sun goddesses of Egypt, they all share similar symbols and totems.

Solar Symbols
CHARIOTS AND BOATS

Numerous cultures envisioned both male and female solar deities traveling across the sky in a golden chariot. The earliest description of the sun goddess's chariot has it drawn by swans; eventually, horses became the predominant animal to transport the sun. In other cases, the goddess's chariot is drawn by pigs.

The sun's connection to the wheel may be why it was envisioned as being transported across the sky in a chariot. The Balts saw the sun as a giant rolling wheel, although later the sun and its goddess rode in a chariot.

In some myths, the sun is transported through the underworld in a boat, while during the day it is conveyed in a chariot. Saule sailed across the sea in a golden boat pulled by swans until she reached the eastern shore and began her journey across the sky-hill in her chariot. In Egyptian myths, the sun was transported through both the sky and the underworld in the *Boat of a Million Years*.

CIRCLES, WHEELS, AND ROSETTES

The earliest representations of the sun were circles that eventually evolved into rayed or spoked wheels set above the heads of figures in primitive art. These images appear on coins and on carved altars and figurines in later times. Wheels and solar circles were commonly drawn on the sexual organs of female solar figures, drawing a connection between the sun and creation, an attribute absent in the portrayals of male sun deities. Clay figurines found in Gaul show goddesses with sun wheels and solar circles on their breasts, womb, and thighs.[25] Statues of Sekhmet portray the goddess in a long dress with rosettes covering either her breasts or nipples.[26]

Sometimes the sun and the sun goddess were envisioned as a wheel. Rather than having a solar wheel drawn on the body or acting as the goddess's symbol, the sun and the sun goddess herself are sometimes envisioned as a wheel. While much of Baltic poetry is dedicated to describing the sun goddess's beauty, in art she is represented by rosettes or a spoked wheel, rather than being shown in human form. The sun itself was envisioned as a rolling wheel in the Baltic mind, and the sun goddess was addressed as *ridolele*, or the "rolling" sun.[27] The Germanic sun is given a similar description.

THE MIRROR

As we have already discussed, the mirror appears in the myths of several sun goddesses. As a symbol, the mirror was used to represent the sun goddess herself. In most religions, a deity is represented by a statue portraying that god or goddess's likeness. The mirror is unique in the fact that it is used in place of a statue to represent the goddess. In Shinto shrines, mirrors are worshiped as if they were the solar goddess herself. They are her earthy representations. According to Patricia Monaghan, "the first polished metal mirrors were fashioned to echo the shape and brilliance of the sun's disc ... Mirrors were invented as a ritual sun-trap to bring the sun goddess to earth, for if the image is the essence, the sunshine in the mirror is the goddess herself."[28]

Monaghan also points out that it would have been easier for ancient smiths to create square mirrors, yet the vast majority of early mirrors were circular, reflecting the shape of the sun.

---

25. Green, *Symbol and Image in Celtic Religious Art*, 39.
26. Remler, *Egyptian Mythology A to Z*, 171.
27. Gimbutas, *Ancient Symbolism in Lithuanian Folk Art*, 148.
28. Monaghan, *O Mother Sun!*, 43.

THE NECKLACE OF POWER

Several solar goddesses possess or are given a necklaces of power that represent either their status or their ability to create order. In Shinto and Egyptian myth, the necklace is shaken to banish spirits or to give blessings. The Baltic sun wore a belt, which she hung in a tree at night and which turned red as she rose into the sun with the dawn. While not a necklace, this seems like a similar theme, as both a belt and necklace are worn around the body and form one of the most common sun symbols: a circle.

THE NUMBER SEVEN

The sun goddess is often connected to the number seven. Hathor manifests as a sevenfold goddess known as the "Seven Hathors," who were portrayed either as seven white cows or as seven sisters. In this guise the Seven Hathors proclaimed the fate of children at their birth; they were called upon to aid in matters of love and to banish evil spirits. According to Cherokee mythology, the sun goddess Unelanuhi was once too close to the earth, making it too warm, until she was moved seven hand lengths above the sky. Unelanuhi's daughter had to be hit with seven rods to capture her spirit from the land of the dead. The Buddhist goddess Marici rode through the sky in a chariot drawn by seven sows. To invoke her favor, Buddhist monks chanted her mantra seven times while facing the rising sun.

TORCHES

Torches are predominant symbols of the sun in Aboriginal myths. The sun goddess is usually envisioned as carrying a torch through the sky in search of her missing child. When the sun visited the underworld, she carried a torch to light her way through the earth, to visit her dead lover.

Solar Totems

Bears

In Native American lore, bears are often connected to the power of the sun or at times keep the sun prisoner during the winter months. Shoshone lore tells of bears being seen walking on two legs like men while performing the sun dance. The Slavey tribe of northwestern Canada tell a story in which the sun refused to shine for three years, leaving the earth in a perpetual winter. Cold and starving, the animals gathered together to see what could be done. Realizing there were no bears present at the council, they suspected a bear had the sun hidden away. So the animals traveled to the upper world, where they came upon a mother bear and her two cubs. The other animals tricked the cubs into telling them that their mother had hidden the sun in a bag inside her den. The other animals then stole the bag and returned the sun to the world.[29]

A parallel seems to have been made between the yearly retreat of the sun and the winter hibernation of bears. In some subarctic regions, the sun, like the bear, disappears during the winter.[30] The myth of the bear stealing the sun also has a striking similarity to the myths involving the sun hiding in a cave, much like the underground den of a hibernating bear.

In Siberia the sun was believed to be carried in the antlers of a celestial elk, who was nightly pursued by a giant bear.[31]

Cats

Many cultures have worshiped the feline and the sun alongside one another. The Tukano Indians of South America believe the jaguar was created by the sun as its representative on earth.[32] Cats were intrinsically connected to the sun in Egyptian mythology. In cat form,

---

29. Vogel, *Weather Legends*, 40.
30. Mitchell, *Following the Sun*, 100.
31. Jacobson, *The Deer Goddess of Ancient Siberia*, 195.
32. Sunquist, *Wild Cats of the World*, 306.

Bast nightly defeated the serpent of chaos, although Ra later took this role. The lioness goddess Sekhmet embodied the destructive power of the sun. In one Egyptian myth, the sun was envisioned as a great cat whose eye was the sun, since a cat's pupil grew larger as the day advanced.[33] During an eclipse, the sun goddess Akewa was said to have been eaten by a jaguar. Thankfully, the sun scalded the jaguar's mouth, and it spit her out. The Mesopotamian goddess Hebat rode atop of a lion, as did the Hittite goddess Wurusemu. In Korea the sun and moon were chased by a hungry tigress. Although she did not appear in cat form, the Buddhist sun goddess sometimes wore the skin of a tiger.

Cows

Although not as common as the horse, cattle have also been held as sacred to sun gods and goddesses. The Greek god Helios had a herd of sacred cattle, which Odysseus and his men had the misfortune of poaching. In Egypt the goddess Hathor was often portrayed as either a cow or a cow-headed woman. In her early mythology, she carried the infant sun in her horns. Ra, the male sun god, was also called the "The Great Wild Bull," a counterpart to Hathor as the divine cow. There is also some indication that cattle may have pulled a "sun wagon" in Neolithic northern European sun lore, similar to the more common horse-drawn sun chariot.[34] When connected to the sun, cattle represent the sun's fertile power.

CROWS AND RAVENS

In early Chinese texts, crows were believed to carry the sun across the sky each day.[35] The Japanese sun goddess Amaterasu's messenger was a three-legged crow. The crow and its cousin the raven were known in many Native American myths as light bearers as well. The Lenape

---

33. Olcott, *Sun Lore of All Ages*, 60.
34. Milisauskas, *European Prehistory*, 204.
35. Yang and An, *Handbook of Chinese Mythology*, 96.

tribe tell a story about the Rainbow Crow, who had feathers in all the hues of the rainbow and who flew up to the heavens to ask the Creator to make the earth warm so that all the animals would not be so cold. The creator lit a stick in the sun's fire and gave it to the Rainbow Crow to bring to Earth. Unfortunately, his feathers were singed black from the heat of the fire. The Haida tribe of the Pacific Northwest tell a similar tale, in which Raven steals the sun.

Both myths give the reason for the crow or raven's black feathers as a result of being burned by the heat of the sun. Ravens are also connected to numerous sun gods as well. Ravens brought the Celtic sun god Lugh messages and were sacred to Apollo.[36] Like the sun goddess, both the raven and the crow were connected to the underworld. The Celts believed that crows and ravens, along with horses, were animals that could move between the worlds, bringing the souls of the dead into the Otherworlds.

FROGS

In some cultures, frogs are closely connected to both fire and the sun. In South America, the frog goddess Nayobo created fire by vomiting.[37] Similarly, in Native American stories the sun is often swallowed by a frog, then vomited up when the frog realizes the sun is too hot to eat.

The Cherokee believed the sun was swallowed by a frog during an eclipse. According to the Maidu, the sun goddess stole children from the earth and ate them. When the sun ate Frog's children, Frog traveled to the sun's house far in the north. When the sun came out of her house, Frog swallowed her whole. But the sun began to swell in Frog's stomach. Trying to contain the sun, Frog grew round and her skin stretched. Soon the heat was too much for her, and the sun burst free from Frog's belly. Although the myth relating the two has been

---

36. Williams, *Callimachus*, 64.
37. Monaghan, *The New Book of Goddesses and Heroines*, xlii.

lost, the Tunica people of present-day Louisiana connected their sun goddess Tach-I with frogs.[38]

While the Baltic sun adored snakes, frogs were denied the sight of the sun goddess.[39] In the beginning of time, when Saule fell in love with the moon god, a frog objected to the marriage, feeling that the sun goddess would neglect her duties and burn up the earth if she had children.

HORSES

The horse is perhaps the most prevalent solar animal in world mythology. Horses are depicted drawing the chariots of sun gods and goddesses through the sky in several mythical traditions. At times the sun goddess rode across the sky in not one chariot but in nine chariots or with multiple teams of horses. The Hungarian sun goddess Xatel-Ekwa traveled across the sky riding three horses simultaneously.

The Christian Bible mentions the connection Pagans made between horses and the sun. King Josiah was said to have removed the horse the kings of Judah had "given" to the sun, after abolishing such Pagan practices. Virtually all the Celtic sun goddesses are connected to the horse. According to archaeologist Miranda Green, "In Celtic religion, horses had a very close affinity with the sun ... Many coins depict a horse associated with the sun symbols and the wheel of a chariot."[40]

Virtually all the Celtic female personifications of the sun doubled as horse goddesses. Like the sun goddess, the horse was also seen as an animal that could travel to the realm of the dead and the underworld. Horses were found in Celtic burial sites along with other animals like ravens and hounds, which were also believed to be able to pass between the realms of life and death. As an animal connected to travel, the horse was believed to convey the soul to the Otherworlds.

---

38. Swanton, *Indian Tribes of the Lower Mississippi Valley*, 318.
39. Monaghan, *O Mother Sun!*, 143.
40. Green, *Animals in Celtic Life and Myth*, 208.

Similarly, in Japan horses were kept at Shinto shrines both to carry small portable shrines and also due to the belief that the solar goddess favored them.

PIGS

Pigs represent fertility, abundance, and at times ferocity. Sometimes pigs or boars draw the solar goddesses' chariot, or she owns a magickal pig or can transform into one. Brighid owned a magickal boar called *Orc Triath*, who granted inspiration to its owner. The abbesses of the Yamdrok Lake monastery in Tibet are believed to be the living incarnations of the sun goddess Marici. One of the abbesses was said to have transformed herself and all the monastery's nuns and monks into pigs during an attack made on the cloister. Circe, the sorceress daughter of the Greek sun god Helios, also enjoyed turning men into pigs, when she wasn't weaving sunbeams for her father.[41]

SNAKES

Because they periodically shed their skin, snakes have come to be associated with renewal and rebirth. The sun goddess also goes through a similar transformation, symbolically dying or entering the underworld at nightfall, to be reborn again with the dawn. Saule was especially fond of snakes. When shown with a cobra on her head, the symbol of the snake goddess Wadjet, Bast was called Wadjet-Bast. In this form she was a protectress of lower Egypt. Ironically, Bast was also said to nightly fight the serpent Apep, a being who embodied chaos. Snakes were also sacred to the Canaanite sun goddess Shapash, who could cure the victims of snake bites. In their morning prayers, Tibetan monks would ask the sun goddess Marici for protection from several things, including snakes.[42]

---

41. Snow, *The Spider's Web: Goddesses of Light and Loom*, 7.
42. Waddell, *The Buddhism of Tibet*, 218.

Spiders

As we have already discussed, the sun goddess is often envisioned as a weaver. As a natural weaver, the spider and the sun are often connected in Native American lore. The Apache believed the strands of a spider's web were woven from sunbeams. If someone killed a spider, the sun would take revenge by weaving a web inside them, eventually killing them.[43] In Cherokee myth, Grandmother Spider Woman pulled the sun to its current place in the sky by carrying it in a basket she weaved; and in Navajo legend, Spider Woman used the rays of sunlight to weave.

Swans

Swans were frequently associated with sun gods during the Bronze Age, while the horse as the sacred animal that pulled the solar chariot became prevalent in the Iron Age.[44] The swan was sacred to Apollo, and according to the poet and scholar Callimachus, the god rode on the back of a swan to the land of the Hyperboreans during the winter months.[45] Swans were sacred to the Irish goddess Áine, who has solar attributes and ruled the month of the summer sun, while her sister Grainne ruled the time of the winter sun. Grainne was also escorted by swans.[46] Saule was said to travel in a golden boat drawn by swans during the night.

---

43. Haley, *Apaches: A History and Culture Portrait*, 71.
44. McGrath, *The Sun Goddess*, 42.
45. Williams, *Callimachus*, 20.
46. McCrickard, *Eclipse of the Sun*, 98.

PART TWO

THE SUN GODDESSES

When someone talks about the moon, we feel the intuitive wonder of Diana. When someone talks about the sun, we feel the heat of passion and the excitement of ardor. We honor the sun women, women who live with their fire energy in delight and fervor.

—Deborah Hoffman-Wade,
Sunshine Woman

It is impossible to say any goddess or god embodies one singular trait. In an attempt to understand the mysteries of the multitude of divinities, we have a tendency to try to categorize them. When you hear the name Aphrodite, you most likely think "goddess of love"; when you hear the name Diana, "moon goddess" probably comes to mind. But is "moon goddess" the epitome of what Diana is? Is she not also a goddess of childbirth and the hunt, the lady of the animals? The gods are complex; like ourselves, they are many things at once. As one of my first teachers liked to say, "The gods are people, too!"

While all the goddesses we will be exploring are associated with the sun, their stories are very different from one another, their natures and personalities differing vastly. They are all goddesses of the sun, but they are not all the same, each bringing to light an aspect of the sun's power.

When I first began my journey with the solar feminine, I was surprised at just how much I was drawn to these goddesses of light. I have always identified strongly with the dark goddess. Through my patron, the Irish Morrigan, I learned that there is strength and beauty in the darker mysteries. But even the Morrigan has a brighter side. At times she is the dark goddess of death and transformation, yet in her triple form she is also the goddess Macha, whom the Irish hailed as the "sun of womanhood."[47] In the end, light is meaningless

---

47. Gwynn, *The Metrical Dindshenchas*, 127.

without the darkness that defines it, and it is the goddesses of light that guide us through the dark.

These goddesses of light and solar fire take on many forms and incarnations throughout the world. Take a moment to imagine yourself standing in a desert. The hot summer sun bakes the earth around you, sapping all moisture from the air. Next see yourself standing in a field surrounded by lush farmlands, the trees and plants reaching skyward toward the sun's light. Now imagine yourself standing on a snowy hill far to the north; as the sun sinks below the horizon, you know you will not see its light again for several months. While the sun is vital to life across the globe, not all cultures viewed the sun, or its goddess, the same way. Although we all gaze upon the same nearby star each day, depending on where we live in the world, the sun affects our lives differently.

Generally, in hotter climates where the sun's heat is strongest, the sun goddess evolved into a patron of war, her rays destroying life rather than nourishing it. We see this destructive side of the sun in goddesses like the Egyptian Sekhmet, whose breath created the desert dunes and who was the wartime protectress of gods and kings. In colder climates she was concerned with bringing fertility to the earth and crops. Thus to the people along the Baltic Sea, she was a loving mother and a goddess of creation. At times she was not only a bringer of light but also its protector, such as the Norse Sunna who was endlessly pursued by a wolf determined to swallow the sun. In the myths of the Middle East, she traversed the dangers of the underworld to bring light and life to the world above.

The sun's personality is not the only thing that varies. In some cultures, she is the actual sun; in others, the goddess pulls the solar orb through the sky in her chariot. Still other cultures saw her as the embodiment of the sun's light rather than the actual sun itself. At times the solar feminine manifests in the form of a sun maiden or a goddess of dawn, who often acts as the sun goddess's maiden aspect.

Other sun goddesses manifest as a pair of sisters, one ruling the hotter summer sun and the other the weaker light of the winter sun. At other times she is a radiant mother figure, while the functions of other sun goddesses revolve around their journeys through the land of the dead and the underworld, where they comfort the spirits of the dead each night before rising to the heights of the sky once more.

While the way the sun and its goddess were viewed differs from culture to culture, what remains constant are the lessons they teach us. The sun women of mythology embrace their inner fires to bring forth inspiration and creation. They burn away and destroy what is no longer useful. While each of the goddesses you will find in this section brings a different aspect of the sun goddess's personality into focus, at the core they all teach us to embrace our own inner fires, to delve into the source of our creativity and strength, and they inspire us to accomplish our dreams and desires.

The goddesses we will be exploring are divided by the regions and cultures in which they were worshiped, along with a brief discussion about how each culture viewed and worshiped the sun. Along with their myths and connections to the sun, you will find spells, rituals, and information on how to incorporate each goddess into your own spiritual practices. Feel free to add to or change any of the rituals, or simply use them as inspiration for creating your own. Also, it is not necessary to work with each goddess in any specific order. If you feel drawn to Sekhmet or Sulis, then work through that goddess's section first.

JAPAN

The ancestor of my ancestors is the Sun Goddess.
The Sun Goddess is the founder of our race ...
the throne is the place of the Sun Goddess.

—Hozumi Yatsuka, *The People's Educations: Patriotism*

It seems only fitting to begin our journey in Japan. The land of the rising sun is home to a goddess whose worship has never died out. From Neolithic times to the present day, Amaterasu has been lovingly worshiped by followers of the Shinto religion. She is the radiant ruler of heaven, the ancestress of the Japanese people, and a goddess of the sun.

Shinto, which means "the way of the gods," is the indigenous religion of Japan. Shinto is primarily based on the worship of *kami*. *Kami* refers to a supernatural being or spirit. It is a broad term, referring to nature spirits; the Shinto gods (who are viewed as the greatest of the kami); and ancestors, who after death become a type of kami. Most Shinto rituals revolve around purification and prayers to keep evil spirits away. It is believed that good deeds and thoughts attract the kami, while evil actions repulse them. There are no set moral codes or commandments in Shinto. "Follow the genuine impulses of your heart" is often quoted as the essence of its spiritual teachings.[48]

---

48. Olson, *Olson's Orient Guide*, 685.

As in most cultures, the sun was seen as a divine ruler of the heavens, and Amaterasu continues to be worshiped as the most powerful of the kami. Her husband was the moon, and her brother the storm god, placing the watery lunar realms in the hands of the masculine. The high placement of female divinities reflects the status of women in early Japanese culture. Women could, like the sun goddess, take on the office of rulership. During the third century, a shaman-priestess named Himiko united and ruled thirty Japanese tribes after eighty years of warfare. Himiko most likely was not her real name, but rather a title. *Hi* means "sun," and *miko* was a term used to describe a female shaman or medium. This would make her a "shaman woman of the sun," both embodying a living representation of Amaterasu as her priestess and ruling on earth as the goddess ruled in the heavens.

Chinese envoys visiting Japan during this time referred to the nation as "Queen Country" because of its habit of allowing females to rule. After Himiko's death she was replaced with a male ruler. The people refused to obey him, and he was later replaced by a female relative of Himiko, a thirteen-year-old girl named Iyo. Not long after Himiko's reign we find another female ruler, Jingu, who was the wife of Emperor Chuai. Jingu often ruled as regent while Chuai was away at war. When her husband died, she ascended to the throne, led a successful invasion of Korea, and ruled for nearly sixty-six years. Eventually, continued relations with China and Korea brought written language to Japan and with it Confucian philosophy, which viewed the masculine principle as superior to the feminine.[49] Although Japan did have several other ruling queens, by 1889 women were forbidden from the office of rulership. Despite women's lowered social and political standing, Japan's emperors continued to claim descent from the sun goddess Amaterasu, who continued to rule the heavens as her queenly representatives had once ruled Japan.

---

49. Sand, *Woman Ruler: Woman Rule*, 196.

Confucian philosophy was not the only thing to migrate from the continent. Buddhism would also find its way to Japan and influence the way the sun was viewed. In 750 CE a monk claimed to have received a divine revelation in which it was revealed that Amaterasu was in fact male, and an aspect of the Buddha. Similarly, in the thirteenth century Amaterasu was masculinized, and her name changed to Ameno-minaka-nushi, the Heavenly Central Lord, a male deity of creation. Neither Amaterasu's name change nor gender reassignment was long-lived or well received by her worshipers.

AMATERASU

A cold winter wind blows across you as you walk through a barren landscape. The trees have long since lost their leaves; the plants and grass around you have become yellowed, dry husks. The few people you see are bundled in several layers of clothes like yourself, attempting to keep warm. Although it is early afternoon, it is as dark as midnight. No sun shines in the sky above. You pass two people with pieces of flint attempting to start a fire. The few sparks they are able to create immediately die, failing to ignite the tinder.

As you continue to walk, the landscape becomes rockier, and the road you walk on spirals up and up a mountain. You climb higher and higher; below you, the houses and people you passed have become small, distant specks. Still higher and higher you climb until wisps of gray clouds begin to swirl around you, and you feel as if you have climbed to the heights of the heavenly realm, the home of the celestial beings of the sky. Just when you feel you cannot climb any farther, you find yourself standing before the jagged opening of a large cave. You step closer and peer into the opening, which is large enough for you to easily step inside without stooping down. Surprisingly, you see a flicker of light. It is only a distant pinprick far in the distance, but clearly visible.

As you watch the distant light flickering and dancing in the dark, the full weight of the cold and darkness of the world weighs heavy on you. You feel it as a deep ache within you, and you try to think back to the last time you felt the light of the sun on your skin or felt the light of inspiration in your heart. Soon you feel an uncontrollable urge to walk toward that spark of illumination, as if it were the only light left in the world.

You take one tentative step inside the cave, then another, and another, until you are submerged in utter darkness. You reach out your hands, touching the rough rock walls of the cave. It is so dark, it feels as if you are floating within the abyss of space. The dancing, flickering light acts as your only guide, and the deeper you travel within the dark, the brighter it becomes. The closer you get to the light, the warmer you begin to feel. After a while you pull off a layer of clothing, and as you do you feel lighter, as if you are not only shedding the fabric but the weight of your problems and the deep sadness that winter has brought as well. You begin to walk faster, moving deeper and deeper into the earth, shedding more layers of heavy fabric, as you move toward the glowing, radiant light.

Soon the darkness around you is almost drowned out by the brilliant light, and you look around you, seeing the light reflect off of hundreds of beautiful gems and crystals that line the cave's walls; they seem to be taking in the light as well, their many facets twinkling in the growing light. Finally you come to a large cavern and the source of the light and warmth. In the cavern's center is a large golden orb of light. It pulses, almost appearing to dance, and you find yourself beginning to sway and hum happily. Something about the light makes you feel alive again. You soak up its warmth and revel in the feel of golden sunlight on your skin. And you know now it is the sun you have found, although why it has retreated from the world to this place you do not know.

The dreariness of winter and the bitter cold of the outside world melt away from your spirit like snow on a spring day. A feeling of joy swells in your heart and slowly you begin to circle around the light, moving your arms, swaying your hips, singing a song full of joyfulness as you move around the cavern. As you do so, you pull off the last few pieces of fabric that cover your body. Free of all that encumbers you, you dance faster and faster. The golden sun pulses faster as if it is dancing with you. You move faster and faster still, laughing with abandon. As you do, the golden orb begins to change. The light shifts and changes until it is no longer a formless orb but a woman glowing and pulsing with the light of the sun. She is dressed in fine silks, her hair a long black waterfall that reaches to her waist. Her face is painted pale, and her full lips a bright red. Her eyes sparkle with joy, yet there is also a sense of agelessness to them, and you know you stand before the goddess Amaterasu, goddess of the sun and divine ruler of the heavens. Silently you wish you could shine as brightly as the goddess before you. You fear when you leave this place, the light and joy you feel now will fade away, the dreariness of the world siphoning it away bit by bit. The goddess smiles kindly at you, and you know she has heard your unspoken thought.

"I am Amaterasu. I rule over all that is, from one edge of the universe to the other. I hold infinity within my golden hands. My light is the expression of my spirit. My will, my joy, my love, my laughter, my capacity for growth and fierceness: this is the core of my light. I am as bright as the sun because I let nothing hinder the glory of my spirit. And so I am the heavenly orb, the sun that illuminates the world. From me all darkness and evil flee. I am the glory of the spirit unhindered."

She gently touches your cheek, and as you look into her eyes you see the burning light of the sun. "Yet even I must at times *take refuge in the womb of the earth, to gather my light again, before I can rise anew. For it is only in times of darkness that we truly learn to shine our brightest. Without plunging into the dark, we never learn to value the light. You have traveled my path, so it is only fitting that you bring my renewed light back into the world above."*

The goddess leans forward and embraces you, and as she does you feel the full force of her light fill you. It radiates from your heart, traveling down through your arms, up to your brow, and down to the tips of your toes, until your mind, body, and spirit are filled with the golden light of Amaterasu. A flash of light fills the cavern, momentarily blinding you. When you open your eyes, the goddess has vanished. You look down and see you now wear the fine silks the goddess had worn moments ago. You look wonderingly at your hands and arms, which now glow with a golden light, and you know the light of the sun burns within you.

Confidently, you turn toward the passageway that brought you here. The cave is no longer dark, the light within you easily illuminating your way as you climb up and up. When you reach the cave entrance, you step out into the world. Reaching your arms up toward the sky, you let your light shine forth into the world, knowing that whenever you feel the darkness of the world suffocating your spirit, you can call upon Amaterasu to illuminate your way, just as she illuminates the world each day.

The radiant Japanese sun goddess Amaterasu is the guardian of agriculture, spinning, fertility, abundance, balance, and order. Her name means "she who shines in heaven" or "great shining heaven." Amaterasu (pronounced *ah-mah-ta-rah-soo*) protected rice fields, invented irrigation canals, and still found time to weave cloth for the rest of the gods. She had a three-legged crow (in some myths he has eight legs) named Yata-Garasu, who acted as her messenger, although in some myths Amaterasu herself could transform into a crow instead. To this day she is considered to be the ancestral mother of the Imperial Household and remains the central divinity in the Shinto pantheon.

There are three different versions of Amaterasu's birth. In one version, the god Izanagi and the goddess Izanami decide to create a supreme deity to rule over the world, and create Amaterasu to fill that role. In a later myth, Amaterasu emerges fully formed from a copper mirror the god Izanagi was holding. In yet another version, the goddess Izanami dies and her husband descends to Yomi, the Japanese underworld, to rescue her. Unfortunately, by the time Izanagi found his wife's spirit, she had already eaten food from the hearth of Yomi and could no longer return to the world of the living. When Izanagi emerged from Yomi, he ritually purified himself in a river. While washing his face, Amaterasu sprang forth from his left eye.

When all the gods were born, Izanagi decided that Amaterasu was the most fit to rule the six quarters: north, south, east, west, the world above and below. He gathered the gods before him and took off his magickal necklace, named Mi-Kura-Tana-No-Kami, and began to shake the beads. Then he placed the necklace around Amaterasu's neck, and by doing so bestowed rulership over all creation to her. Amaterasu's magickal necklace was said to be made of jade *magatama* beads. Magatama is a type of curved bead with a flaring tail that dates back to Neolithic Japan. They represent the spirit and were generally worn for good luck. In this case the magatama necklace takes on part of Izanagi's essence, symbolized by ritually shaking it. By putting his essence or spirit into the necklace, he conferred his own power to Amaterasu.

Despite ruling the heavens, Amaterasu didn't always get along with the other gods, and many of her myths revolve around the disputes and quarrels she has with them. Like many sun goddesses, she weds the god of the moon, Tsuki-yomi, but ultimately his actions force them to part ways. Her brother, the storm god Susano-o, also attempts to make the sun goddess's life difficult with his wild behavior.

One of Amaterasu's first tasks as the ruler of heaven was to provide humanity with food. To do so, she asked her husband, the moon god, to search for Ukemochi, the goddess of food. When Tsuki-yomi found Ukemochi, he asked her to give him enough food to feed all of humanity. Immediately, Ukemochi began vomiting fish, rice, and animals. Then she began pulling more food from her nostrils and rectum. Although she had an odd way of preparing the food, everything she placed before the moon god was exceptionally delicious. Disgusted by the manner in which Ukemochi created the food, Tsuki-yomi drew his sword and killed her.

Appalled by his violence, Amaterasu ordered him to be eternally separate from her, and this is why the moon only comes out at night when the sun is no longer in the sky. Then Amaterasu set out to find Ukemochi's corpse. In death Ukemochi's body had transformed into various types of food. Beans grew from her nose and rice from her belly, and her eyebrows transformed into two silkworms. Amaterasu placed the worms in Ukemochi's mouth and began to spin thread; with the strands, she invented weaving.

While the moon god abides by Amaterasu's wishes, her interaction with her brother is more volatile. Their constant quarreling reflects the battle between chaos, represented by Susano-o's erratic behavior, and order, represented by Amaterasu. In one story, Susano-o came to Amaterasu after having caused a great deal of trouble in heaven. Susano-o claimed his intentions were good, but wary of her brother's antics, Amaterasu made him submit to a ritual test in order to prove his good intent. Susano-o said he would give birth, and if the children were males, it would prove his intentions were peaceful. Susano-o took five of Amaterasu's jewels and cracked them open with his teeth, and five gods jumped out of them. Amaterasu complained that he did not succeed since he created the gods from her jewels, but Susano-o was so pleased with his creations that he tore through the world, destroying rice fields and leaving his feces on Amaterasu's throne. At first the goddess ignored her brother's antics, but when he tossed a skinned horse through the roof of her weaving room, which frightened one of her ladies-in-waiting to death, she decided to take action. Enraged by her brother's behavior, she shut herself in a cave, leaving the world cold and dark without the light of the sun.

Without the sun goddess, the outside world was plunged into a perpetual darkness; plants withered; and people died from the bitter cold. All of the eight million gods gathered outside the cave and pleaded with Amaterasu to return, but she refused to leave her cave. In their desperation, the other gods left presents outside the cave to lure Amaterasu out, but nothing they offered her enticed her to return to the world. Finally, the shaman Uzume, the goddess of merriment, took action. She hung a mirror and a magatama necklace (it's unclear whether this is the same necklace given to Amaterasu by her father or a different one) on a tree branch in front of the cave, then she stood on top of a washtub and began to dance.

Her dance turned into a comical striptease, with the shamaness revealing her vulva, and all the gods began to laugh. Inside the cave, Amaterasu heard their laughter and called to them, asking what was going on. Uzume replied that they had found a more beautiful goddess to take her place. Curious, Amaterasu cracked open the door to the cave and saw her reflection in the mirror. Having never seen her reflection, Amaterasu was dazzled by the brilliance of her own image. While she was distracted, the other gods tied a rope to the cave door to hold it open, preventing the sun goddess from retreating back into the cave. The mirror Amaterasu saw when she emerged from the cave is said to be the one housed in her shrine in Ise, and remains one of the most treasured relics of the Shinto religion.

Magatama beads were used in early Japanese shamanic practices and were believed to be able to either house a spirit or to help draw a spirit into a shaman.[50] The beads could also be used to call upon the spirit of the deceased in order to bind or banish them.[51] With this in mind, we can view Uzume's dance as a shamanic rite. She uses the magatama necklace to call Amaterasu's spirit back from the dead and to bind it to the world of the living.[52] Amaterasu's retreats to the cave can be seen as a symbolic descent into the underworld. She leaves the world in a state of darkness and cold, much as the weak light of the winter sun heralds the cold, dark half of the year. This also gives significance to Uzume's striptease. She exposes her vulva in a symbolic act of rebirthing the sun. When Amaterasu emerges from the cave, she is leaving the symbolic womb of the earth to be reborn, making Uzume's dance an act of sympathetic magick.

As punishment for having made the sun goddess retreat from the world, Susano-o had his fingernails and toenails torn off and was banished from the heavens. Despite being banished, one especially rainy night Susano-o went to the houses of each of the gods and begged for lodging. Unwilling to anger the sun goddess, all of the other gods turned him away. Finally he came to Amaterasu's door and begged for lodging. Assuming he came to cause more trouble, and finally having had enough of her brother's mischief, Amaterasu prepared herself to face Susano-o. She tied her skirts to the sides of her legs so that they resembled trousers, wound her hair on her head with jewels, and took up three swords and a quiver of fifteen hundred arrows. With a bow in one hand and a sword in another, she danced, singing spells and incantations and kicking up the soil around her. The sight was so terrifying that Susano-o ran from her and never set foot in the heavens again.

---

50. Matsumae, "The Heavenly Rock-Grotto Myth and the Chinkon Ceremony," 18–19.
51. Ebersole, *Ritual, Poetry and the Politics of Death in Early Japan*, 96.
52. Ibid., 98.

Amaterasu is the ultimate multitasker. She rules the heavens and takes care of her rice fields. She's innovative, inventing spinning and weaving; she makes all the clothes for the multitude of gods; and she has to deal with the antics of her brother. Like most sun deities, she displays an abundant nature. She provides the gods and humanity with food; she gives them the gift of weaving and shows them how to irrigate their fields, but Amaterasu's greatest lesson is that of renewal and harmony.

In some ways Amaterasu is trying to do too many things all at once; the stress becomes too much and she needs to leave the world behind. Like Persephone, she needs to travel to the inner darkness of the earth, to the realms of the underworld, to be renewed. It isn't until she has emerged from the darkness of her cave that she finds the strength and resolve to finally deal with Susano-o. While patient and lenient with her brother in the past, she emerges from the darkness with a new fire, taking on the guise of a warrior goddess and challenging her brother. She no longer allows herself to be stepped on and pushed around by Susano-o. It isn't until she stands up for herself that he finally leaves the heavens and she is free of his destructive antics. Amaterasu is only able to bring harmony back to her world when she has restored her own inner balance.

WORKING WITH AMATERASU

Amaterasu can help us restore our own inner harmony and bring balance into our lives. We all have encountered our own personal Susano-o, a person who drags us into their self-made drama and causes havoc in our lives. Amaterasu teaches us how to stand up to these individuals and how to claim our own inner fires. As a goddess of abundance and agriculture, she can also be called upon for prosperity and to ensure successful endeavors. As a mother goddess and the inventor of weaving, she teaches us that we are all connected, that we are all threads in the tapestry of life that she weaves.

Amaterasu's primary symbol is the mirror, making her an excellent goddess to invoke for mirror magick. When invoking this goddess or when creating an altar dedicated to her, a mirror can be used in place of a statue to represent Amaterasu. The sword and necklace are also her symbols. When she sent her grandson, Ninigi, down to rule the earth, she gave him the mirror that had coaxed her out of her cave, her jewels, and a sword named Kusanagi. She then instructed Ninigi to adore the mirror as if it were her.[53] The necklace or jewels that Amaterasu wears are symbols of abundance and spiritual power. When Izanagi gave her his necklace, she became the ruler of heaven, and it's from her jewels that Susano-o births his divine creations.

A beaded necklace, especially one with magatama beads, can be worn to call upon Amaterasu's authority and power. Her magatama necklace takes the place of a crown, for she is the queen and ruler of heaven. The necklace is somewhat reminiscent of the *torc* (a woven band of metal) worn by Celtic kings and queens as a symbol of sovereignty. Both the mirror and necklace form a circle. After all, a necklace is a circle, simply a malleable one, that encircles the neck, and most mirrors are also made in the shape of a circle. The circle or wheel is a common symbol that we will find connected to the solar feminine, symbolizing the connection to the life cycle and the sun's yearly cycle. Both symbols imitate the shape of the sun and reflect Amaterasu's connection to order and balance.

As is the case for many of the solar goddess, we will be exploring, horses, particularly white ones, were sacred to Amaterasu. The sacred stables at Amaterasu's shrine at Ise still house horses that are led before the central sanctuary three times each month.[54] Japan's emperors, who claimed descent from her, traditionally rode a white horse on special occasions.[55]

---

53. Leeming and Page, *Goddess: Myths of the Female Divine*, 57.
54. Eidelberg, *The Biblical Hebrew Origin of the Japanese People*, 16.
55. Volker, *The Animal in Far Eastern Art*, 102.

AMATERASU INVOCATION

Use the following invocation to call upon Amaterasu in your darkest hour or whenever you need a little sunshine in your life. Ideally, you should dance or simply sway back and forth as you say the invocation, as it was Uzume's magickal dance that enticed the sun's return.

> *Amaterasu*
> *Great lady of heaven*
> *My heart is heavy*
> *I dwell in darkness*
> *It is as if you have returned to the cave*
> *I yearn for your light,*
> *For the warmth of the sun*
> *Amaterasu, hear my prayer*
> *Shine your golden rays upon my sorrows*
> *I am dancing for you, Amaterasu*
> *I am dancing*
> *as Uzume danced for you*
> *Amaterasu, bring the dawn!*

. . . .
AMATERASU SUN DEVOTION

The following is based on a daily devotion still performed in honor of Amaterasu in Japan today. Practitioners face the east and greet the sun by clapping twice, saying prayers and offering the goddess gifts of water and rice at the beginning of each day.[56]

To connect with Amaterasu and draw upon her blessings, you can do this devotion each morning for several days. You may wish to wake at sunrise to honor her, but performing the devotion when you wake up is also fine. I prefer to pick one thing in particular I wish to

---

56. Kinsley, *The Goddesses' Mirror: Vision of the Divine from East to West*, 87.

ask Amaterasu to bring into my life and perform the devotion each morning for several days with my intended goal in mind.

If you wish, you may leave Amaterasu an offering as part of your morning devotion. The traditional offering of water can be poured outside after the devotion. Offerings of incense or rice would be appropriate.

Stand facing the east with your feet slightly apart. If possible, stand near a window where you can see the light of the sun. Take a deep, cleansing breath. Clap twice. Then, holding your hands palms upward in the goddess position, say:

> *Amaterasu*
> *Great kami of the sun,*
> *Whose radiance illuminates both heaven and earth*
> *Shine your blessing upon me*
> *Bless me with (patience, health, etc.) this day!*

See the light of Amaterasu filling your body with each breath. When you are ready, clap your hands twice again. Leave your offering to Amaterasu on your altar.

. . . .
MIRROR AND CANDLE SPELL

You Will Need:
1 white candle
4 small mirrors

For this spell you will be using the mirror's reflective qualities to amplify your magick. The size of the mirrors are not important. Small mirrors are the easiest to work with, are inexpensive, and can be found in your local craft store. A mirror used for everyday tasks would not be ideal for magick. Mirrors have long been considered doorways to the spirit realm and can retain the vibrations of those who touch and look into them. The mirrors you use for spellwork should never be used for anything else.

The next part will differ depending on the type of spellwork you are doing. If, for example, you want to attract prosperity, make an infusion of basil and wash the surface of the mirror with the water. Then leave the mirror outside in a sunny spot or on a windowsill where it can catch the light of the sun, for at least an hour. By doing so, you are charging the mirror with the sun's energies, as well as the energy of the herb. If you are doing a spell for winning a court case, you could use an infusion of bay leaves; for love, chamomile; for any kind of psychic work, eyebright. The trick is to use an herb connected to both the sun and the desired outcome of your spellwork. For a list of herbs connected to the sun, see page 271.

Place the candle in the center of your sacred space. If you wish, inscribe it with your desired goal. You could also anoint it with the same infusion you used on the mirrors or with corresponding oil. If you are drawing something to you, anoint the candle from wick to base. To banish something, anoint it from the base to the wick. Place the mirrors around the candle, with one in each cardinal direction, so that when lit, the candle's flame will reflect in the mirrors. (Most craft stores sell small plastic stands that can be used to prop the mirrors up. Stands made for holding decorative plates will work just as well for your magick mirrors.) If you wish, cast a circle. Ground and center, then invoke Amaterasu by saying:

Amaterasu, who shines in the heavens
Ruler of the six directions
Most brilliant Lady of the sun
Cast upon me your loving gaze
Let my will and yours be one!

Light the candle and visualize your desired goal. Visualize the sun's light shining through the mirrors, filling the candle with the vital, life-giving power of the sun, adding to your will and fueling your magick.

Let the candle burn out. Store the mirrors in a place they will not be disturbed. Before using the mirrors again, wash them with salt water to cleanse them.

To cleanse the mirrors, wash them with an infusion of angelica, then wrap them in fabric and put them somewhere they will not be disturbed.

....
CREATING AMATERASU'S MIRROR
You Will Need:
1 small mirror
1 small bowl of sake
1 bowl of water
1 small bowl of rice
1 soft cloth

When Amaterasu gave humanity her sacred mirror, she instructed people to worship the mirror as if it were herself. Today in Shinto temples and home shrines, mirrors are used in place of statues to represent the great kami. Besides being a sun symbol, the mirror reminds us that the divine dwells within each of us. Just as Amaterasu was mesmerized by the radiance of her own image when she emerged from her cave, when we gaze into Amaterasu's mirror we must remember to see ourselves as part of her divine being.

Dedicating a mirror to Amaterasu is very similar to blessing a statue of a god or goddess. The mirror can be used on an altar to represent the goddess. It can also be used for mirror magick to draw upon her energy. Finding the right type of mirror for your needs is essential. Some people prefer to use a decorative mirror that can be hung on a wall. There are many inexpensive fantasy mirrors on the market that can be both beautiful additions to your home and an excellent tool for magick. Some also have candleholders or ledges attached that can serve as a combination altar and magick mirror. As with the magickal mirrors in the previous spell, the mirror you choose to dedicate to Amaterasu should not be used for anything else. Think of it as choosing an altar statue; while not the likeness of the goddess, it will act as a representation of the divine. A small portable mirror will work just fine and can be placed on an altar to represent Amaterasu. Your mirror does not have to be fancy; a plain mirror purchased from a craft store will work just as well as an ornately decorated one.

You may also wish to decorate your mirror. On the back of my mirror I wrote Amaterasu's name along the border. You could also draw her symbols, such as the sword or phoenix, with a permanent marker on the back or front of the mirror. As Amaterasu's necklace of power is prominent in her myths, I also have a magatama bead necklace that I drape around my mirror during rituals.

Once you have selected your mirror, you will need to bless and charge it. To do this, take the mirror, the small bowl of water, and the bowl of sake to a sunny place outside. Hold the bowl of sake in your hands and lift it toward the sun. See the light of the sun filling the sake. Then, using the cloth, gently wash the surface of the mirror with the sake. Next take the bowl of water and hold it up to the sun, seeing its light fill the water. Using the cloth, gently wash the surface of the mirror with the water. Finally, hold the mirror toward the sun, so that its light touches the mirror's surface. Say:

Amaterasu, gaze upon your brilliance
As you first did when the gods beckoned you to leave your dark cave
Queen of the Heavens
Goddess of the sun
I bless this mirror in your name,
That when I look upon it I shall see your radiant face

Leave the mirror where the sun can shine upon it for at least an hour. Pour any remaining water and sake on the ground as an offering to Amaterasu. Place the mirror on your altar, or wrap it in soft fabric until you wish to call upon Amaterasu's power.

Amaterasu Mirror Divination

You Will Need:
1 mirror
A bowl of water or sake

Sit comfortably in front of your mirror (ideally this should be a mirror dedicated to Amaterasu or one that you use for magick). Relax and take three deep breaths. Take a moment to consider your question. Hold it clearly in your mind, or state it out loud. Gaze into the mirror and softly chant Amaterasu's name. Try not to concentrate on any one particular thing within the mirror; just allow your gaze to be relaxed. It is perfectly okay to blink. You may see images within the mirror or simply have a sense of knowing the answer to your question. When you are done, pour the bowl of water or sake outside as an offering to Amaterasu.

Amaterasu Incense

2 parts cedar
½ part lavender
½ part rose petals

Amaterasu Correspondences

Animals: crow, horse
Symbols: necklace, mirror, sword
Colors: gold, yellow, green
Stone: jade

THE BALTS

Part of the area along the Baltic Sea, now modern-day Lithuania and Latvia, is unique in the fact that its people held onto their Pagan traditions longer than any other region in Europe. Early attempts to convert the Baltic people to Christianity were met with little success. In 1009 CE, missionary Bruno of Querfurt was beheaded for destroying statues of the gods and violating a holy forest. By the twelfth century, the Pagan Balts stood wedged between the Orthodox East and the Catholic West. After a failed campaign in the Holy Lands, Pope Alexander III declared a crusade against the Pagans of northern Europe in 1171 CE, beginning three hundred years of holy war against the stubbornly Pagan Balts.

While their neighbors embraced the new religion, Lithuania remained the last Pagan nation in Europe, until 1386. Christianity officially became the state religion of Lithuania when Grand Duke Jogaila was baptized as a condition of his marriage to the princess of Poland. Western Lithuania fervently resisted the new state religion and remained Pagan until the early 1400s. In the countryside, Pagan practices were never fully suppressed and at times were practiced alongside Christianity. Catholic chroniclers throughout the seventeenth and eighteenth centuries complained of the Lithuanians' lack of interest in the new religion. Although they baptized their children, Lithuanians continued to honor the old Pagan holidays and their folk traditions.

Fortunately, the Baltic people's resolve to hold on to their customs has preserved a rich tradition where the feminine sun holds particular importance. Although Baltic Paganism was primarily an oral tradition, its myths have been preserved in the form of folk songs and hymns, called *dainas*, which recount the exploits of the Baltic gods. Within the dainas, the sun goddess Saule and her sun-maiden daughter are spoken of often and with great fondness, attesting to the love and esteem the Baltic people held for the sun.

In Baltic mythology, gods of the sky and earth were of primary importance. Like the Baltic people who were primarily farmers, the sky gods farmed and made their homes on the hill of the sky. And it is this hill that the sun goddess Saule climbed each day as she moved across the sky realm.

Fire was believed to be inherently feminine and particularly sacred, making it no surprise that the Balts should envision the sun, the ultimate source of fire, as feminine as well. The Greeks described Balts as "pyrolatrians," or fire worshipers, for a grove or place of worship was not complete without its sacred flame. Several times a year, the sun maiden Auszrine was said to visit family hearths, and there were many superstitions concerning fire. Fire was regarded as a living thing; it represented not only warmth and light but was also symbolic of the ancestors, who were believed to watch over the family beside the hearth.

A bowl of clean water was left near the hearth fire so that the spirit of the fire could wash herself, and offerings to the gods were thrown into the hearth fire. Sacred fires were tended by priests atop hills and alongside rivers. Hearth fires were never allowed to go out, except at midsummer when they were extinguished and ritually relit. Kicking, stomping, or spitting into any kind of fire was considered disrespectful and could incur bad luck.[57] Eventually, as Pagan shrines were destroyed, the home hearth became the focal point for religious practices.

The sun goddess was especially honored during the festival of Lingo, the summer solstice, when Saule was believed to dance for

---

57. Balys, *Treasure Chest of Lithuanian Folklore*, 39.

joy in the sky. During the festival, women wore folk costumes with beaded coronets and streaming ribbons to symbolize the rays of the sun. While in this garb, they were called Daughters of the Sun and became the embodiment of the sun goddess upon earth.[58] During Kaledos, the winter solstice, images of the sun were carried through the fields to encourage the sun's fertile blessings.

In more recent times, the folk traditions of the Baltic people have seen a notable renaissance, particularly after the dissolution of the Soviet Union. Under the name *Romuva*, Baltic Paganism was officially recognized in 1995 as a legitimate religion by the Lithuanian government. Like their ancestors who greeted the sun each morning and sang loving songs in her honor, the sun goddess remains an important divinity within the Baltic Pagan revival.

SAULE

You find yourself standing on the edge of a cliff. Below, the ocean waves gently crash against the rocky cliff face. As the sky darkens, you watch as the sun dips low on the horizon. It is a rosy orange color, and you think for a moment you can discern shapes at the heart of the orb's light. For a second you think you see horses with manes of fire and a woman standing tall in a chariot. But as you blink, the image is gone.

You watch the sun sink lower and lower, but as it just touches the horizon and the ocean waters, something unexpected happens. The sun's light falters, and falls in on itself until it is a fiery comet falling from the sky—down, down into the waters. You hear a loud roar as the comet hits the water, and you see a faint orange glow deep in the waters as it falls through the depths. Darkness descends around you. There is a heavy feel in the air. It is a night that will never end, without a sun to rise anew to chase away the shadows. All seems lost until you notice

---

58. Benjamins, *Dearest Goddess: Translations from Latvian Folk Poetry*, vii.

something twinkle upon the shore below. It is faint, but there is a shimmering of light.

Slowly you climb down to the beach. It is a slow descent, but finally your feet touch cool, wet sand. The small twinkling light is brighter here. Just where the sea foam meets the shore, a small amber stone gives off a faint light. You pick it up in your hand and realize it is amber. An amber teardrop, a tear of the sun goddess Saule. You cup the stone in your hands and bring it close to your lips, and whisper the goddess's name. It comes out half a prayer, half a plea: "Saule."

As soon as the name leaves your lips, the sand begins to move. It spirals around your feet, falling in on itself, forming a pit like a tunnel deep within the earth. You peer down, holding out the teardrop for light, and see that there are spiral steps leading down into the dark. You know where this must lead. The realm deep within the earth is the place of the dead, and that is where you must go to rescue the sun.

Tentatively you place your foot on the first step. The stone is cold and solid on your bare feet. Step by step you descend into the deep. Soon, true darkness, darker and deeper than the one in the world above, envelops you. But the farther down you travel, the brighter the amber teardrop begins to glisten and shine. After what seems like hours, you come to the end of the stone stairs. It opens to a small chamber with a large door. Feeling compelled to move forward, you stand before the door and touch the surface. It is made from bone-colored stone. It feels cold and smooth under your hand. But soon you realize there is no handle. You push and try to pull at the carved surface to no avail.

Just when you feel you will never get past the obstacle before you, you hear a sound. The earth is shifting and reforming behind you. You turn in time to see a figure emerging from the very earth itself. Her skin is the color and texture of freshly turned soil; her eyes glisten as if made from a thousand precious gems; and her clothes are twisted vines and roots. She smiles at you and says, "Do not fear. I am the very earth, mother to all that grows and draws breath in the world above. I am the guardian of those who are laid to rest in the realms below, and I am the first of the children of Saule. I too am a daughter of the sun, and I know why you have come."

She touches an earthen hand to your shoulder and turns you toward the door once again. "Know this: everything that passes through the land of the dead changes, even the sun. And no road traveled within this realm can be trod a second time. You will not be able to come back the way you came, but I promise there is a way to return to the world of life above if you can find it."

She extends a hand, and you see a key of white stone in it. She gives you the key, and when you look up again, she is gone. You stand alone again, deep within the earth, at the threshold of the doors of death. When you look at the door again, you see there is a keyhole. Unwavering in your resolve to bring light back to the world, you unlock the door.

As soon as the key slides into place, the door, key, and cavern vanish. You find yourself instead standing on a grassy lakeshore. You blink, your eyes adjusting to the light. It is bright as day here. You look up and see you are in a vast underground cave. The ceiling high, high above is covered in stalactites. Ahead a vast lake reaches out as far as you can see. There are distant shores in either direction; on them wispy forms gather in groups by the water's edge. They seem excited about something. Some point enthusiastically toward something in the middle of the water, and you see that this is where the light is brightest.

As you squint, trying to see the source of the light better, something nudges your arm. With a start you see a pair of horses standing patiently beside you. One mare snorts and stomps an impatient hoof. The pair are harnessed to a golden chariot. The chariot and the horses shine with a light that radiates from within, casting them in a golden halo of light. This is the chariot of the sun, the same one Saule rides across the sky each day. They must have fallen with the goddess into the ocean. The horse that nudged you gestures with a regal head to the empty chariot. If anyone can help you find the missing goddess, surely it would be these two.

As soon as you step into the chariot, the horses take off toward the lake. As their hooves touch the water, both they and the chariot begin to transform. The chariot is now a golden boat gliding through the water, pulled by a pair of huge swans. Soon the shore is gone and the sunlight grows brighter as you come to the source of the light. On a small sandbar in the center of the lake stands Saule. Honey-colored hair falls in waves around her face. Her silken, embroidered dress glitters and dances like living flame. Her face is motherly, and as she looks at you, there is no doubt within you that you are her child and that she loves you. Everything about her radiates this love.

As the boat slides upon the sandbar, you call to her to come with you. You tell her you have come to free her from this place. Expecting her to come to the boat, you are confused when she stands still and looks out to the shadowy figures that have gathered on the distant shores to see her light. "These are my children too. How can I leave now? They have been away from my light for so long, and they have welcomed me so lovingly. I cannot abandon them."

You begin to tell the goddess what the world above is like now without her presence; you plea for all the life that will die without her light; and you tell her the reasons you need her light in your life. She considers your words, and finally nods and steps into the boat. The swans pull the boat toward the other end of the lake. The ghosts follow your progress and wave, calling out to the sun goddess as she passes.

Finally, you come to a rock wall. There is no shore here; the dark waters lap against the rocky wall that stretches ever upward, and for a moment you worry you will be trapped in the land of the dead forever. Then Saule steps to the bow of the boat. She reaches down into the water, and it froths and swirls at her touch. "I am Mother to the universe, to the earth and the stars of heaven. I am consort to the moon and sky. I am the spark that kindles new life. I burn away, and I stir that which is stagnant to renewal. All flows from my light, and to all I will light the way, in death, in life, in times of joy and times of trial. I am the light that guides the spirit, forever into eternity." The water spirals upward, imbued with the light of Saule, and as it crashes against the stone it carves a tunnel, a tunnel that reaches upward, flowing with light-filled water.

Saule looks out to the shades and ghosts on the shore. "I have passed through life to death and will pass thusly each day. I will ride my chariot through the sky and bring my light to the world of the living during the day, and at night I will pass into the world of the dead and be the light in the darkness to all who have passed."

The golden boat bears you upward in a rush of water and light. And as you explode into the world above, the swans and boat transform again to the mares of Saule and the chariot of the sun. It launches into the sky, and the world is filled with the brilliance of dawn. As you ride with Saule, you know that you will always have Saule's light within you. And you know that no matter what trial you face, what place you find yourself in, the goddess of the sun will always be there to bring light and energy into your life.

To the Balts the goddess Saule (pronounced *SOW-lay*) was a loving and radiant mother who watched over her earthly children as she journeyed across the sky each day. As a goddess of creation, light, and agriculture, she plays a central role in the mythology of the Latvians and Lithuanians. She is lovingly mentioned in hundreds of dainas, traditional folk songs. She is the patroness of orphans and the unfortunate. She is not only mother to humanity but also a cosmic mother who gave birth to the earth. All life could trace its origins to her.

Saule's name translates simply to "sun," connecting her directly to the sun and its energies. She is said to have created the world from an egg-shaped mass, which she warmed with her golden light. Each day she was attended by her daughters, the evening and morning stars, who may be different aspects of herself. She watched over orphans and was called upon to find lost livestock. When she wept, her tears turned into amber or red berries. One daina describes how a peasant pleaded with a particularly cruel overlord not to be whipped until the sun was in the sky so that Saule could weep for him, and presumably avenge him.[59] In this aspect, she, like many solar deities, is a divine eye in the sky. She sees all wrongdoing and can find that which is lost or hidden, not unlike the Celtic Sulis, who was petitioned for similar reasons.

The Balts envisioned the sky as a mystical sky-hill where the gods lived and built their homes. Seeing the sky as a hill explained why the sun began her journey low in the sky, presumably at the bottom of the sky-hill, and rose as she climbed toward the top. It was across this sky-hill that Saule rode her golden chariot each day. She had two horses, one made of gold, the other of diamonds, who never tired. At times she was said to drive nine chariots pulled by one hundred horses. The large number of horses drawing her chariot is considered by some to show the importance of the sun goddess, as other important sky gods in the pantheon are also said to have chariots driven

---

59. McCrickard, *Eclipse of the Sun*, 108.

by numerous horses.[60] The number of horses and chariots may also represent the heat of the summer sun, as opposed to the weaker rays of the winter sun when Saule rides in a single chariot, which may represent winter. When she tired, Saule rested in the branches of a rowan tree (or a birch tree, depending on the version). While she rested, the sun stood still in the sky, explaining why at noon the sun appears still in the sky.[61]

Saule had many children, but it was Auszrine and Wakarine, the morning and evening stars, that helped their mother on her journey each day. The sisters looked after her house and accompanied Saule through the underworld during the night. The morning star lit Saule's fire at dawn, and was considered both a goddess of dawn and the hearth. Wakarine, the evening star, lit Saule's fire during the evening and prepared the goddess's bed.

At the end of the day, Saule washed her horses in the sea and tended her apple orchards far in the west. Sometimes she was said to sleep in the branches of the apple trees. Then she sailed in a golden boat pulled by swans to the east to begin her journey again. In some stories, Saule falls into the ocean as she descends from the sky-hill and drowns. The evening and morning stars plead with the earth goddess, who also ruled over death, to allow the sun to return to the world. Feeling pity for her mother, the earth gave Saule's daughters the keys that allowed entrance to the land of the dead, and they soon rescue their mother from the underworld.

In the beginning of time, Saule married the moon god Menesis. The moon was only one of Saule's husbands, as she was also married to the sky god Dievas and the storm god Perkunas (also called Perkons). They were happy for a time and once moved across the sky together. In some stories they grow unhappy with each other and divorce, but each wants custody of their eldest daughter, the earth. They cannot come

---

60. McGrath, *The Sun Goddess: Myth, Legend and History*, 41.
61. Varner, *The Mythic Forest: The Green Man and the Spirit of Nature*, 63.

to an agreement so each visits the earth separately, the sun by day and moon by night.

In another version, Menesis falls in love with the morning star, whom Saule had promised in marriage to the twin sons of Dievas. Sometimes the moon rapes the morning star; other times she is his willing lover. When Saule discovers her husband's adultery, she falls into a rage and slashes him with her sword. The scars left from her sword can still be seen on the face of the moon today. In some versions it is the storm god Perkunas who slashes and dismembers the moon, explaining the way in which the moon shrinks each month, as the god is hacked into smaller and smaller pieces.

In other stories, Saule banishes her daughter from the heavens for becoming lovers with the moon. No longer welcome in her mother's realm, the morning star traveled to the earth to preside over the family hearth as a goddess of fire. In this version, the union between the morning star and the moon seems to be consensual.

Most likely Auszrine and Saule are two aspects of the same goddess. Auszrine doubles as both a star goddess and a sun maiden. Stars after all are distant suns, and the morning star's light is treated as a weaker, younger version of her mother, the sun. Some stories say that Saule grows weary of her daily travels across the sky on the winter solstice and steps down from her position in favor of her daughter. This explains why the sun's light grows weaker and weaker up until the day of the solstice, when it is reborn and the days grow steadily warmer.

One folktale tells of a young man who saw two suns in the sky at dawn and dusk, but only one during the day. He traveled to the home of the sun goddess and discovered the second sun he had seen was her daughter, the sun maiden Auszrine, attending her mother. It is clear from this story that Auszrine was also considered a sun goddess as well.

It is also significant that the twin sons of Dievas court Auszrine. If she was a dual goddess, embodying two different natures, it would make sense that the man courting her would appear in a similar form, bearing two faces just as the sun goddess does. The fact that both Saule and Auszrine are the moon god's lovers also hints that they may be the same goddess. The moon god taking the young sun maiden as his lover may reflect the cycle of the seasons. He is consort to the young sun from the winter solstice through spring, while he is husband to the mature sun mother during summer and fall, remaining at her side throughout her ever-renewing cycle.

At times Saule is referred to as either the "sun virgin" or "sun mother," emphasizing her dual aspects. Other descriptions Saule was given are *balta saulele*, meaning "dear little white sun," and *skaisti saulele*, meaning "dear little red sun." White represented joy and goodness in general to the Balts, and it is this color they associated with Saule as the mother sun. The "little red sun" seems to refer to her younger self, as either Auszrine or Wakarine, who represented dawn and sunset when the sun turned a rosy color.

Saule's marriage to Perkunas seems happier than her relationship with the moon. The connection between sun goddesses and storm goddesses is common in many cultures. The Japanese sun goddess Amaterasu's brother, and the cause of most of her problems, is also a storm god. But unlike the mischievous Japanese storm god, Perkunas is a benevolent god who ruled over thunder and rain. He is associated with fertility, as the rain he brought fertilized the land and made the crops flourish. Thunder was said to be the rumbling sound of his goat-drawn chariot as he went across the cloud-filled sky. At times Saule and Perkunas are at odds. He is said to make her laundry, the clouds, dirty. And his dark storm clouds obscure Saule's radiance. In folk songs Saule is called upon to banish the work of her husband, and to send storms and foul weather elsewhere in the world. The cold of winter was believed to be caused by evil spirits, and each year

Perkunas helped the sun overcome the cold of winter by smiting the winter spirits with his axe. Bonfires were also lit at this time to help the sun goddess recover from the darkness of winter.[62]

The Christian missionary Jerome of Prague, who visited Lithuania in the early fifteenth century, recounted a story in which Saule was once rescued by the signs of the zodiac with a giant hammer. Jerome had found the locals worshiping a hammer, which they told him was the very same weapon used to free the sun goddess. In the story recounted by Jerome, Saule was captured and held in a tower by a powerful king. Like the mythology of other sun goddesses, Saule retreats from the world, or in this case is held prisoner. The signs of the zodiac rescued Saule, using a giant hammer to free her from her prison. This myth most likely explained why the sun's light grows weaker in the winter. Once the imprisoned sun is freed, her light once again warms the earth, bringing with it the fruitfulness and warmth of summer.

Little is mentioned of Saule's relationship with her third husband, Dievas. He is a god of the sky and at times is either confused with or given as another name for the moon god Menesis.[63] His twin sons courted Saule's daughter the morning star and were sometimes depicted in the form of two stallions pulling Saule's chariot. At other times they pulled the chariot of the moon through the sky. The twins sons of Dievas are sometimes described in folk songs as the morning and evening stars, roles Saule's daughters Auszrine and Wakarine also fill. Saule and Dievas each appear to form a kind of trinity. Auszrine represents the maiden sun who rules over dawn, Saule the mother sun, and Wakarine the waning setting sun. Dievas and his sons may represent the waxing and waning of the moon, if he is in fact another aspect of Menesis, or another triple form of the god that mirrors Saule's changing faces.

---

62. McGrath, *The Sun Goddess: Myth, Legend and History*, 37.
63. Ibid., 40.

WORKING WITH SAULE

Unlike the more destructive sun goddesses of warmer continents, Saule's personality is that of a mother goddess. She is the patroness of orphans and the unfortunate, a celestial mother always looking down lovingly at her earthly children. In general it seems sun goddesses of temperate climates take on this role more often than their sisters closer to the equator. In warmer climates the sun goddess takes on a more warlike face. Saule's warrior side only appears when her children are wronged, as when she strikes Menesis with her sword after he defiles their daughter. Even in her fiercer aspects, her anger is directed at righting wrongs and protecting those she loves, especially her family.

Saule is an excellent goddess to work with when dealing with family problems. When family members fight or when tensions run high between you and a loved one, invoke Saule's loving energy to shine reason on the situation and bring loving energy back into the household. While we like to think of our families as the people who will always be there for us, all too often women and children become victims of an abusive spouse or parent. Like Saule, those who are closest to us can sometimes be the source of great pain and betrayal. For those who are dealing with an abusive family member or are coming to terms with abuse dealt to them at the hands of a parent, Saule and her daughter can be figures of healing and rebirth. When betrayed, Saule takes the situation into her own hands. She stands up for her daughter and for herself and severs her ties to Menesis. She moves on with her life and finds love again. She is a goddess of action; she does not sit and wonder why bad things happen to her, instead taking the necessary steps to reshape her life.

Saule's sacred animals are the horse, swan, and snake. *Žaltys* (pronounced *zhal-TEES*), a kind of grass snake, were kept in homes, usually near hearth fires, and were considered particularly sacred to the sun goddess. Saule was said to cry amber tears at the site of a dead žaltys. It was also believed that if a snake was given a fatal blow, it would not die until the sun had set. In 1604 a Jesuit missionary de-scribed the practice of keeping these house snakes, claiming the Balts had gone mad: "The people have reached such a stage of madness that they believe that deity exists in reptiles. Therefore they carefully safeguard them, lest someone injure the reptiles kept inside their homes. Superstitiously they believe that harm would come to them, should anyone show disrespect to these reptiles."[64]

Saule's animal companions reflect her nature. The horse is a com-panion to many sun deities and represents Saule's fertile nature, while the snake embodies her capacity to be reborn again and again. Saule is reborn many times. She rises from the dead after drowning, and she rises from the ashes of a destructive relationship to rebuild her life. Like the sun, she is constantly renewing herself, shedding the remnants of the old day to begin anew as she rises each dawn, much like a snake shedding its skin.

Saule was said to dance on the silver hill of the sky on the summer solstice, which is why the festival was called Ligo, meaning "swaying." During rituals to Saule, dance can be used as a way to raise energy and honor the goddess. There is no particular type of music you have to use to honor Saule. Pick something that reminds you of her love of life and loving nature. See yourself as Saule, feel the goddess within you as you dance. Your entire ritual could simply be a dance dedi-cated to the goddess.

Saule's colors are red, white, and silver. In some dainas she is de-scribed as a golden apple, and both her chariot and boat were made of gold. When she dances at midsummer, she wears silver shoes. When working with Saule as the mother sun, light white candles to repre-sent the goddess. The color red is connected to the younger sun or her virgin aspect as the sun maiden Auszrine. Berries, amber, and apples would be appropriate offerings to Saule. The Baltic people used wheels, rayed circles, and rosettes to represent Saule, making these symbols ex-

---

64. Gimbutas, *Ancient Symbolism in Lithuanian Folk Art*, 33.

cellent altar decorations for rituals involving her. These symbols can also be carved into candles to invoke Saule's energies.

· · · · · · · · · · · · · · · · · ·

SAULE INVOCATION

Saule, Mother Sun
Amber-weeping goddess
Across the sky you ride each day in your golden chariot,
Attended by your daughters
As the sun sets beyond the horizon,
You make your bed in the branches of your apple trees
Your sacred serpents twine around your arms
In your swan-drawn boat you pass through
the underworld to begin a new day
Your warmth brings life and light to the world
Your spirit shines with radiance
You who are the mother of all life
The earth, your eldest daughter,
And the stars, your innumerable children.
Cast your loving gaze upon me, O Mother Sun
Comfort me in my times of sorrow
Fill me with strength in times of need
Hail Saule!

· ·

TEARS OF THE SUN SPELL

You Will Need:
1 piece of amber
1 cup or chalice
Apple cider or mead

Saule is no stranger to sorrow. When Saule weeps, her tears turn to amber, but although life sometimes makes her weep, she always transforms her current situations into new and better things. Use this spell to start a new phase in your life.

Go to your sacred space. If you wish, cast a circle, but it is not necessary. Fill the chalice with the cider or mead. Hold the chalice in your hands and visualize the things you wish to remove and banish from your life in the chalice. The things, emotions, or people holding you back from achieving your goals or that which is no longer useful in your life—see these things filling the cup. Then visualize Saule standing before you. When you are ready, say:

This chalice holds all that is no longer useful in my life
I banish these things from my life and offer them to Saule

Turn the chalice over, pouring its contents on the ground. If you cannot do this ritual outside, you may want to have a bowl you can pour the liquid into, which can be poured outside after the ritual. Another alternative would be to not use the cider and simply see the things you wish to banish fill the empty chalice. See the things you wish to banish flowing away from you, allowing you to start a new phase in your life. Put the chalice back on the altar and hold the piece of amber in your hands. See all of the new and positive things that you wish to fill your life with. Take as long as you need, until the picture is clear in your mind. See the image filling the stone. When you are ready, say:

Mother Saule,
Weeping tears of amber
I feel your sorrow
Look down upon your daughter/son
Shine your light upon me
I hold your golden tears in my hand,
to remind me that out of darkness and despair
can come new life and light.

Saule, wash away my sorrow
Fill my life with new and better things!

Thank Saule. Carry the stone with you or keep it on your altar to attract positive energy into your life.

. . . .
SAULE PROSPERITY SPELL

As a mother goddess, Saule is connected to the fertility of the land. She is described in several traditional folk songs as lifting her skirts and walking through farmers' fields. When she dropped her skirts, it was time for the harvest. Saule's light brings growth and abundance to the earth, making her an excellent goddess to call upon to draw wealth and success into your life. As the Balts who worshiped her were mainly farmers concerned with the health of their crops, she would also be an ideal goddess to call upon if you are an avid gardener.

. . . .
FINDING THAT WHICH IS LOST SPELL

Saule was called upon to find lost livestock by the Baltic people. As the sun goddess she rode high in the sky and could see all that happened below her. If you lose something and just can't seem to find it, visualize holding the object in your hands and see Saule's golden light shining upon it and bringing its location to light. Say:

Saule
Noble lady of the sky
All-seeing fiery eye,
Riding in your golden chariot across the sky
Reveal to me that which I have lost

····················

SAULE INCENSE

2 tablespoons amber resin
1 tablespoon myrrh
½ tablespoon apple blossoms
1 tablespoon rose petals

····························

SAULE CORRESPONDENCES

Animals: horse, snake, swan
Symbols: rosette, wheel
Herbs/Plants: apples, rowan, birch
Colors: white, red, silver, gold
Stone: amber

FINLAND

Like the folklore of neighboring Latvia and Lithuania, the concept of a feminine sun was predominant in the mythological land-scape of Scandinavia.

The mythology of the Finnish people was primarily preserved through an oral tradition. Parts of Finnish mythology were eventually written down during the seventeenth century, although the majority of it continued to be passed down through word of mouth. During the nineteenth century, folklorist Elias Lönnrot traveled across Finland collecting traditional songs, poems, and folklore. Intending to ignite a sense of national pride by giving the Finnish people a national epic akin to the *Iliad* or *Beowulf*, in 1835 Lönnrot compiled the existing folklore with the material he collected on his travels into a series of fifty poems, known today as the *Kalevala*, detailing the deeds of the Finnish gods.

Finnish cosmology is unique in that it recognizes both the sun and moon as female. Unlike other sun and moon deities, rather than being at odds with one another, these sisters worked together, weaving the threads of fate, bestowing riches on those they favored, and making the crops and plants fertile. In many ways they were seen as two parts of the same whole. One creation myth tells how the world was created when the goddess Ilmatar accidently broke an egg a bird laid on her as she floated in the vast primordial ocean. Half of the eggshell became the sky, while the other half became the earth. The egg yolk became the sun and the egg whites became the moon, suggesting the light of both luminaries were from the same essential source.

Unfortunately, these sisters were often abducted or their light blocked from the world, and several stories within the *Kalevala* revolve around the adventures the other gods embark on in order to return light and warmth to the earth. At times it is a person who steals the sun and moon; in other cases, the forces of nature prevent their light from shining on the earth. One story tells how an oak tree began to grow and grow until it reached so high into the heavens that it blocked out the sun and the moon. No one could cut the tree down except for a tiny man who appeared out of the sea. Once the oak was cut down, the crops, animals, and forests flourished in the renewed light.

PÄIVÄTÄR

You find yourself standing before a cold, towering mountain. All around you the world is cold, and the wind chills you to the bone. At the base of the mountain you see a large gate. You walk up to it quickly and knock. The doors open, although you see no one within. The doors lead into a passageway chiseled out from the mountain itself. The walls feel rough as you run your hands over them. After a while, you notice a faint light shining farther down the tunnel. It reminds you of the sun and the warmth that has fled the world outside. Eager to find warmth and light, you walk faster toward the faint glow.

Soon the passageway ends, and you find yourself in front of a door with a large lock on it. The light shines from behind the door, seeping out from its edges. Beside it stands a stooped hag. The woman wears many furs, and although her eyes are glazed over with age, she looks straight at you. You ask the hag what this place is, and she tells you this is the prison of the sun. Taken aback that anyone would hold the sun prisoner, you tell her how the world is cold and barren outside, and how much the world needs the sun's light and warmth. She seems unaffected by your pleas. "It is not I who holds the sun in her prison. If you want the sun returned to the world, you must release her." You look at her perplexed, and this seems to amuse her. Looking at the locked door, you tell the hag you do not have the key.

She smiles. "Oh, but you do, my dear! Many have brought keys; even great magicians have forged magickal keys to open that lock. Fools! You all possess the key. It cannot be forged, only found."

You think about her words for a while. Then you walk up to the lock and hold it in your hands. It is as cold as ice, and then you know what you need to do. You close your eyes and bring to mind the warmth of a summer's day. You think of the sun's light falling between the leaves of a wooded glen. You draw that feeling of light and warmth into yourself, then into the lock. Soon it begins to warm, until finally it glows with a faint light. Then with a satisfying click, it unlocks and the cell door flies open.

The light of the sun shines through the cell, washing everything in a warm light. A woman stands at the center of the light. She is a tall youth with pale-gold hair and silver-white robes.

And you know you are gazing upon the sun goddess Päivätär. She smiles, and as you look beside you, you see the hag is gone. And you wonder if she ever really was there at all; perhaps this has all been a test.

"Even when it seems as if my light has gone from your life, know that I am within you. You are the only one who can bring that light, that vital spark, back into the world and your life when others lock it away and try to extinguish it. You must be your own light, and when you draw that light within to the surface, it will ignite that same fire in others."

The image of Päivätär begins to fade and finally vanishes. Quickly you make your way outside to see the sun high in the

sky, her light and warmth transforming the lands. You smile to
yourself, knowing the same light dwells within you.

Fairest Sun, from rock arisen,
Like the golden cuckoo rise you,
Like the silver dove arise you … resume your former journey.
—*Kalevala: The Land of the Heroes* (W. F. Kirby, trans.)

In Finland, the sun goddess Päivätär spent her days perched on a
rainbow, spinning sunlight. With her magickal silver reed, she wove
the thread of fate, and with a golden shuttle she wove golden cloth.
Her companion was her sister, the moon goddess, who was another accomplished spinstress, and wove the thread the sun spun.
Throughout the poems of the *Kalevala*, she is a benevolent force,
aiding those who call upon her, bringing with her light wealth and
good fortune.

Päivätär's troubles begin when Väinämöinen, a magician and the
god of song and poetry, began to sing while playing his magickal
harp. His music drifted up to the heavens and was so enchanting that
both the sun and moon strained to hear it. The moon maiden settled
in the branches of a birch tree and the sun sat on the branch of a fir
to listen to the lovely music. While they were distracted by the music,
the hag Louhi captured both the sun and moon and brought them to
her icy home in the far north. Singing a magickal incantation, Louhi
imprisoned the sisters in an iron prison deep within the mountains.
The earth was left in utter darkness. There was no light or warmth for
year upon year. Life became dark and dismal; frost covered the crops;
people and cattle died of starvation. Soon, even the stars began to
lose their luster in the absence of the sun and moon.[65]

---

65. Crawford, *The Kalevala*, 702.

Eventually the gods grew tired of the dark and cold state of the world and asked Väinämöinen and the smith god Ilmarinen to free the sun. Ilmarinen felt the solution to their problems was to create a new sun and moon. It is unclear why he favors this course of action. Perhaps he felt Louhi was too dangerous a foe. She was often involved in conflicts with the Finnish gods and was both a shapeshifter and a powerful sorceress. Regardless of the reason, Ilmarinen began forging a metal sun and moon. He placed the moon on the highest branches of a fir tree and the metal sun in the branches of the tallest pine tree, but despite his skill they did not shine.

Finally Väinämöinen decided to take action. He cut three strips of bark from an aspen tree and used them to divine where the sun was hidden. He then traveled to the far north and demanded that Louhi release the sun. When she refused, he challenged her men to a contest of arms. With his magickal sword he easily defeated Louhi's warriors and went to where the sun and moon were imprisoned. The prison was guarded by serpents and adders, and after destroying the snakes he found nine doors each with three locks. Unable to open the doors, he returned to Ilmarinen's forge, where he asked the smith to forge keys to open the sun's prison.

Louhi, nervous that the gods might actually be able to free the sun, transformed into an eagle and went to spy on the smith. She flattered him with compliments and asked what he was making. Not fooled by the sorceress's disguise, Ilmarinen told her, " 'Tis a collar I am forging for the neck of wicked Louhi, toothless witch of Sariola, stealer of the silver sunshine."[66] Fearful the gods would imprison her, Louhi flew back to the north and released the sun and her sister. Disguised as a dove, a bird connected to good luck, Louhi returned to the smith. He asked her what tidings she brought, and she pointed out that the sun was rising and he no longer needed to continue his work. As the sun rose above the hills, Väinämöinen sang a song praising the sun and imploring her

66. Ibid., 713.

to bring her blessings to the cold and barren earth: "Rise, thou silver Sun, each morning; Source of light and life hereafter; Bring us, daily, joyful greetings; Fill our homes with peace and plenty; That our sowing, fishing, hunting; May be prospered by thy coming."[67]

Although the details of her daily journey across the sky are not mentioned in the *Kalevala*, Väinämöinen's song does mention the sun's resting place: "End thy journeying in slumber; Rest at evening in the ocean; When thy daily cares have ended."[68] Like the Balts, who envisioned their sun goddess gliding across the sea in her boat or sinking beneath the waves at the end of the day, the Finnish sun also rested in the ocean. It is unclear if she had to travel through the underworld in order to rise the next day, but Päivätär was believed to be able to look into the realm of the dead.

When the hero god Lemminkainen vanished, his mother searched tirelessly but could not find him. Finally, in desperation, she asked the sun goddess if she had seen her son. Päivätär tells her that Lemminkainen had drowned in the river of Tuonela (the Finnish underworld). The god had been attempting to capture the black swans that lived there in order to win the hand of Louhi's daughter. Lemminkainen's mother then dredged the river for her son's body. She found him in pieces and sewed his body back together. When she was done, she asked Päivätär to shine brightly for three days to lull the world—even Tuoni, the god of death and ruler of the underworld—to sleep with the sun's excessive heat: "Thou sun ... shine out hotly for a spell, dim and sweaty for a while, and a third time full with blazing. Lull to sleep the peevish people ... Let the power of Tuoni slumber."[69]

Sitting in the low-hanging branches of a birch tree, Päivätär did as the woman asked. While the god of death slept off the heat wave, Lemminkainen's mother used three drops of magickal honey to restore her son's life.

67. Lönnrot, *The Kalevala*, 715.
68. Ibid., 716.
69. Friberg, *The Kalevala: Epic of the Finnish People*, 129.

While still an infant, Päivätär's own son met with an unfortunate accident, perhaps making her sympathetic to the plight of Lemminkainen's mother. While she was rocking the child on the edge
of a rainbow, he grew so hot that he burned through the cradle and
fell through the sky, down to the earth, where he was swallowed by a
magickal fish.[70] He was later rescued, as Ilmarinen required the child's
fire to forge the metal sun the gods attempted to use as a replacement
for the stolen sun goddess.

Despite being a mother, Päivätär is often described as a "fair maid."
She is mentioned infrequently by name in the poems of the *Kalevala*,
instead being referred to by the title "sun-daughter." A number of the
Finnish gods who embodied elemental forces are referred to in a similar manner; the moon goddess Kuutar is called "moon-daughter." It
is similar with other primordial deities, such as the creation goddess
Ilmatar, who is simply referred to as "water-mother" in one poem instead of by a proper name. Here the use of "daughter" is simply to
assign gender to an inherently genderless force, and does seem to emphasize that she is a maiden goddess. In her myths Päivätär is quite determined to remain unwed and retain her independence, giving suitors
impossible tasks to avoid marriage.

When the god Väinämöinen sought her hand, he tries to woo her
by telling her of all the benefits of marriage. Unfortunately, his description of marriage mostly revolves around having someone to bake
him honey cakes and brew his beer for him, so it is perhaps no surprise that Päivätär isn't too impressed by his offer. She replies to him,
"Bright a summer day but a maid's state is brighter ... daughter-in-law
in a husband's house is like a dog on a chain."[71] Then Päivätär goes on
to tell him she will only marry a man who can carve a boat from her
spindle, a seemingly impossible task. Väinämöinen attempts to do so

---

70. Monaghan, *The Goddess Path: Myths, Invocations, and Rituals*, 221.
71. Lönnrot, *The Kalevala*, 81.

but is so zealous to complete the task that he becomes clumsy and nearly cuts off his toe with his axe.

Like those of many sun goddesses, Päivätär's story speaks to us of a seasonal cycle. Her imprisonment and release mark the shift between the dark and light halves of the year. Her myths have many similarities to those of Amaterasu and Saule. Like Amaterasu, Päivätär is hidden from the world and the gods must find a way to return the sun to the dying world. Although Päivätär does not go willingly, as Amaterasu does, they both retreat into the earth, one in a mountain prison, the other into a cave. Päivätär's imprisonment is reminiscent of Saule's mythology, where she is imprisoned in a tower and rescued by the signs of the zodiac.

The hag Louhi also plays a similar role to Cailleach, another hag goddess, who yearly imprisoned the Welsh goddess Bride in a cave in order to bring about winter. The fact that it is not the gods but Louhi who releases Päivätär in the end suggests that this story represents a seasonal cycle. Even though the gods trick Louhi, ultimately even the power of the gods cannot hold back the cycles of nature. Louhi lives far to the north in a frozen, wintry land. This imagery suggests that she is the embodiment of winter, and only she can decide when her season of influence is over. Although winter is harsh, it is a natural part of the earth's yearly cycle, and spring cannot come until the proper time.

Louhi also possessed a magickal object called the *sampo*, which brought wealth and good fortune to its owner. The sampo was envisioned as a magickal mill of plenty. When it turned, it simultaneously ground flour, created salt, and produced money. The sampo has also been interpreted as a symbol for the celestial realm, revolving around the central axis of the world tree.[72] This magickal object was a source of great conflict, as the other gods often attempted to steal it from Louhi, just as they battled her to reclaim the sun. As the winter hag,

---

72. Dorson, *Peasant Customs and Savage Myths Volume 1*, 175.

this is a fitting object for Louhi to win. If the sampo represents the heavens and the mill's turning, its cycle through the year, then it is insinuated that Louhi controls the world's cycles of abundance and bareness, just as she controls when summer and the sun may return to the world.

Like Amaterasu and Saule, Päivätär and her sister are accomplished spinners. Päivätär weaves both the sunlight and the thread of fate. As the sun marks the days and the seasons, she also measures out the length of our lives by weaving the thread of our destinies. Päivätär's spinning is also linked to wealth. Another story within the *Kalevala* describes a poor woman who happens upon Päivätär and her moon sister while they were spinning their thread. Upon seeing the goddesses, she asked the sisters to give her a portion of their wealth: "And began to ask them gently ... Give you of your gold Kuutar, and your silver give Päivätär, to the maiden poorly dowered, to the child who now implores you!"[73] The sisters give the woman silver and gold, and she returns home happy. The sun's connection to wealth is also alluded to in the song of praise Väinämöinen sings upon the sun's return. He asks the sun to fill their homes with plenty and to make their farming and hunting expeditions successful, making the sun not simply a bringer of warmth but also a catalyst for bringing about the abundance of the earth.

WORKING WITH PÄIVÄTÄR

Päivätär teaches us to be independent and to draw on our inner light during times of darkness. She defies social norms and stays a maid, making up her own mind as to how her life should be. Päivätär's maidenhood is less about a sexual state, as she bears a child, than retaining her freedom. When you feel constrained by social norms, or if you feel the need to find your voice and assert your own independence, invoke Päivätär.

---

73. Kirby, *Kalevala: The Land of the Heroes*, 43.

Päivätär is also an excellent goddess to work with to lift the spirits and reignite our inner fires. Like Päivätär, life can sometimes make us feel trapped. Our inner fires cannot shine through our despair and diminish. We lose sight of our goals and lose faith in our dreams. As a goddess who weaves the thread of fate, Päivätär can aid us in bringing positive change into our lives, and as a goddess of the sun she can also aid us in rekindling purpose and hope in our hearts. All too often we may ask for change and work toward it in our magick practices, but if we fail to rekindle our inner fires, if we continue to believe we are not worthy of change or that nothing will change our situation, we sabotage ourselves and our work. The change Päivätär offers us transforms us within and without. Päivätär knows that true change must begin within us before it can manifest in the outside world.

Although most sun goddesses are connected with gold or described as appearing golden, Päivätär is connected to silver, while her sister, the moon, gives gifts of gold. The *Kalevala* describes Päivätär wearing white garments while she weaves, holding her silver reed: "On the sky's collar bow; upon heaven's arch; shimmered in clean clothes; and in white garments; cloth of gold she is weaving; of silver she is working...with a silver reed."[74] A white altar cloth, preferably one with silver along the hem, can be used to decorate an altar dedicated to Päivätär. White or silver candles are appropriate for spells and rituals invoking Päivätär.

Päivätär often rests from her journey across the sky in the treetops. She reclines on a tree branch when listening to Väinämöinen's enchanting music. In other parts of the *Kalevala*, she is described as moving among or bending down toward pine trees in particular.[75] The metal sun Ilmarinen forges is also placed in the highest branches of a pine tree. Pine branches can be used to decorate Päivätär's altar, and pine incense would be an appropriate offering to this goddess.

---

74. Lönnrot, *The Kalevala*, 79.
75. Kirby, *Kalevala: The Land of the Heroes*, 449.

....
PÄIVÄTÄR INVOCATION

Päivätär
Sun-daughter sitting upon the arch of the sky
Spinning the sunlight like thread
Your sister at your side
Reed and shuttle darting across your loom
Together you weave the threads of our lives
Päivätär, fill us with your blissful light
Weave the thread of fate kindly
Fill our hearts with joy,
Our homes with your warmth
Let your radiance shine through all that we do!

....
PÄIVÄTÄR INCENSE

2 parts pine needles
1 part cedar
½ part juniper berries

....
PÄIVÄTÄR AND KUUTAR PROSPERITY SPELL

You Will Need:
1 silver candle
1 gold candle
A piece of silver or gold jewelry

In this spell you will be calling upon the energies of both the sun and moon to bring prosperity into your life. You will need a piece of jewelry made from gold or silver. If you do not have something made from gold or silver, something that has those colors on it will do. In the past I've used a ring that was made from pieces of silver and gold twined together for this spell, while a friend of mine chose to bless a gold ring and a silver necklace she is fond of wearing.

Before beginning the spell, consider what kind of prosperity you wish to bring into your life. In the *Kalevala*, the sun and moon are called upon for various types of wealth. A poor woman calls upon them to give her silver and gold because she lacks a dowry. When the sun returns from her prison, she is asked to bring good fortune to hunting and joy to the people's lives. Wealth isn't always the amount of money in your bank account. You could ask the sun and moon sisters to bring a better job, to enrich a relationship, to bring you a wealth of creativity. The possibilities are endless.

On the silver candle carve Päivätär's name, and on the gold candle carve Kuutar's name. Then place the silver and gold candles next to each other on your altar. Light the silver candle, saying:

I call to this place Päivätär of the silver sunshine!

Light the gold candle, saying:

I call to this place Kuutar of the golden moonlight!

Hold the jewelry in your hands. See Päivätär's and Kuutar's light filling the jewelry, drawing the prosperity you desire to you like a magnet. When you are ready, say:

> *Päivätär of the silver sunshine,*
> *Spinning with your silver spindle*
> *Kuutar of the golden moonlight,*
> *Weaving with your golden shuttle*
> *Sun-daughter, give to me of your silver!*
> *Moon-daughter, give to me of your golden!*

If possible, take the jewelry outside and hold it up to the light of the sun and later the moon. Wear the piece of jewelry until your desire has manifested.

. . . .

Renewing the Inner Fires Ritual

You Will Need:

1 white or silver candle

Päivätär incense (see page 97)

Like Päivätär, at times we feel trapped. Our inner fires, our will and creativity, can be stifled by the trials and difficult events we face in life. Whether we want to renew our creativity, fight depression, or just bring a little sunshine into our life, Päivätär can help us kindle the fires within.

If you wish, cast a circle. Light the white candle and incense. Sit quietly for a few minutes. Think about your inner fire, that force within you that is your creative nature, your will and determination, the power that fuels your spirit. Take a moment to consider what has stifled this inner fire, and why you wish to rekindle this force within yourself. When you are ready, say:

Päivätär, Lady of the sun
Päivätär, who was imprisoned by dark Louhi
I am chained, as you were chained in your icy prison
My heart is frozen, as you were frozen in your mountain cell
Break my chains, beloved Päivätär
Kindle the fires within
That I may rise like the sun, above all that hinders me
Fill me with your silver light, Päivätär
Let my inner fires shine!
Let my spirit burn as bright as the summer sun!

See Päivätär standing before you. She is young and exuberant and glows with a brilliant light from within. Flames dart along her skin, giving her an aura of brilliant fire. Päivätär steps closer. Tell her why you wish to rekindle your inner fires; ask her to help you burn away the barriers preventing your inner light from shining. Päivätär places a hand upon your forehead and the other over your heart. You feel her fire filling you, melting away fear and doubt. Soon you glow as bright as Päivätär.

When you are ready, extinguish the candle and thank Päivätär. Relight the candle and see Päivätär's light filling you whenever you need to replenish your inner fires.

PÄIVÄTÄR CORRESPONDENCES
Symbols: spindle, shuttle, thread
Herbs/Plants: fir and pine trees
Colors: white, silver
Stone/Metal: silver

NORSE

The Norse pantheon has been long described as the exception to the solar norm of male/sun and female/moon. Victorian scholars went as far as to call the reversal in the so-called solar myth "norm" as proof that the Norse were a barbaric culture. But as we have already seen, the Norse were certainly not alone in their thinking.

What we think of as Norse mythology comes from the myths and folklore of northern Germanic peoples who inhabited northern Europe and Scandinavia. Starting around 700 CE, the Norse migrated in search of new lands, eventually settling parts of Britain, Iceland, and Greenland. Following in tandem with their views of their celestial deities, their word for *sun* was feminine, while *moon* was masculine.

Most of their surviving mythology centers on the Norse gods and their interaction with various other beings, such as humanity and the *jötnar*, a race of beings that lived in one of the nine realms on the world tree. Most of the stories that remain to us today come from the *Poetic Edda* and the *Prose Edda*, a collection of prose and myths compiled in the thirteenth century in Icelandic, although it contains material from earlier traditional sources, reaching into what we think of as the Viking Age.

SUNNA

You find yourself standing in a large golden chariot. One hand grasps the curve of richly carved metal, the other holds a pair of reins made from a rope of knotted gold threads. A pair of white horses pull the chariot through the air. Although you know you must be high up in the sky, it is hard to see the world below. The chariot, the horses, and even you yourself give off a brilliant light that shines down to the world in great waves.

After what seems like hours, you reach the height of your journey. You pull on the reins and bid the horses rest for a moment. Jumping off the chariot, you find you can stand quite well, and you spend a few moments feeding the horses and giving them water. As they toss their heads, sparks rain down through the sky. All is peaceful and calm until one of the horses rears up. You look around, searching for what could have scared the mare so. Then you see it. It is a dim, gray shape behind you, but as it runs across the hill of the sky it becomes bigger and bigger. Soon, in the few moments that you watch, its shape becomes clear. It is a gray wolf, but not the kind you would find in the forest. This wolf is enormous; his great maw hangs open, teeth bared. He could easily swallow you and the horses whole. You know this must be Sköll, the son of the monstrous wolf Fenris and grandchild of the trickster god Loki.

Quickly you leap back into the chariot and urge the horses onward. The horses run faster and faster. Soon their legs are just a blur. But no matter how fast they run, the wolf gains ground and comes closer. Soon you can hear the wolf's heavy footfalls just behind you. You turn to look behind you, just as a giant paw knocks you from the chariot. The horses run onward, too startled to stop. The great maw comes down around you so fast that you don't realize what has happened until it's too late.

You blink in the darkness. As the wolf Sköll is not a normal wolf, being trapped in his belly isn't a normal experience either. You float suspended in the darkness. Occasionally you hear a howl in the distance, but nothing more. As you take in your surroundings, you realize you are not the only one the wolf has devoured. To one side you see a woman clothed in golden regalia. She glows softly in the dark with the same light that radiates from you. You realize this must be Sunna, the goddess of the sun, whose chariot you have been driving across the sky. You walk over to her, and she puts a shining hand over yours. "I have been trapped her for some time. Even light must give way to dark at times. But I am glad you are here. Together we might bring light back into the world."

She smiles; she takes your hands in hers. You feel Sunna's light flow through you, and your light, the spark of your very being, flowing into the goddess. Together the light grows and grows until the darkness of your prison is filled with a brilliant flame. The edges of that flame burn and lick at the edges of the wolf's gut. Far away you hear a painful yowl. The darkness around you shakes and rolls. With another great howl of pain, you and the goddess are thrust from the prison and back into the sky, as the wolf coughs you both up.

A horse nuzzles your shoulder, and you look up to see the chariot horses standing beside you. The wolf is nowhere to be seen. "He'll be back one day," Sunna tells you. She stands in her chariot again, her light burning brighter than before. "Light will always be tested by the dark. The Sköll wolf has his role to play, and I have mine. Without our chase, if he did not take me prisoner from time to time, my fire would diminish. All things must walk through the dark to truly know the light. And it is only in the dark that we learn how to shine and bring forth the best parts of ourselves."

The scene fades, and you find yourself in your own body
again, knowing the light of Sunna will always be with you when
you find yourself in a dark moment in life.

From the Norse pantheon we have perhaps the most well-known sun goddess, Sunna (also called Sól). While Victorian scholars saw her as an anomaly, she falls very much in line with the myths of other solar goddesses. In Sunna we see the story of the sun's decline and rebirth, and triumph over forces that endanger all of life.

Both of the names Sunna and Sól mean "sun," making her function in the celestial order clear. In the poem *Alvíssmál*, the god Thor questions the dwarf Alvíss about the sun, asking what the sun's many names are in each of the nine worlds. Alvíss gives several responses, including "Ever-glow" by the jötnar, "All-Shining" by the Æsir, and "Fair Wheel" by the elves.[76] The idea that the sun was a wheel that rolled across the sky is common among several cultures. Similarly, the goddess Saule was given an almost identical epithet.

In both the *Poetic Edda* and the *Prose Edda*, which chronicle the stories of the Norse pantheon, she is described as the sister of the god moon, Mani. When the world was formed from the body of the giant Ymir, the sun, moon, and stars were made from the sparks that shot forth from Muspellsheim, the land of fire. Each day Sunna drew the chariot of the sun across the sky, drawn by her horses *Allsvinn* ("Very Fast") and *Arvak* ("Early Rising"). Sunna's brother also rode the chariot of the moon across the sky.

In some stories, Sunna and Mani do not originally have their celestial posts from birth. In this version of the creation of the sun and moon, they were the children of Mundilfari, who compared the beauty of his two children to the sun and moon and named the children after the celestial bodies. But unfortunately, the gods were an-

---

76. Hollander, *The Poetic Edda: Volume 1*, 316.

gered by Mundilfari comparing the splendor of anything they created to his offspring. So the gods placed the two children in the heavens, having them escort the celestial bodies they were named for across the heavens.

Unlike other brother/sister pairings of the sun and moon, Sunna and Mani coexist peacefully. They do not pursue each other as do the solar and lunar deities of other pantheons, but instead they are the ones being chased by the wolf Sköll, the son of another monstrous wolf and son of Loki, Fenris. At times the wolf gets close enough to take a bite out of the sun, causing an eclipse.

At *Ragnarok*, the Norse end of the world, it is believed that Sunna will finally be swallowed by the wolf Sköll. But although the current world ends, the Norse envision a new world forming after the great battle of the gods at Ragnarok. Although the sun is swallowed, as Sköll devours the sun Sunna miraculously will give birth to a daughter. This daughter, it was believed, would take her mother's place lighting the world.

Like the Baltic Saule, Sunna's daughter takes her mother's place. Although it is at the end of the world rather than as a shift between the seasonal cycles of the sun, the sun's connecting with renewal and rebirth remains embedded in her mythology.

WORKING WITH SUNNA

Sunna's story speaks to us of renewal and an ability to come out of an overwhelming situation reborn. Even though the wolf does devour Sunna, the outcome of this struggle is her daughter's birth and the young goddess acting as a younger reborn version of the goddess. Even though it seems like Sunna loses this battle, really she emerges in a new form, one where her pursuer is no longer a threat.

. . . .
SUNNA INVOCATION
Beautiful Sunna
Lady of warmth, heat, and passion
Riding through the heavens with your horses Allsvinn and Arvak
Set your gaze upon me, most beloved sun
Bless me with your light
Guide me through my journey each day

. . . .
SUNNA SPELL FOR OVERCOMING OBSTACLES
You Will Need:
Pen and paper
1 gold or red candle

Use this spell to call upon Sunna and to overcome difficult situations, especially ones that have you feeling worn down. On the paper, draw a large sun. It can be a circle with spokes or a more detailed drawing, depending on your artistic skills. In the center write the situation or obstacle you face. Light the candle and place it over the center of the sun drawing. Say:

Sunna, who rides through the heavens each day
Pursued but never overcome
Ever fleeing, ever overcoming the task before you
Sunna, help me overcome the challenges before me
Guide me through the task at hand

Let the candle burn down or light it for a few minutes each day. When the situation has resolved itself, burn the paper.

. . . .
Sunna Incense
1 part sandalwood
1 part frankincense
1 part amber

. . . .
Sunna Correspondences
Symbols: solar wheel, chariot
Animal: horse
Color: gold

THE CELTS

The sun, like the mothers, was acknowledged as having
powers or regeneration, renewal ... and the penetration of
the sun's rays into the dark womb of the earth gave scope in
the imaginative Celtic mind in the visual linking of these two
crucial religious themes.

—Miranda Green, *Symbols and Images in Celtic Religious Art*

In no other culture was the sun goddess more prevalent than in the myths and traditions of the Celts. The people we know today as the Celts consisted of tribes and clans who migrated across Europe, eventually making their way as far west as Wales, Scotland, England, and Ireland. They shared the belief of a feminine sun, but because they were not a unified people, we find numerous Celtic goddesses connected to the sun and its light, with each of the many solar goddesses in this tradition representing different aspects of the sun's energies.

In Ireland she was seen in the guise of Brighid, and Áine and her sister Gráinne. Áine, who was honored each year with bonfires and a torch-lit procession on the summer solstice on her sacred hill, ruled the summer sun, while her sister Gráinne, whose very name translates to "sun," ruled over the winter aspect of the solar year. Even the Irish Macha, who is most well known as a goddess of battle, had hints of solar attributes. In the *Dindshenchas*, a collection of myths surrounding Irish place lore, she is called the "sun of womankind."

In Britain the sun was Sulis, who brought healing through her thermal waters. The Welsh goddess Olwen, whose name means "Golden Wheel," a title similar to the ones given to Sunna and Saule, may also have had a solar nature.

While the Celts worshiped numerous goddesses connected to the sun, the way in which they viewed these solar goddesses differed from their counterparts in neighboring cultures. Although goddesses like Sunna and Saule were envisioned quite literally as the sun itself or as carrying the solar orb across the sky, the sun goddesses of the Celts were not seen literally as the sun, but rather as the being or the force behind it. They are often compared to the sun and its light or bare names that translate to "sun," making their connection to the solar orb clear. Perhaps the Celts did at one time envision a god or goddess carrying this heavenly orb through the skies, but if so this imagery has been lost to us today. Some have speculated that the Celtic sun goddesses may have begun as beings representing the deification of fire, who later came to represent both the power of fire and the sun.[77]

Although they were greatly outnumbered by their female counterparts, the Celts did honor male gods connected to the sun as well, such as Lugh and Belenos. Likewise the Celts did not see a need to make the moon exclusively male or female. Sun goddesses stood alongside sun gods without any conflict. Furthermore, there is no evidence that the Celts ever attempted to masculinize their sun goddesses. Although they did not adhere to strict gender assignments to the sun and moon, the Welsh and Irish words for sun, *haul* and *ghrian*, are both feminine, suggesting that in the Welsh and Irish pantheons the sun was inherently a symbol of the feminine.

The connection between fertility and the female sun seems to have been especially prevalent in the Celtic mind. An altar found in southern Britain shows a group of mother figures under a gabled

---

77. Amber K and Azreal Arynn K, *Candlemas*, 24.

niche decorated with a large sun-wheel.[78] Several pipe-clay figurines found in central Gaul portray goddesses with sun wheels and solar circles on their breasts, wombs, and thighs, indicating a connection between the sun and the fertile powers of the goddess. As archaeologist Miranda Green puts it, "Solar wheels ... with sun motifs on her breast, belly, and thighs. Both the abundance of sun-images on this statuette and their position on the sexual parts of her body may be significant in interpreting the importance of the solar image for fertility."[79] These figurines were found in shrines, healing springs, domestic settings, and graves, illustrating not only the sun's connection to fertility during life but also the ability to regenerate the dead, giving them the gift of rebirth.

The concept that the sun traveled through the underworld at night to comfort the dead is found worldwide. It is one of the most predominant themes in the myths of the solar feminine, and it should come as no surprise that the Celtic sun had a strong connection to the land of the dead.

Cairns and burial mounds were constructed to align with the sun's movements. In Ireland, sites like Newgrange and the Dowth passage tomb in County Meath were situated so that the sun would shine within their chambers on certain days of the year. In Ireland it was believed that the souls of the dead entered the afterlife by flying toward the setting sun. According to author Christopher Winn, "In more simple times it was believed that the souls of those about to die flew towards the dying embers of the sun as it set in the west, and there they would enter the Underworld."[80]

The dead were also buried with images of the sun, suggesting the sun goddess guided the spirits of the dead to the Otherworlds. In the Dowth passage tombs, several of the chambers are decorated with spirals and rayed circles. As Miranda Green writes, "The sun

---

78. Green, *Symbol and Image in Celtic Religious Art*, 37.
79. Ibid., 39.
80. Winn, *I Never Knew That About Ireland*, 259.

was perceived to penetrate the dark, infernal regions ... Celtic communities in Europe sometimes buried their dead with solar amulets, to comfort them in their sojourn in the Underworld."[81]

During Christian times in Ireland, it was customary to carry the dead around the graveyard prior to burial, a symbolic act representing the sun's journey through the sky. Nineteenth-century author and Catholic priest John O'Hanlon noted the practice in his book *Lives of the Irish Saints*: "An old custom is preserved here at funerals ... of carrying the dead around the graveyard. This is said to be of Pagan or Druidical origin, as representing the course of the sun round the earth ... and the dead was buried to face the east, thus meeting the rising sun; just as Christians are now, because we are told that the Sovereign Judge will come with the rising sun."[82]

The Celts also drew a connection between water and fire. While these two elements seem to represent polar opposites, the majority of Celtic deities associated with fire and the sun also have a strong connection to water. Considering that solar deities in other cosmologies have a tendency to rest during the night in the ocean or other bodies of water, the connection between water and fire seems less out of place. Patricia Monaghan has hypothesized that the basins found within burial tombs like Newgrange may have acted as primitive mirrors to catch the light of the sun.[83] If this is true, it draws a strong parallel between the myths of the Celtic sun and solar goddesses from other cultures that were also connected to mirrors and caves. Their mirrors were not made of polished copper, but were instead sacred wells, where water reflected the light of the sun as the polished surface of a mirror reflects light.

Similarly, Brighid and Sulis are connected to sacred springs, which would have reflected and "captured" the vital energy of the sun and its goddess. This would certainly explain the connection the Celts saw

81. Green, *Celtic Myths*, 47.
82. O'Hanlon, *Lives of the Irish Saints*, 701.
83. Monaghan, *O Mother Sun!*, 81.

between water and fire, and why so many of their solar deities also ruled over sacred wells and springs. The goddess Sulis is connected to thermal waters in particular, suggesting that the sun's warmth could penetrate the earth and warm the waters deep below the ground.

BRIGHID

You find yourself walking along a grassy path. The sun is just set-ting, and you watch the beautiful colors that dance across the sky as it sets. In the distance is a burial mound with spirals carved into the stones that line a passageway that goes deep into the earth. As the last of the sun's light vanishes below the horizon, you watch as a spark flies from the sky and passes into the mound's passageway. A few heartbeats later, you hear a sound emanating from the mound. It sounds like the blows of a hammer.

Slowly you make your way to the mound. As you reach the passageway, you peek inside and see a light shining from deep within the mound. The sounds of hammer blows become louder now. Curious, you make your way into the mound. Its roof and passageway are made of slabs of rock that have been carved with spirals and solar wheels, and your fingers brush against them as you continue through the passage.

You walk deeper and deeper into the earth, and the light begins to grow. Finally you come to the center of the mound. It opens to a great chamber. The light is so bright, you must shield your eyes with the back of a hand. All through the chamber, sparks fly as a woman stands over a large forge. In her hands is a great hammer. As it strikes again the anvil, it rings out with a musical quality.

The woman sees you and beckons you over to the forge. The light in the chamber, you realize, comes from the woman rather than the forge fire as you first thought. The woman's hair is a halo of red that falls around her kind face in a way that makes you think she is no stranger to hard work. She wears simple green robes, the sleeves rolled up to keep her hands free. Even so, she has an air of royalty and sovereignty about her.

She smiles and tells you she is pleased that you have followed her here. "I am Brighid. I am the forge flame, the fire of the sun high above. I am the fire in the head that ignites and inspires. I am the spark that brings life to all things and sets all things into motion. I am the healer and the shaper. My forge shapes the souls as easily as the spear or sword. I am the well of inspiration that cools and tempers. I am always in motion, always burning." She takes a spearhead from the anvil and plunges it in the well you notice next to the forge. Steam rises as she does, and fills the chamber. The scene begins to fade, but you still hear the goddess's voice say, "You are the sword on the forge; you are the song that rings through eternity. You are shaped, reformed, and ever remade on my forge."

Brigit, ever excellent woman,
golden sparkling flame …
the dazzling resplendent sun.
—St. Ultan hymn to St. Brigit, *Thesaurus Palaeohibernicus*

From the time of the Celts to modern times, Brighid remains one of the most revered goddesses of the Celtic pantheon. Her worship stretched from continental Europe and spread with the emigrating Celtic tribes to Britain and Ireland. In England she was Brigantia; in Scotland she was hailed as the maiden Bride; and in Ireland she was Brid or Brighid. In many ways, her worship never truly died out; the love and devotion the Irish people felt for her eventually transformed Brighid the goddess into the Christian Saint Brigit, who remains a beloved figure in Ireland today.

Brighid appears at times a paradoxical figure. She is goddess of both fire and water, a patron of healing and battle, a virgin saint who was once a goddess of fertility. Her myths have become an amalgam of what remains to us in *Lebor Gabála Érenn*, which details how the Tuatha Dé Danann (the Irish gods) came to Ireland, along with the Irish glosses, and the many legends that surround Brigit the Christian saint. Whether or not there was an actual Saint Brigit is debatable. Perhaps an Irish nun by the same name did exist, whose story eventually merged with that of the goddess, but it is generally accepted by scholars that many of the attributes and characteristics of Brighid the goddess were eventually endowed to the saint. According to Phillips Barry, "By the times when biographies of Saint Brigit had come to be circulated, she had been connected in legendary lore with a group of beliefs that belong to the category of solar mythology … Waiving the debatable question, whether elements of Irish Paganism have filtered into Irish Christianity."[84] What remains constant in Brighid's mythology is her connection to the vital creative force of the sun.

Brighid's name comes from the root *bríg*, meaning "high" or "exalted," making her the "exalted one." As a sun goddess, it is also fitting for her to be held on "high," as the sun dwells high above. When the Romans invaded Britain, she was equated with Minerva, and in one inscription she was hailed as *Caelestis Brigantia*,[85] or "Heavenly Brigantia," again suggesting she inhabited the sky or heavens. Her name also hints at her connection to sovereignty and rulership. In the *Lebor Gabála Érenn*, Brighid is a queenly figure, daughter of the god Dagda, one of the kings of the Tuatha Dé Danann. She later married the god Bres, who eventually ruled over the Irish gods. The Welsh word for king, *brenin*, is thought to mean "consort of Brigantia," Brighid's counterpart in Britain, mirroring her role as a great queen and goddess of sovereignty in Ireland. We find similar themes

---

84. Barry, *Bridge of Sunbeams*, 86.
85. Ireland, *Roman Britain: A Sourcebook*, 193.

in the stories of Amaterasu, Hathor, and the Hittite *tawanannas*, who were also connected to queenship.

In her guise as one of the Tuatha Dé Danann, Brighid was known as a triple goddess of healing, smithcraft, and the patroness of poets. Cormac's glossaries describe her as "the goddess whom poets adored, because very great and very famous was her protecting care. It is therefore they call her goddess of poets by this name. Whose sisters were Brigit the female physician [woman of leechcraft], Brigit the female smith [woman of smithwork]."[86] She was also credited with inventing keening, having cried out when seeing her slain son on the battlefield.

Numerous sacred wells across Ireland, Wales, and Britain were dedicated to Brighid and believed to have healing powers, especially involving the curing of eye ailments. As Patricia Monaghan has suggested, these wells may have acted as ancient mirrors that absorbed the sun's sacred light.[87] Celtic solar goddesses are often connected to water along with the fire of the sun. As a smith, Brighid's fire shapes metal (or symbolically the soul), and her sacred waters cool and temper it, giving it substance and form, completing a cycle of transformation initiated by her sacred fires.

In Wales Brighid was called *Bride*, and shared almost identical qualities with her counterpart in Ireland. In Scotland Bride was yearly imprisoned in a cave by the hag goddess Cailleach, who may be another aspect of Bride. According to folklorist Lady Augusta Gregory, one half of Brighid's face is youthful and the other withered and old, likely indicating a dual nature. During the spring and summer months Bride ruled, while Cailleach tended to the winter months. Cailleach was called the "daughter of the little sun," most likely referring to the weaker sun of winter.[88] Cailleach was often unwilling to give up her hold on the land, and Bride had to escape the hag each

---

86. Stokes, *Sanas Chormaic*, 23.
87. Monaghan, *O Mother Sun!*, 81.
88. Monaghan, *The Encyclopedia of Celtic Mythology and Folklore*, 69.

year. In some stories, Cailleach's son falls in love with the beautiful Bride and helps her escape. Enraged, Cailleach tosses boulders at the lovers, accounting for the many large rocks scattered across the Scottish landscape. She held off spring throughout March and April with storms as she continued her pursuit, until the time of Beltane, when Bride and spring emerged triumphant. In other versions, Cailleach travels to the well of youth, and as she drinks from the sacred waters she transforms into Bride, bringing with her the spring. She repeats the process at Samhain when she drinks the waters again, transforming once again into the hag.

As Saint Brigit, she is said to have performed several miracles that have curious parallels to the traits attributed to Brighid the goddess. The legends that surround her birth are especially interesting. Brigit's mother was the slave of a chieftain named Dubthach. Incidentally, Dubthach was also the name of a legendary warrior in the Ulster cycle and the name of a legendary poet, making it likely that her father also began as a figure in Pagan tradition that was later adopted and reshaped within Christian cosmology. Dubthach's wife became jealous of the slave girl and threatened to leave her husband, along with her large dowry. Dubthach then brought the girl to live with a Druid who delivered a curious prophesy about the unborn child. He told Dubthach that "the offspring of your wife shall serve the offspring of the slave, and the slave shall bring forth a radiant daughter who will shine like the sun among the stars of heaven."[89]

Brigit was born on the first day of spring just as the first rays of the sun lit the sky, as her mother walked across the threshold of the house, holding a pail of milk, which she used to wash the babe.[90] Thresholds and other locations that were between places such as river shores where land and water meet were considered doorways to the Otherworlds, signifying Brigit's less-than-ordinary status. Her connection

89. Meehan, *Praying with Visionary Women*, 12.
90. Gregory, *A Book of Saints and Wonders*, 8.

to the sun is apparent in the time of her birth, at sunrise, and that the Druid prophesizes she will shine like the sun. Being born on the first day of spring is also significant, as this would have corresponded to Imbolc, which was a sacred day connected to the goddess Brighid, eventually being adopted as a holy day for her saintly incarnation as well. Imbolc was a time to celebrate the shift in the yearly cycle when the sun once again regained strength and brought with it the warmth and fertility of the summer months. It is also the day the Welsh goddess Bride escapes her winter prison and returns to the world.

As an infant, Brigit's connection to the sun and fire continued. One day when Brigit's mother was returning home, she was horrified to see the house was on fire. Running inside to save her child, she discovered the house was not in fact on fire but that the light was emanating from the infant, who appeared to be wreathed in flames. Other accounts speak of a flame burning from between Brigit's brows.

As the child grew, the only food she could abide was the milk of a cow with white and red ears given to her by the Druid her mother served. It was also said that everything she touched increased; the animals she laid her hands on produced more milk; and the thread she wove became endowed with healing properties. Animals with red and white ears are often attested to being otherworldly, or belonging to the faeries in Celtic stories, again hinting at the fact that Brigit is no mere mortal. Brigit's connection to cattle is also emphasized in other legends surrounding the saint. Her mother bathes her in cow's milk when she is born; in other stories Brighid uses cow's milk to cure illnesses or gives the animals to the poor. In one story, she gave away her mother's entire store of butter (a product made from cow's milk), which was miraculously refilled after she prayed fervently. On another occasion when she did not have food to feed visiting bishops, she prayed as she milked her cattle and produced enough milk to fill a lake.[91] Similarly, the goddess Brighid was said to have two

---

91. Gregory, *A Book of Saints and Wonders*, 10.

magickal oxen, *Fe* and *Men*, as well as the king of boars, *Torc Triath*, and the king of sheep, *Mag Cirb*.

Cattle in Celtic culture were symbols of prosperity, and Brighid's connection to the animal, both as a saint and goddess, is symbolic of the fertility and prosperity she brings. As a solar goddess, it represents the fertility the sun brings with its warmth. We find the connection between cattle and the sun's fertile power in other cultures as well, such as the Egyptian Hathor, who appeared as a cow, and the Cattle of the Sun in Greek mythology, which were attended by the sun god Apollo.

On one occasion Brigit came inside from tending her sheep and laid her cloak on a sunbeam, which she had mistaken for a hook, to dry. A bishop, having seen this, told his servant to hang his cloak on another sunbeam, but each time he tried, it fell to the ground.

Like the goddess, Brigit the saint was also able to cure blindness. Given the connection often made between the sun and the eye, this is not surprising. On one occasion Brigit and a nun named Daria (sometimes Dara), who had been blind since birth, sat talking about their love of Jesus as the sun went down. The hours quickly passed as they talked, and the sun once again began to rise. The beautiful light of the sun as it washed across the land was so lovely that Brigit sighed. Saddened that Daria could not see its beauty, she touched the woman on the brow, and she was miraculously able to see. After gazing upon the world for a time, Daria asked Brigit to restore her blindness, claiming that seeing the world so clearly with the eyes made God less visible to the soul.[92]

Another story, from the eighth-century *Irish Life of Brighid*, or *Bethu Brigte*, tells how Brigit blinded herself to deter a suitor, having decided never to marry. Despite her making it clear she did not wish to marry, her brother informed her that whether she liked it or not, the pretty eyes in her head would soon be betrothed to a man. She

---

92. O'Hanlon, *Life of St. Brigid*, 246.

told him it was unlikely that any suitor would want a blind girl and proceeded to gouge out her own eyes. Afterward she restored her sight with the aid of a stream created by her own staff. All attempts to force her to marry were subsequently ceased, but not before she caused her brother's eyes to burst from his head for his part in attempting to arrange the undesired marriage. Her ability to restore eyesight, blind the wicked, and restore her own sight is significant. The sun is often referred to as an eye, and the ability to cure blindness is a common theme found in the stories of other solar goddesses, including the British Sulis, who also was called upon to cure ailments related to the eyes.

As a saint, Brigit is most well known for establishing an abbey in what is now Kildare. The Gaelic name for Kildare is *Cill Dara*, meaning "Church of the Oak." A site sacred to the Druids seems like an unlikely place for a Christian abbey, but when we consider Brighid the goddess's assimilation into Christianity, it appears to be a deliberate attempt to convert a site sacred to the goddess into a sacred place connected to the saint. Legend says Saint Brigit went to the king of Leinster with four of her maidens to ask for land to build the abbey. The king refused, after which Brigit requested that he give her as much land as her cloak could cover. Laughing, he agreed. Brigit then told each of her maidens to take a corner of the cloak, and they began walking east, west, north, and south, and as they did so the cloak stretched for miles and miles until it covered the entire piece of land Brigit wished for the abbey.

The Welsh chronicler Gerald of Wales visited Kildare in the twelfth century and described how Brigit and nineteen of her nuns took turns tending a sacred fire, which had been burning for some six hundred years at Kildare. The fire never went out, and the ashes never needed cleaning, as they never increased. The fire was said to be surrounded by a hedge that no man could cross, lest he go mad. After Brigit's death, the nuns, each in turn, continued tending the flame. On the twentieth day, Brigit's spirit was said to watch over the flame. The tradition continued until Henry de Loundres, the archbishop of Dublin, ordered it to be extinguished in 1221 CE, as he considered the practice to be "too Pagan." It was soon relit by the locals, and then extinguished again during the Reformation during the reign of Elizabeth I. In 1993 it was finally relit by Mary Teresa Cullen, then the leader of the Brigidine Sisters, at the opening of a justice and peace conference.

WORKING WITH BRIGHID

Brighid will always remain in my mind as one of the most quintessential of sun goddesses, perhaps because she was the first solar deity I encountered in my practices. I first met the sun goddess in the most unlikely of places: a college art class. As most of my money went to paying for my classes, many of my ritual tools were the products of open-ended art assignments. This particular assignment was to make something out of clay, and as it was almost Imbolc and Brighid was both connected to the holiday and to crafts, I decided whatever I would make should be dedicated to her. As I molded the clay, I asked Brighid to inspire my work, and as I kneaded and shaped the clay, the image of a rayed sun began to form. I knew Brighid was connected to fire, and as fire and the sun went hand in hand, it seemed like a fitting symbol.

After carving the many variations of her name in the ogham on the sun disc I had sculpted and adding indents to hold candles, I was quite pleased with my work. As far as my art class was concerned, it was a nifty candleholder, and as far as I was concerned, I had a new centerpiece to place on my coven's Imbolc altar. When I brought my art to the Imbolc ceremony for the group I was working with at the time, it came as quite a surprise to be told I had chosen the wrong symbol to represent Brighid, and that it was a symbol for the god and the masculine, not the goddess. Ultimately, that experience sparked my search for the sun goddess, and taught me to see Brighid in a new light. I had worked with her for years, yet had never made the connection between her and the sun.

Brighid has so many aspects that it is little wonder that the Celts envisioned her as triple-faced. When beginning to work with this goddess, it may be beneficial to work with each of her three aspects for a period of time. You could, for example, work with her aspect as the poet for a month, then take time to work with her other two faces. Afterward you may wish to take time connecting to her as a goddess of the sun and fire, or even connect to Brighid the saint.

Taking time to work with the element of fire is also beneficial when working with Brighid. Fire fuels everything that Brighid does, as both a goddess and a saint. If you have ever visited a replica of an old-fashioned forge, you'll know that fire and heat were an integral part to a smith's work. Fire and willpower combined melted and shaped weapons, jewelry, and everyday tools. This may not seem amazing to us today, but it would have seemed magickal to our ancestors, a divinely inspired act that transformed the raw substance of the earth into works of art. On a metaphorical level, it is the fire of Brighid's forge that shapes us and transforms us.

BRIGHID INVOCATION

Smith, harp bearer, song weaver
Lady of fire, eternal undying flame
Strike the hammer,
Inspiration tame
Mother keening for a son
Lady of the healing well and cleansing flame
Brighid, I call your name!

....
Brighid Mantle Spell

You Will Need:
1 white candle

This spell can be used to bless and protect a new house or to renew the protection on a home, and it can even be cast over a person for protection.

Sit comfortably, preferably in the center of your home. Light the candle. Take a moment to see the borders of your house clearly, as if you were looking at them from a bird's-eye view. If you are protecting a person, take a moment to see that person in your mind's eye. When you have the image in your head, see Brighid standing before you. Around her shoulders is a thick green cloak. She takes it off her shoulders and spreads it over the house (or around the shoulders of the person). It expands until it covers the entire house in green, glowing light that no unwanted person can pass through. When you are ready, say:

In the oak grove, Brighid's fire the priestesses tend
You whisper to the heart of victory, strength, a summer without end
The hammer that strikes the soul
The flame above the head
Brighid, your protection bestow!

Hold the candle up at brow level, and say:

Brighid's mantle above us

Hold the candle down toward your knees (or place it on the floor for a moment), and say:

Brighid's mantle below us

Bring the candle to chest level:

> *Brighid's mantle surround us*
> *Safe, protected, and whole*

If you wish, you can also walk around the house or area to be protected holding the candle in your hands and seeing Brighid's protective light encasing your home. Thank Brighid and extinguish the candle.

KEEPING BRIGHID'S FLAME

You Will Need:
1 red or orange pillar candle
Brighid incense (see next page)

Tending Brighid's flame is both a sacred act of devotion to this goddess and an excellent way to connect with her many mysteries and aspects. In Kildare, her flame was tended by nineteen priestesses over the course of nineteen days, with the goddess herself tending the flame on the twentieth day. There are several ways to approach tending the flame. If you are working with a group, you could have a designated person tend the flame for a period of time (perhaps three days each) after the candle is initially blessed. If you are working alone, you can light the candle for a few minutes each night and meditate on Brighid. When I do this practice, I pick an aspect of Brighid to connect to for each night, and I leave an offering around the candle for that particular guise of Brighid. By the twentieth day, the altar where I keep the candle representing her flame is colorfully adorned with offerings of flowers, images of her sacred symbols, and even some devotional poetry. On the twentieth day I will light the candle and let it burn out completely, letting Brighid's energy fill my working space and house.

Burn the incense and pass the candle through the smoke. Hold the candle in your hands for a few minutes. See the nineteen priestesses in your mind's eye. Perhaps they wear the garb of Pagan priestesses, or they are dressed in the habits of nuns; both have tended her flame through the years. See in your mind's eye the flame they tend. Hold the image clearly in your mind, then draw the flame toward you. See it cupped in your hands and flowing into the candle you hold. Take as long as you need to do this. When you feel ready, place the candle (preferably in a fireproof container; candles in glass jars are perfect for this kind of devotional) on the altar or in the space you have set aside for this work. Say:

> Brighid's flame within me
> Brighid's flame without
> Holy fire burning eternal
> Flame of the smith, shape me
> Flame of the poet, burn within me
> Flame of the healer, flow ever through me,
> as I tend this, your sacred flame

This chant can be repeated each day as you light the candle, or you may choose to have a different chant for each day.

. . . .
BRIGHID INCENSE
1 tablespoon rose petals

½ tablespoon cinnamon

½ tablespoon sandalwood

1 tablespoon blackberry leaf

3 drops sandalwood oil

3 drops dragon's blood oil

· ·
BRIGHID CORRESPONDENCES

Symbols: Brighid's cross, sun wheels

Animals: ox, cow, boar

Colors: red, white

Stone: garnet

SULIS

You find yourself standing in a lush valley. Hills rise up around you in a green crescent of life and vegetation on one side; and on the other in the distance you see the sunlight glistening off of the waters of a river. As you continue to look around, you see a dirt road not far off with small groups of people talking and laughing as they make their way deeper into the valley. You feel compelled to follow them, so you make your way to the road. Soon there are people on either side of you. They welcome you, recognizing you are on the same journey.

Although you are not sure where you are being led, you continue onward with the others. Soon the dirt path changes to wood logs that have been laid out to form a road over the marshy soil. Finally the road brings you to a spring. Water bubbles to the surface, filling a large area with a pool that smells pleasantly of something unidentifiable. You breathe in the scent. It is neither fresh water nor the briny smell of sea water; instead it smells of minerals from deep within the earth.

Still uncertain where you are, you ask the woman next to you. "This is the spring of Sulis," she tells you. She points to the sun high above. "When she dips below the horizon and the sun travels below the earth, she heats the sacred waters. Sulis is fire and water made one."

As you watch, people gather around the spring. Some throw offerings into the water; others drink from the spring and offer prayers. Some ask for healing, others for the righting of wrongs and the catching of thieves, others for the Goddess to watch over

them as they bring their children into the world. There is a still-
ness in the air, and you feel as if the Goddess is listening.

Slowly you come to stand beside the sacred waters. You notice
wisps of steam wafting up into the air. As you dip your hands in
the water, it is pleasantly warm, and as it touches your lips you
taste a faint hint of iron. You close your eyes and send a silent
prayer to Sulis. And as you close your eyes, you see the image of
a woman in your mind's eye. She is tall and regal yet there is a
loving, motherly quality to her. The type of woman who would
let you cry on her shoulder, yet also take up a sword in your de-
fense. Surprised by the vision, you open your eyes, but when you
do, you see that your surroundings have changed. The spring is
ringed with stones, and beyond it is a large complex where the
wooden road had been. A small, Roman-style temple stands to
one side, with a bathhouse ringed with Roman columns attached
to it. You can hear water running into the baths and see people
slowly, ritualistically entering the water.

Uncertain how you have arrived here, you make your way
to the temple. Others come and go, but they seem unaware of
your presence. In the temple you see other stone-lined pools, all
fed by the sacred spring by some feat of Roman engineering. As
you wander deeper into the temple, you come to a large room
with a copper statue of a woman. It has the same face as the
woman in your vision. The copper seems to make her shine with
an otherworldly light. Here too you see devotees bring offerings
to the Goddess. Sulis remains ever-present, and you know you
are being given a glimpse of another time. You feel reassured
that these people around you still call out her name and offer up
prayers and gratitude to her.

Walking closer to the statue, you kneel before it and again
send a silent prayer to Sulis. You ask for her waters to heal you.

Perhaps it is a physical healing you ask for, or one of the soul or heart. You ask for her blessing to wash across you.

When you look up, you see Sulis standing before you, no longer a vision or a statue but flesh and blood. As you continue to kneel before her, she reaches out a hand and lovingly caresses your cheek. Like her statue, a faint glow surrounds her; it makes you think of the sunlight streaming through the trees on a summer day. It is warming and reassuring, rather than scorching or burning. She cups her hands together, and as you watch, they fill with water. "Drink. I am of the waters, and of the force that imbues them. I am the fire within the earth, and the fire of the sun that dances on the surface of the spring. I am the fires and the waters within you."

She touches her cupped hands to your lips and you drink. The water is sweet and cool, yet full of a fiery power at the same time. You feel as if you are drinking sunlight. As the power of Sulis flows through you, you feel it wash away all that ails your spirit and body. It soothes you, then ignites within you something new. Dreams and goals you have given up on come to the forefront of your mind, and everything seems possible.

"Fire and water seem at odds with one another, but they are both my allies. My waters wash away and heal, and my fire sparks new life into the old, and inspires the mind and heart. When we keep these forces in balance, we can transform ourselves and those around us. Whenever you feel your balance slipping, when you need rest and healing, come to me. Drink of my waters, and know that my spring, my sacred waters, flow within you."

With that blessing, the temple and the scene blur and fade, and you find yourself back in your body, knowing that the sacred waters of Sulis flow within you.

At the bottom of the Avon Valley in Britain, the Romans replaced the humble grove of a local Celtic goddess with a Roman-style temple and bathhouse that remains a place of pilgrimage to this day. The modern city of Bath is named for the bathhouse fed by the healing waters of the hot springs sacred to the goddess Sulis. Although she is best known as a goddess of this thermal spring, she was a goddess of far-reaching sight who punished thieves, watched over women in childbirth, and infused her sacred waters with the healing power of the sun.

It is estimated that the hot springs at Bath have been in use for the last 10,000 years, first by the Neolithic tribes of Britain, and later by the Romans. In pre-Roman times, a manmade causeway led across the marshy ground to the hot springs. Archaeologists have discovered numerous Celtic coins, as well as other offerings, indicating the site was being used extensively by the Celtic tribes prior to the Romans adopting the site. When the Romans invaded Britain around 43 CE, they converted the Celtic shrine into a bath and temple complex. Equating Sulis with the Roman Minerva, they built a temple to the reimagined goddess Sulis-Minerva. The bathing complex was fed by a constant flow of water from pipes and a reservoir that still functions today. In Roman times, visitors could view the sacred springs from the main hall of the baths, and the waters of the River Avon beyond. Once the Roman legions departed in the early fifth century, the baths and temple fell into decline, until they were rediscovered in the seventeenth century.

There are several interpretations of Sulis's name, with several overlapping meanings, but each lends clarity to her character and the mysteries she ruled over. One meaning comes from the Old Irish *súil*, meaning "eye" or "vision." *Súil* may be derived from the Proto-Celtic word for sun, *sūli*.[93] Her name may also be related to the Proto-Celtic *silīn*, meaning "to look" or "gaze." The same root has been related

---

93. Zair, *Reflexes of the Proto-Indo-European Laryngeals in Celtic*, 120.

to the goddess Adsullata, whose name means "She Who Is Gazed Upon," possibly making Sulis "Upon Whom We Gaze." No matter the translation, they all hint at a deity who is either the sun itself or who resides in the sky. At first this seems odd for a goddess connected to healing water and hot springs. The sun's solar fire seems at odds with the sacred waters Sulis rules over, but when we consider that the sun was commonly thought to travel underground at night or enter the earth through sacred mounds, a solar deity heating water beneath the ground makes sense.

As in other cultures, the concept of the sun being an all-seeing eye in the heavens in firmly rooted in Sulis's name. The oldest known inscriptions refer to her as Sul, later becoming Sulis, and finally becoming known as Sulis-Minerva when the Romans equated her to one of their own goddesses after they conquered the British Celts. Only one inscription of her name has ever been found outside of Bath, indicating she was a local deity, connected primarily the hot springs that became central to her worship.

Most of the inscriptions and artifacts dedicated to Sulis are in the form of *defixiones*, or curse tablets, a kind of tablet with the petitioner's name inscribed on it as well as the goddess's with a request for a blessing or aid in an endeavor, such as "*PRISCVS TOVTI F LAPIDARIVS CIVES CARNVTENVS SVLI DEAE VSLM* [Priscus, son of Toutus, stonecutter of the Carnutes tribe, to the goddess Sul, willingly and deservedly fulfills his vow]."[94] There is some evidence that Sulis may have been a triple goddess. One inscription invokes Sulis as the *Sulevi*: "*SVLEVIS SVLINVS SCVLTOR BRVCETI F SACRVM F L M* [To the Sulevi, Sulinus Scultor, son of Brucetus, willingly and deservedly made this sacred offering]."[95] Over a hundred and thirty defixiones have been found dedicated to Sulis. Some also give us an alternative name, Sulla, which could perhaps be an older form of her

---

94. Ireland, *Roman Britain*, 185.
95. Ibid., 186

name or, if she is a triple goddess, could refer to one of her three faces. It is also interesting to note that there were three springs, within close proximity of one another, from which Sulis's sacred waters sprung.

One defixio found at the baths reads: "To the most holy goddess Sulis. I curse him who has stolen my hooded cloak, whether man or woman, whether slave or free, that … the goddess Sulis inflict death upon … and not allow him sleep or children now and in the future, until he has brought my hooded cloak to the temple of her divinity."[96] Sulis was also petitioned to find lost objects and to witness oaths, as well as to catch thieves. The concept that the sun could see all from its lofty position in the sky, thus being able to catch criminals, is a trait Sulis shared with other sun goddess. Similarly, in Lithuania, Saule was also called upon to find thieves, and the Canaanite Shapash could see all that transpired on the earth and in the land of the dead.

Other offerings left for the goddess include coins, shoes, and amulets, but some of the most common were molds or images of solar wheels. In Sulis we see again the connection the Celtic people drew between the sun and water. A solar wheel would be an odd symbol to be associated with a deity only connected to water, but in the Celtic mind Sulis was both the eye of the sun and the keeper of healing waters. The fact that the water she is associated with is a hot spring that rises from the earth's heat may have also helped foster the connection between the sun and this spring in the minds of the Celts. Many cultures believed the sun traveled underground during the night before it emerged again the next day. It is possible they believed Sulis heated her sacred waters as she made this nightly travel, as well as warming them from her vantage point in the sky.

From her association with the healing thermal waters at Bath, it is fairly certain that Sulis was considered a goddess of healing. The renown for Bath's thermal water regained a new height during the

---

96. Ireland, *Roman Britain*, 186.

Victorian era, when the well-to-do flocked to the city for the healing waters and high society. Inscriptions also link Sulis to a local school of midwives, suggesting she may have protected woman during childbirth.

WORKING WITH SULIS

Several years ago I had the chance to visit Bath and Sulis's temple. Walking into the Roman baths, which is now a museum, was like stepping back through time. Although no one is allowed into the pools, Sulis's sacred water still flows into the baths and other pools in the complex. As I walked around the central pool and listened to the sound of the water flowing, Sulis's presence was palpable. Although the bronze statue of the goddess is no longer in what remains of the temple (only the head remains in the museum), I could see a beautiful bronze statue in my mind and devotees gathered around whispering Sulis's name and laying offerings before the goddess's image.

Although I had never worked with this goddess before, what struck me was how enduring she was. Given enough time, water will wash away all that obstructs its path, and I felt that is what Sulis had done. She went from being worshiped by the Celts to being re-imagined as a face of Minerva by the Romans; then after centuries of her temple being buried, she emerged again to be rediscovered. And today she remains with us. Through all the centuries of people coming to Bath to see and partake in her sacred waters, she most certainly meant many things to different people across the long span of time. She has been worshiped, and at times visited simply as a relic of the past, but still she remains.

Sulis teaches us to bring balance and healing into our lives. She is both the sun and the healing waters. She holds these seemingly opposites forces in a sacred balance. Call on Sulis for any type of healing, for ease through pregnancy, and to bring justice to a situation. A small fountain, found in many craft and home goods stores, is an excellent way to bring Sulis's energy to your home. A fountain can be used in place of an altar for this goddess, and offerings placed in or beside the fountain.

······················
SULIS INVOCATION

Sulis
In you, earth and sky meet as one
You are the flowing waters from the heart of the earth
You are she who is gazed upon,
the fiery solar eye
You are the soother, the bringer of justice
Heal me, Sulis
Avenge me, Sulis
Be within me, Sulis

······························
SULIS'S HEALING WATERS

You Will Need:
1 clear glass or bowl
Bottled or purified water

To bless water with Sulis's energy, take a bowl (or clear-colored glass) and fill it with bottled or purified water. Sit comfortably with the bowl in front of you. See Sulis standing before you. She glistens as rays of sunlight illuminate her features and radiate from her. See her essence filling the water, then say:

Sul, Sulis, Sulla
Eye of Vision
She who is gazed upon
Shine your eye upon me
Cleanse my spirit

Enliven my body and mind,
As the sun blesses your sacred waters from on high

If possible, set the water outside in a sunny place for at least a half-hour. You may wish to cover it with plastic wrap so nothing is blown into the water. You can use this water to bless objects or an area, or simply drink some every morning when you feel a cold coming on or when doing any kind of healing work.

....
SULIS BATH SALTS

You Will Need:
1 cup Epsom salt
3 bay leaves
¼ cup chamomile
¼ cup orange peel
⅛ cup honey

The sacred water at Bath was fed from rainwater from the Avon Valley and surrounding hills that sunk deep into the earth's crust through a fault line beneath the city. It took some six thousand years to be forced back up to the surface through fissures in the limestone. This ancient rainwater steamed and bubbled up from three springs. This rust-colored steaming water is teeming with more than forty minerals, including calcium, sodium, and iron.

Creating your own bath salts and infusing them with Sulis's energy is a wonderful way to call upon her as a goddess of healing. Pour the salt in a large bowl. Break the bay leaves in half and mix with the salt. Then add the chamomile and orange peel. Mix all the dry ingredients until they are evenly distributed, then add the honey. Mix the honey in with a large spoon until thoroughly mixed together. You will end up with a sticky mixture. Take a large spoonful and roll the mixture into a ball in your hands. This can either be left on a sheet of wax paper to dry and used at a later time or can be tossed into a hot bath for immediate use.

. . . .
SULIS INCENSE
1 part frankincense
1 part rosemary
½ part Irish moss

. . . .
SULIS CORRESPONDENCES
Colors: blue, white
Symbols: solar wheel, wells, cups

RHIANNON

You find yourself on a dimly lit path. All around you the world is steeped in twilight. You try to see your surroundings, but nothing is clear. You could be outside or in a vast cavern; it is impossible to tell. As you continue onward, the darkness begins to feel heavier. It weighs you down and makes your shoulders sag. You find yourself wondering why you even continue onward. What's the point? The darkness grows thicker and your thoughts bleaker. Dark shapes along the path flit by, whispering the things you fear the most and prodding you as you walk. You begin to slow; your feet grow heavy.

When you are just ready to give up and let the shadowy figures do what they will with you, you see something moving toward you on the path. It is a blur of purest white, moving at first too fast to discern its shape or appearance. It begins to slow as it approaches you, and you realize it is a large white mare. As it passes by you in a blur of white, you reach up. Grabbing a handful of mane, you pull yourself on her back.

Although you still feel the weight of the darkness, it feels somewhat lighter now that the mare carries you. But the weight is still there and you realize the darkness here is of your own making; it is bound to you, and only you can unbind it. As you think this, you hear a voice in your mind. It comes from the mare. Although the voice does not speak out loud, you hear her clearly: "Give me your sorrows, give me your burdens. I can bear them with you."

Not knowing why, you feel compelled to stretch out across the mare. You lean down and bury your face into her mane. As you do, a strange sensation comes over you. When you close your eyes, you begin to see through the mare's eyes. Slowly you feel yourself melting away, becoming one with the mare as she runs faster than seems possible.

The weight feels like a yoke around your neck. But as the mare, you see these weighty shadows differently. While in your own form they seemed like chains, things you had no control over, you see now that you have made them so. Deciding they were chains made them bound to your spirit. Now you see you have only to shrug them off. It is a choice, nothing more, whether or not to change your life. And so you do just that. With a great bucking motion, you heave the shadows off of you.

As they slip away, left behind in the darkness, you feel amazingly free. You run faster and faster, until your surroundings blur. When you finally do stop, you are no longer in the dark underworld but in the world above next to a great, grass-covered mound. You see a small passage in the mound and know it leads back to the underworld. In the distance the sun is just beginning to rise.

Again you begin to feel yourself changing. You are yourself again. When you look over to the mare, you see that a woman stands in her place. Her chestnut hair is arranged in many braids, and she wears a regal dress of beautiful yellow silks that catches the light of the rising sun.

You realize this is Rhiannon, the horse goddess who emerged, as you just did, from the Otherworlds. Rhiannon smiles at you. "You have made your way through the underworld, as I do each day. From this world to the Otherworlds I travel, as the sun does each day. My path is ever fraught with troubles. They come from so many directions, they can overcome us. They become a yoke that drives us down. But know that I am ever at your side. Bring to me your burdens, place your sorrows before me. I have known them all, and I have risen like the dawning sun each day above them. Let me be your strength, and I will carry you farther than you thought possible."

They saw a lady, on a pure white horse of large size, with a garment of shining gold around her.
—Lady Charlotte Guest, *The Mabinogion*

The Welsh goddess Rhiannon stands by each of us in our darkest hours. She is the light within that guides us through life's many trials and obstacles. Wearing many guises throughout her mythology, she is a goddess of the underworld, a horse goddess, and a radiant goddess of the sun all at once.

You're probably thinking to yourself, "Wait a minute, isn't Rhiannon a moon goddess?" Many modern sources do call Rhiannon a moon goddess, but let's take a moment to examine why exactly that is. First, there is nothing within Rhiannon's mythology that connects her to the moon. She is connected to the horse, a solar animal, both through the way in which she meets her husband, Pwyll, riding an uncatchable white horse, and in her punishment after being accused of killing her son, where she is made to carry visitors on her back like a horse. When she first emerges at dawn from the Otherworlds, through a sacred mound, she is described as wearing "golden" silks, bringing to mind the color of the sun. Like the sun, which was thought nightly to visit the underworld, she emerges from a sacred mound—a place connected to the Celtic Otherworlds and the land of the dead due to the fact that such mounds were usually ancient burial sites.[97]

So where does the moon come into play? Modern sources have connected Rhiannon to the moon by drawing a connection between the white color of her horse and the pale color of the moon. Like so many goddesses, she is labeled a moon goddess simply because we have been led to believe that the divine feminine and the moon instantly go together. Considering that the color white and white animals represented death in the Celtic mind, her white horse seems more likely to indicate Rhiannon's role as an underworld goddess and a psychopomp, rather than mark her as a moon goddess.

Rhiannon's story begins when Pwyll, the prince of Dyfed, visited the Mound of Arberth. Pwyll was told that if he spent the night on the mound, he would either suffer blows or see a wonder. Unafraid, he slept on the mound, and as the sun rose, a woman dressed in golden robes, riding a white horse, appeared from the mound. Immediately enchanted with the woman, Pwyll sent one of his men to find out who she was. But no matter how fast the man ran, he could not catch up to the woman.

The next day Pwyll and his men again waited on the mound. As the first light of the morning sun filled the sky, the woman again appeared from within the mound. This time Pwyll sent a man on horseback to pursue her, but again he could not catch the woman and her horse. On the third morning, Pwyll himself pursued her on the fastest horse he could find. No matter how fast his horse ran, the woman seemed no closer to him than when he first started his pursuit. Finally he called out and asked her to wait for him, which she did, after scolding him for driving his horse to exhaustion.

---

97. Paxson, "One of Ten Thousand," *SageWoman Magazine*, issue 73.

The woman told Pwyll she was Rhiannon, the daughter of the Otherworldly king Hyfaidd Hen, and that she was being forced to marry a man against her will. She also informed him that she had heard of Pwyll's great deeds and wished to marry him instead. Pwyll instantly fell in love with Rhiannon, and the two planned to meet in a year and a day to be wed. On the appointed day, Pwyll rode with one hundred of his horsemen to the house of Hyfaidd Hen, where a wedding feast was being prepared. During the feasting, a man asked Pwyll to grant him a request. Being in a happy mood, Pwyll foolishly told the stranger he would grant any request he asked. Unfortunately, the stranger was Gwawl ap Clud, the man Rhiannon had originally been engaged to. Gwawl demanded Rhiannon's hand in marriage, which Pwyll by his own oath could not refuse him.

Determined to marry the man she loved, Rhiannon managed to postpone her wedding with Gwawl. A year and a day later, Pwyll attended the wedding feast armed with a magickal bag given to him by Rhiannon. Disguised as a beggar, he asked Gwawl for enough food to fill his small bag. Gwawl agreed, but no matter how much food was placed in the bag, it never filled. Finally, Pwyll told the astonished guests that the bag could only be filled when a nobleman trampled the food within. Gwawl attempted to do so, but as soon as he placed his feet in the bag, Pwyll pulled the bag up and trapped him inside. In exchange for releasing him, Gwawl consented to Pwyll marrying Rhiannon.

Pwyll and Rhiannon wed and lived happily for a time. Eventually, Rhiannon gave birth to a son, but on the night of his birth he vanished. Fearful they would be punished for falling asleep when they were supposed to be watching the infant, Rhiannon's handmaidens killed the puppies of a hound that had also given birth that night. The maids smeared the dog's blood on Rhiannon's hands and left their bones beside her. When Rhiannon woke, the maids swore she had devoured her own child. As punishment, Rhiannon was forced to sit beside a mounting block and carry all who visited the castle on her back for seven years.

Rhiannon's son was later found by a vassal of Pwyll's in his stables, lying beside a newborn colt. As the boy grew, his resemblance to Pwyll became unmistakable and he was returned to court and Rhiannon was exonerated. Upon his return, Rhiannon named him Pryderi, which means "worry" or "anxiety."

When Pwyll died, Rhiannon married Manawydan, the Welsh version of the sea god Manannán mac Lir. Their union draws on the connection the Celts saw between water (represented by Manawydan) and fire (Rhiannon). During a celebration, a magickal mist descended on the land. When the mist lifted, the land, Rhiannon, her husband, her son, and his wife were the only people left in the country. One day while out hunting, Manawydan and Pryderi followed a white boar to an enchanted castle. When Pryderi entered the castle, he found a golden cup. Unfortunately, as soon as he touched the cup, he found he could not remove his hand. Later Rhiannon chastised Manawydan for not coming to Pryderi's aid and attempted to rescue her son, but as soon as she touched the cup, she was also entrapped, and both Rhiannon and her son vanished.

In their absence Manawydan takes up agriculture, but his crops are beset by an army magically transformed into mice. Eventually, Manawydan discovers that all of their misfortune was caused by Llwyd, a friend of Gwawl, as revenge for Rhiannon refusing his affections. Manawydan bargains with Llwyd, and the enchantment on the land is lifted and Rhiannon and her son set free. During her imprisonment, Rhiannon and her son lived in Llwyd's court, where Rhiannon was forced to carry hay and wear a horse's halter around her neck.[98]

Like most Celtic sun goddesses, Rhiannon is not described as the physical sun, making her connection to the sun seem obscure at first, but if we know where to look, there are many hints to Rhiannon's solar

98. Markale, *Women of the Celts*, 88.

origins within her mythology. She appears from the mound of Arberth as the sun rises, and she wears golden garments that shine like the sun: "They saw a lady, on a pure white horse of large size, with a garment of shining gold around her." [99] It seems unlikely that a moon goddess would be wearing such garments. That the color of her garments are emphasized is significant. She is not simply described as wearing finely made clothes; they are always golden in color.

One of the most prevalent myths connected with the solar feminine is her nightly descent to the underworld. While the entrance to the underworld changes (in Rhiannon's case, it's a sacred mound), the journey the sun takes each night remains the same. Sacred mounds were often ancient burial sites and were connected with both the ancestors and the realm of the dead, making them fitting entrances to the underworld. That Rhiannon appears specifically each day at dawn also suggests a connection to the sun's light. When she emerges, she brings the sun with her.

Rhiannon's imprisonment in Llwyd's court may also be symbolic of the sun's journeying to the underworld. While the land is under Llwyd's enchantments, it is empty and barren. Llwyd magically steals Rhiannon away, depriving the land and her family of her light. It is not until her husband begins planting that she is released. The barren period here may represent winter, when the sun is weakest and the land made infertile. Her husband's agricultural venture signals a turn in the seasons; the sun is returned and the spell on the land is broken. When Rhiannon returns, the land is rejuvenated and fruitful again, representing the summer sun and bright half of the year.

Her totem, the horse, is also another clue to her role as a sun goddess, as the horse is an animal associated with the sun and other sun deities. On Celtic coins, horses appeared with stylized images of the sun and spoked sun wheels. As Miranda Green puts it, "In Celtic religion,

---

99. Guest, *The Mabinogion*, 345.

horses had a very close affinity with the sun … many coins depicted a horse associated with the sun symbols and the wheel of a chariot." [100]

The horse also had a very close connection to death. It was an animal that could travel between the worlds, and horses have been found in Celtic burials, presumably to escort the souls of the dead to the Otherworlds. Likewise, the goddesses the Celts connected to the horse also fulfilled a similar function. Rhiannon also owned magickal birds, whose singing eased all sorrows and could bring back the dead. Again her role as a psychopomp is made clear, by restoring the dead to life. Saule, the Baltic sun goddess, also owned magickal birds and made a similar nightly journey to the underworld. Rhiannon's difficult love life is also reminiscent of Saule's troubles with her husband.

Working with Rhiannon

Of all the goddesses in the Celtic pantheon, Rhiannon is perhaps the easiest to relate to. Life isn't easy for Rhiannon. She endures many trials before achieving happiness. She is betrayed by those she thought were her friends (the maids who accuse her of killing her son); she escapes an abusive relationship (getting out of her betrothal to Gwawl); and she is widowed. But she learns to find love again. We can relate to so much of Rhiannon's story, from escaping an unhealthy relationship, to experiencing betrayal, to opening ourselves up to new relationships with others. Despite all the trials in her life, Rhiannon always perseveres and emerges triumphant. Like the sun, she is reborn again and again, and rises renewed.

Rhiannon leads us through the dark, as the sun who journeys through the darkness of the underworld, knowing at times we must retreat into the dark to heal and grow. Call upon Rhiannon to overcome obstacles or whenever you feel the weight of the world on your shoulders. She reminds us that we have the ability to reinvent our lives

---

100. Green, *Animals in Celtic Life and Myth*, 208.

if we so desire, and that if need be she is with us to help carry our
burdens.

···························
RHIANNON INVOCATION

Rhiannon
Lady of renewal and spring
Clothed in the golden sun you ride,
Unbridled, untamable, uncatchable
Swift as the wind
Rhiannon
Mare Mother
Mistress of golden sunshine,
Whose birds chase away all sorrow
And wake the dead
Rhiannon, I call to you this day
No prince could catch you,
No hero, god, or king
Only to those who call,
Does sweet Rhiannon,
Her blessings bring

································
A LIGHT IN THE DARK SPELL

You Will Need:
1 gold candle
Sun water (recipe on page 272)
Pen and paper
1 fireproof bowl

For this spell you will need a space to work where, if not all, at least
most, of the light can be turned off. The idea is to make your working

space as dark as possible, as you will be mimicking the sun's journey from the dark underworld to the light-filled world above. Although only one candle is necessary, you may use as many as you wish. I've used several candles to form a large circle around my sacred space for this spell in the past, so as to be "encircled" by Rhiannon's light. Before you begin, write down on a piece of paper the problems and burdens you wish to overcome.

Begin by walking clockwise around and sprinkling the sun water on the space you will be working. If you wish to cast a circle or call the elements, you may do so.

If you have not done so already, turn off as many lights as possible. Sit comfortably in the center of your working space and take three deep, cleansing breaths. Hold the paper in your hands while bringing to mind whatever it is that is weighing down your spirit—the obstacles and burdens in life that you face. Whatever they are, see them clearly in your mind and in as much detail as possible. When you are ready, light the candle, saying:

> *Rhiannon, lady of the golden sun,*
> *Who treads the shadowed halls of the underworld each night*
> *I suffer as you have suffered*
> *Rhiannon, ride forth*
> *Bring the light of a new day*
> *Bear my burdens with me*
> *Renew me this day!*

See Rhiannon standing before you. Her golden robes shimmer like rays of the sun. She holds out her arms and embraces you, and as she does she fills you with her radiant light. You feel uplifted; the weight of your burdens eases. Her light and your own grow brighter and brighter until your obstacles and burdens are dim shadows.

Take the paper and light it in the candle's flame, saying:

Rhiannon rides with me this night
In her name I banish all sorrow and plight

Place the paper in the fireproof bowl and let it burn out. Scatter the ashes outside after you are done. When you are ready, thank Rhiannon. Light the candle for a few minutes each night until it burns out completely.

....
RHIANNON INCENSE
2 parts amber
½ part cedar
1 part honeysuckle
½ part rose petals

....
RHIANNON CORRESPONDENCES
Animal: horse
Colors: gold, white

EGYPT

Egyptian mythology is complex and often confusing. As Egypt became unified, local deities merged with the identities of similar gods and goddesses found throughout the Egyptian empire. In one myth a goddess may be considered the mother of a particular god, only to be called his daughter or wife in another. Like the Romans, who often fused together the identities of their own pantheon with those of the people they conquered, such as with Sulis-Minerva, we find similar mergers in the Egyptian pantheon with gods such as Amen-Ra and Wadjet-Bast. To the Egyptians, the mergers between their gods complemented rather than detracted from the god's power.

One thing is quite clear: the Egyptians held the sun to be especially important. In no other pantheon is there such a plethora of sun deities—so many, in fact, that the Egyptians had different gods who represented the dawning sun, the afternoon sun, and the setting sun, along with goddesses who represented both the gentle and fierce aspects of the solar orb. From this pantheon emerges three goddesses who, while often confused for one another, represent distinctly different aspects of the sun's power. In the mother goddess Hathor, we find the sun's creative, fertile force; in her alter ego, Sekhmet, we see the sun's ability to destroy; and in Bast we find a fierce protector who shows both motherly and warrior attributes.

While the stories of theses goddesses differ from their cousins in other pantheons, there are several patterns that remain universal in the myths of all sun goddesses regardless of the culture from which they originate. As in the Shinto and Celtic traditions, the sun goddess is connected with both the eye and the mirror. Hathor's worship in particular was connected to mirrors. All three of the Egyptian sun goddesses we will be exploring were given the title "Eye of Ra" or "Eye of the Sun."

As in the myths of other solar goddesses, these three accompany the sun below the horizon and into the underworld. Both Hathor and Bast nightly visited the underworld, with Hathor rising in the morning to give birth to the sun god Ra and subsequently the new day, while Bast rode in the sun god's boat, protecting him from his enemies as he sailed nightly through the underworld. Like Amaterasu, they arise from the underworld renewed, bringing with them new light. Bast and Sekhmet were both connected to snakes, an animal associated with many sun goddesses, including Sunna and Unelanuhi. Bast's identity was even merged with the snake goddess Wadjet, to form Wadjet-Bast, a goddess who was the protectress of Lower Egypt. Bast also battled the serpent Apep, who nightly attacked Ra's solar barge.

Although Ra eventually emerged as the supreme sun god in Egyptian mythology, all three of the goddesses we will be exploring plays a vital role in the sun's daily cycle. Most likely, the large number of Egyptian deities connected to the sun came from the merger of numerous local sun divinities into a larger pantheon. Each is a sun god or goddess is their own right, simply a personification of the sun's power unique to a certain region.

While Egyptian sun deities could be either male or female, the moon was always viewed as male. Thoth is both the god of wisdom and the moon. Khonsu and Lah (sometimes called Yan) are also moon gods. In the *Papyrus of Ani*, a spell invokes Lah: "O One, bright

as the moon-god Lah; O One, shining as Lah."[101] With the influence
of the Ptolemies (a dynasty of Greek kings who ruled over Egypt
from 305 BCE to 30 CE), the gender of the sun and moon became
somewhat altered, and goddesses who had never previously been
connected to the moon were given lunar attributes.

The Egyptian sun goddess is fiery and colorful; she rules over the
dance of life and joy as Hathor and Bast. As Sekhmet she is the devourer, a goddess of death, yet also a goddess of healing and change,
tearing and devouring our inner darkness to reveal the light within.
She embodies the fullness of life and its cycles, both creative and
destructive.

HATHOR

*You find yourself standing in a marsh. Although you stand on a
dry patch of land, all around you there are tall reeds and grasses
and channels of water flowing through them. You hear the sounds
of herons and other water birds as they go about their day. As
you take in your surroundings, you hear a faint cry. Searching
for the source of the sound, you move through the reeds until you
find a woman lying on a dry bit of land. You can see she is in the
middle of childbirth, and feeling compelled to help her, you take
her hand and speak soothingly to her.*

*With another cry, the child is born. And as you hold the in-
fant in your hands, you notice the child glow with an unearthly
light. As you stare, the child begins to rise up and change into a
fiery ball of light. You look back to the woman and see she has
changed, too. Where the woman was now stands a golden cow,
her horns falling to either side in large crescents. She walks up
to the orbs of light and scoops it up in her horns. Not knowing
why, you put a hand on the cow's shoulder, and as you do, you
suddenly find yourself with the cow high above in the heavens.*

---

101. Budge, *The Papyrus of Ani*, chapter 2.

The sun rises up and fills the sky, and the cow transforms again into the beautiful woman. Black, braided hair falls on either side of her face. She wears white robes that fall to her feet, and on her brow you see a headdress with the solar disc cradled between crescent horns. You know now that you are in the presence of the sun goddess Hathor.

"The sun has many faces," she tells you. "I am both the mother of the solar child, and I am the Eye of Ra." She begins to glow, and you see the light of the sun burning from deep within her. "I am the sun above you and the mother who bears it into the heavens."

She reaches out a fiery hand, and tentatively you clasp it in your own. Immediately you feel the fire of the sun flowing through your veins. In your mind's eye, you see the path of Hathor. You see the power of the sun pass through her each day. She is the power that fuels the sun, one of its many manifestations. She brings light into the world, and you see her bringing that light through the underworld, protecting it and taking it within herself to be reborn anew with the dawn.

"My fire burns within you as well," she tells you. "You are all my children. Call upon me and I will guide the light within you. I will ignite it as I guide the sun each day." As she says this, you feel Hathor's power flowing through you. A feeling of contentment and renewal flows through you, and new ideas spring forth in your mind. In the light of Hathor all seems possible.

Ra says the beauty of your face, glitters when you rise . . .
One is drunk at your beautiful face, O gold, Hathor.
—Jeanette Ellis, *Forbidden Rites*

In Hathor we find both the nurturing and destructive aspects of the sun. She is a primordial goddess of creation who brings joy to life through the gifts of love, music, dance, sensuality, and drunkenness. She assists in childbirth and declares the fates of newborns. Yet when angered, she transforms into the lioness goddess Sekhmet, ruthlessly slaying her enemies and sopping up blood like wine. Like the sun, Hathor can be a benefactor, illuminating our lives, or she can be the harsh heat of the desert that bakes the earth and withers away all life. To the Egyptians, she represented the full spectrum of life, and the many traits of the sun.

Hathor's worship dates to pre-dynastic times, making her one of the oldest goddesses in the Egyptian pantheon. Throughout Egyptian history she remained a popular goddess, her worship extending from the common people to the royal elite. In her earliest depictions she does not appear as a woman at all, but as a divine cow carrying the sun disc in her crescent horns. At the dawn of each day she gave birth to the sun and carried it into the sky between her horns, making her a goddess of the sky as well as of rebirth. In her guise as the Celestial Cow, she is often pictured towering over the young Pharaoh, nourishing him with her life-giving milk. In this form she was believed to have given birth to the universe, which may be why one of her titles was "Lady of the Limit," with *limit* referring to the universe.

Hathor's nature is very dualistic. She is often equated with Aphrodite, ruling over beauty and sensuality, yet she is also responsible for nearly destroying humanity. There are several Egyptian poems and hymns that beseech the goddess to intervene in matters of love. Her festivals involved ritual inebriation and ecstatic dance, where "singers, vital and beautiful, are intoxicated by speedily moving their legs out before them." [102]

At times Hathor appeared as a seven-fold goddess. The Seven Hathors acted as divine midwives—attending the birth of children— and determined the child's fate. They also were petitioned in matters

---

102. Graves-Brown, *Dancing for Hathor*, 67.

of love, and it was believed the red ribbons they wore could bind evil spirits.[103]

When Hathor showed her fiercer side, she underwent a very literal transformation. In the "Book of the Divine Cow," Ra sends his "eye," Hathor, to destroy humanity, which he believed had been planning to overthrow him. But when Hathor begins her task, she transforms into the raging lioness Sekhmet. Soon Ra regretted his decision and took pity on humanity, but unfortunately Sekhmet was consumed with bloodlust and refused to stop her slaughtering. Her slaughter only ended when Ra tricked her into drinking beer that had been dyed red. Thinking the beer was blood, Sekhmet began drinking it with gusto and soon became too drunk to continue her bloody rampage. Sated, Sekhmet once again transformed into the gentle Hathor.

Eventually Hathor's worship became so widespread that her identity merged with that of several other goddesses, including Isis, Mut, and Bat, accounting for some of the conflicting roles she plays in Egyptian mythology. She is at time the god Horus's wife, yet in other myths she is his mother, a role she shares and perhaps absorbed from Isis. Similarly, she is at times the sun god Ra's mother, wife, or daughter, despite her worship predating Ra's. As Egyptian religion evolved, so did Hathor's myths. While the type of familial relationship with Ra or Horus changes from myth to myth, her connection to the sun remains. Both Horus and Ra represent the masculine sun, while Hathor's connection to them implies she is the feminine aspect of the sun. This is clear in her connection to Ra, where she is his "eye" and dwells in the sun god's forehead. Dwelling within the sun god, or the sun god dwelling within her womb as her son, implies that they represent both the masculine and feminine aspects of the sun. Either way, one lives within the other, showing a deep connection between the two.

---

103. Remler, *Egyptian Mythology A to Z*, 77.

Hathor was given several titles, including the Lady of the West, Mistress of Jubilation, the Lady of Light, and the Mistress of Life. But the title that is continually repeated in ancient Egyptian prayers and texts is the *Golden One*. Her radiance is so bright that "the gods turn their heads away in order to see her better." [104] When comparing her to a king, we are told he "shinest like Hathor," [105] and according to the Stone of Palermo, she was worshiped in "the sun temple," [106] making her status as a solar goddess unmistakable.

As is the case for Amaterasu and other sun goddesses, mirrors played a role in her worship. A painting in the grave of Mereruka shows women dancing in honor of Hathor, bearing mirrors and votive objects, most likely depicting a ceremony called the "Time of Mirrors" when mirrors were left as offerings to the goddess. [107] In her temple in Dendera, a Pharaoh is shown offering Hathor a mirror fashioned by the gods Ptah and Sokaris. [108] This seems to parallel Amaterasu's story in which the gods left offerings, including a mirror, at the entrance to Amaterasu's cave. In Hathor's case, it is the king offering her the mirror, although it was created for her by other gods. Her face was also a popular subject to be carved on the handles of mirrors.

Another parallel between Hathor and other solar goddesses is her connection to the eye. The sun was regarded as a cosmic eye in the sky in several cultures, regardless of gender. This is very apparent in Egyptian mythology. Both of Horus's eyes were connected to celestial objects—one being the sun, the other the moon. Hathor along with Bast and Sekhmet were given the title "Eye" of Ra. The Egyptian word for "eye," *iret*, is feminine, making it likely that the Egyptians first envisioned the sun as female. An inscription on the wall of Hathor's temple in Dendera describes how Hathor was born from Ra's

---

104. Bleeker, *Hathor and Thoth*, 26.
105. Ibid., 26.
106. Monaghan, *O Mother Sun!*, 50.
107. Ibid., 27.
108. Bleeker, *Hathor and Thoth*, 53.

eye. Her birth is surprisingly similar to the conception of the Japanese goddess Amaterasu, who was born when her father washed his eye in a river.

In the inscription, Ra opens his eye at the moment he rose from the Nun (primordial waters). Fluid (it is unclear if this is some of the primordial water he rose from or a tear) fell onto the earth from his eye and transformed into the beautiful Hathor. This most likely was a later myth, as she was Ra's mother in her incarnation as the Celestial Cow, rather than his daughter. Still, her frequent connection with the eye in the Egyptian mind is important. Like Amaterasu, Brighid, and many other solar goddesses, the relation between the sun and the eye is emphasized in their mythology. While other Egyptian goddesses wear the solar disc above their heads, Hathor is the only one born from a divine eye, or referred to as shining or golden like the sun.

Hathor was also called the Lady of the Malachite, acting as a patroness of those who mined for the semi-precious stones and also referring to her role as a goddess of beauty, as malachite was ground up and mixed with makeup that was worn around the eyes. Although this probably says more about her role as a goddess of beauty, it is interesting that the stone she is connected to was used in connection to the eyes.

Hathor's name also hints at her role as a solar deity. One translation of Hathor's name is "House of Horus." As a sky goddess, this could refer to the sky being the sun's home or that she carried the sun god in her womb, or "house." As the "House of Horus," her name was represented with hieroglyphics showing a falcon within a square. This representation of her name seems to have been predominant during Egypt's Late Period, while during the earlier Middle and New Kingdoms her name was spelled using different hieroglyphics. An alternative translation proposed by Egyptologist C. J. Bleeker is "My House Is the Sky." This seems like a fitting name for a sun goddess. If Hathor is the sun, then her home would be the sky. Given that her worship predates that of Horus, and that his role as her son was a later evolution within her mythology, this seems a more likely translation of her name.

The way in which Hathor was depicted in Egyptian art is also another clue to her status as a sun goddess. She is the only Egyptian goddess to be depicted in full profile, with her head facing the viewer directly. Egyptian art traditionally depicted figures from the side, showing only half of their face. There are hundreds of examples of Hathor's face shown in full profile with the ears of her totem, the cow, decorating the tops of pillars or the handles of mirrors. Here her face becomes a stylized sun symbol in itself.

As the Lady of the West, Hathor greeted the souls of the dead and was the guardian of the Theban necropolis. In the Egyptian *Book of the Dead*, she is shown emerging, in cow form, from tombs in the Libyan mountains. She was also said to join Ra as he disappeared below the western horizon each day. If beseeched properly, she would carry the dead safely on her back, and possessing her outer garment, or *tjetsen*, granted souls safe passage through the dangers that awaited them in the land of the dead. In the shade of her sacred tree, the sycamore, she would greet the dead, offering them food as they traveled to the underworld. One story tells how Hathor (or Isis, depending on the version) healed Horus's blindness using milk from a sycamore. Against we see the connection between Hathor and the eye.

WORKING WITH HATHOR

The beauty of working with Hathor is that she encompasses so many of the sun's attributes. When angered, she is the raging warrioress Sekhmet, yet she is also a goddess of jubilation and love. She both greets us at our births, determining our fates, and guides us through the realm of dead when we breathe our last. She encompasses all of life.

Hathor teaches us to enjoy all life has to offer. Invoked as the goddess of pleasure, she teaches us to revel in our senses, whether that means listening to a beautiful piece of music or enjoying the touch of a lover's hand or the taste of good food and wine. An excellent way to honor her is through dance and music. If you play an instrument (even something as simple as the harmonica or tambourine), dedicate a song to Hathor. Dance is another wonderful way to honor Hathor. Put on one of your favorite songs and sway and move to the beat of the music, while asking Hathor to join you. Sacred dance helps ground us to our bodies and become more in tune with our physical forms. While much of spiritual work leads us to explore that which is outside of the physical, we can never really find true balance if we do not become in tune with the sacred forms the gods have given us during this lifetime. When honoring Hathor through dance, begin by becoming aware of your body and honoring the sacred within you, and know Hathor dwells within you.

As a patroness of the necropolis and the greeter of the dead, Hathor can also help us navigate the realm of the ancestors and the beloved dead. Hathor is an excellent goddess to work with to overcome the grief of a loved one's passing, and also to call upon to aid a loved one's journey to the next life.

....
HATHOR INVOCATION

For this invocation, choose your favorite song or piece of music or something that reminds you of the goddess. Michael Levy's "Hymn to Hathor" from his CD *Apollo's Lyre* would be a good choice, as would any of the music from Gerald Jay Markoe's *Meditation Music of Ancient Egypt*. If calling upon Hathor for matters of love, you could also use your favorite love song; for invoking her joyful nature, pick something upbeat that puts you in a good mood. Take a few minutes to feel the rhyme of the music. Close your eyes and let yourself sink into an altered state, while remaining aware of the music. When you are ready, begin to move and sway to the music while saying:

I sing your praises, O Hathor
Hear me, O golden one,
You one who thrusts back the darkness and brings the new day
You are the Lady of Jubilation
Hathor, who illuminates the soul
Lady of Dance, Mistress of the harp playing
I praise your majesty each day
I sing your name, Golden Hathor, I dance as you dance
I move as you move, with the ebb and flow of time
Beloved daughter of Ra
Mistress of music, dance with me
Speak with my voice
Move through me this and every day

....

HATHOR, SEKHMET CHANT

Hathor, Sekhmet
Ladies of light and love and fire
Destruction and creation joined as one
Golden Hathor, you are the mother of life
The Mistress of jubilation
Goddess of joy and passion,
Your face shining as the rising sun
Hail, Mother of Life!

Fierce Sekhmet, you who are the avenging Eye of Ra
You are the raging heat of the desert,
The chaos that cleanses the soul
Devouring the darkness within,
You shatter and rend so we may be reborn anew
Hail, Mother of Destruction!

Hathor, Sekhmet
Creation, destruction
Bless us with your light
Cleanse us with your fire

....

HATHOR MIRROR SPELL

You Will Need:
1 small mirror
1 medium-size bowl
Sand

This spell is best done outside on a sunny day, as you will be reflecting the sun's light with the mirror. But if it is a cloudy day, you could substitute a candle for the sun's light or simply visualize a ray of the sun shining on the symbol you will use to represent your desired goal.

If possible, sit in a sunny place. Place the bowl in front of you and fill it about halfway with sand. Take a few moments to visualize what you wish to manifest. See it clearly in your mind. Before you begin the ritual, you should select a symbol (the simpler the better) that represents what you wish to draw into your life. When you have a clear picture of what you desire in your mind, begin to draw the symbol in the sand. Take the mirror and angle it so the light of the sun is shining on the symbol. See the golden light of Hathor filling and infusing the symbol with intent. See Hathor bringing it into manifestation in the world. When you are ready, say:

Golden light of Hathor, creative forces of the sun
My will is manifest, as this spell is done

If you wish, leave the bowl outside in the sunlight for the rest of the day or grab a handful of sand and scatter your intent into the wind to be manifested in the world.

. . . .
Hathor's Scrying Spell

You Will Need:
1 small mirror
1 golden candle

Prior to beginning any scrying, take the mirror and wash it thoroughly. If desired, you may wish to rinse it with sun water (see page 272). Then place the mirror in a sunny spot where the sun's light will shine on it for at least three hours. Afterward, wrap the mirror in a soft, dark cloth until you wish to use it for scrying.

Place the candle in the center of your working space. Hold your hands over the candle and see Hathor's light filling it. Light the candle and place the mirror in front of it so the candle's light will reflect on the mirror's surface. Make sure you place the mirror where you can comfortably sit and gaze into it. When you are ready to begin, pass your hand over the mirror and say:

> *By the rays of the sun, this spell has begun*
> *Second sight, inner light ignite*
> *By golden Hathor my will be done*
> *No truth remains hidden, no path unlit*

Gaze into the mirror as long as you wish. You may wish to have a piece of paper and pen handy to write down any impressions or messages. Your gaze should be comfortable; don't forget to blink! Some people see actual images form in the mirror when scrying, while others see images in their mind's eye. The mirror simply acts as a tool to focus your inner sight, so don't be disappointed if images don't immediately appear in the glass. As with anything, the more you practice, the more skilled you will become.

. . . .
SEVEN HATHORS' SPELL TO BLESS A CHILD

You Will Need:
A permanent marker,
1 foot of red ribbon
Hathor incense (see page 162)

Use this spell for blessing a newborn or for a general blessing for a child of any age. You will need a length of red ribbon, which can be purchased at a craft store, preferably an inch in width. Pass the ribbon through the incense. Take the marker (preferably a gold-colored one) and write the names of the Seven Hathors on the ribbon: *Lady of the Universe, Sky-Storm, You from the Land of Silence, You from Khemmis, Red-Hair, Bright Red*, and *Your Name Flourishes Through Skill*. After you have written their names, write (on the same side if you have room or on the opposite side of the ribbon) the name of the child. Then draw an oval around the name with a horizontal line on one end to resemble a cartouche. Royal names and the names of kings were encircled in this way. When you are done, hold the ribbon above the altar. See the Seven Hathors standing before you, and say:

> *Seven sisters*
> *Seven Hathors*
> *Ladies divine*
> *Who rule all time*
> *Bless and protect* [name]
> *Seven hands hold her/him,*
> *Seven eye behold her/him*
> *Seven goddess enthrone her/him*
> *And shield her/him from all harm*

See the Seven Hathors take the ribbon from you and infuse it with their blessings and protection until it glows with light. Take as long as you need to do this. Thank Hathor and, if you wish, leave her an offering. Tie the ribbon on the post of the child's bed or place it somewhere in his or her room. It can also be tied around the neck of a stuffed toy that is kept in the child's room—a stuffed cow or lion would be a good choice!

....
BLESSING FOR ONE WHO HAS PASSED
You Will Need:
1 white or gold candle
A picture of the person who has passed, if possible
Lotus oil
Lotus incense or an incense of your choice

This blessing can be done right after a loved one has passed or on the anniversary of their passing as a way of honoring them.

Arrange a picture or mementos from the one who has passed around the white or gold candle. Light the incense and pass the candle and picture (or other items) through the incense. When you are ready, say:

> *Golden lady who greets and comforts the dead,*
> *In the shade of your sacred sycamore, you offer succor and rest*
> *Beloved Hathor, wrap your tjetsen over* [person's name]
> *Guide* [person's name] *through the Duat**

*Duat (pronounced *DO-AT*) was the name the Egyptians used for the land of the dead or underworld. It was through this realm that the sun (regardless of gender) traveled during the night to bring warmth and light to the dead.

Anoint the candle with the lotus oil.

Golden Hathor, guide him/her safely through the dark.

Anoint the picture/object (this works best if it is in a frame; if the oil will damage the picture or object, simply place your hand on it).

Golden Hathor, stand beside him/her for all time.

Let the candle burn out or relight it for a few minutes each night. If you have anything you wish to say to the person who has passed, sit in front of the candle and speak what is in your heart. You may also wish to leave offerings of food or wine for the deceased.

....
HATHOR OIL
2 parts myrrh oil
2 parts rose oil
1 part sandalwood oil

....
HATHOR INCENSE
5 parts orrisroot
3 parts myrrh
4 parts rose petals

....
HATHOR CORRESPONDENCES
Animals: cow, lioness
Symbols: sistrum, mirror, menat necklace
Herb/Plant: sycamore
Colors: red, blue
Stone: malachite

SEKHMET

You find yourself standing on a sand dune. The heat of the desert washes over you in waves. Everywhere you look there is only sand. There is no vegetation or wildlife, just the heat of the sun and the ocean of sand before you. You begin to walk, each footfall sending sand trickling down the side of the dunes.

After what seems like an eternity, you see something in the distance. It is almost the same color as the sand, but as you come closer you see it is a temple. Excited, you begin to travel faster toward it. Soon you walk through a long promenade of statues. As you look up, you see that each statue is of a woman with the head of a lion carved from black stone, and you know you have come to the temple of Sekhmet, lady of the desert, goddess of the sun and of divine justice.

You walk up the steps and into the temple. Large columns rise up around you, and images of lionesses decorate the walls. Soon you come to a larger statue of the goddess. Like the other statues you passed on the promenade, this too is carved from black stone. The goddess stands with an ankh, the symbol for life eternal, in one hand, and the other hand is outstretched as if beckoning you.

Feeling compelled, you walk closer to the statue. Although you didn't notice it before, there is a low altar below the goddess's statue. You see seven large jugs filled with what looks like wine on the table. You reach out a hand and hold one of the vessels. It is made from a thick ceramic. The dark red liquid smells delicious, and without thinking you put the jug to your lips and start to drink deeply. Before you know it, the jug is empty. You immediately reach for another and begin drinking it down. It doesn't taste like wine; it tastes like the most delicious thing you have ever tasted. It fills you with a feeling of elation, as if you were drinking in all of life. Soon you have consumed the contents of all the jugs.

You feel as if fire flows through you, as if all of life courses through your veins.

You close your eyes, and in your mind's eye you see Sekhmet standing before you. Her body is that of a lithe woman in scarlet robes. Her head is that of a lioness, although the eyes that look into your own are human. "You know me as the lady of the desert, the bringer of destruction, but I am much more. All of life lives within me. To know me you must burn with my sacred fire, to fill your veins with all of life. To know that to destroy is to only make way for new beginnings."

She holds up a cup filled with blood-red wine. "I am the spark that engulfs, I am rage, and I am laughter. There is nothing I cannot conquer. I drink deep of life's bloody wine, the blood of the slain, the blood of death, the blood of birth, and the blood of the womb that flows freely from the thighs. These all belong to me. The blood of life flows through me; it fills my veins like fire. From my crimson-stained maw I drink, and drink, and drink."

Sekhmet offers you the cup, and again you drink the wine of Sekhmet. You feel her fire filling you. Within you, you offer up all that is no longer needed in your life to the fire of Sekhmet. All that no longer serves your purpose in this life is consumed by her holy flame. And as Sekhmet's fire burns away these things within you, you feel it also empowering and uplifting you. The fire of the unconquerable goddess burns within you, and you know there is nothing you cannot accomplish.

Sekhmet, the Mistress of Dread, who gives life eternally.
—Inscription from a temple statue

Of all the Egyptian sun goddesses, Sekhmet burns the brightest. She is the embodiment of the midday sun and the scorching heat of the desert. Her nature is like the fire of the sun she represents, being both beneficial and destructive at times. Sekhmet rules over the inner fires that fuel our lives, our drives, and our aspirations. While embodying the warrior side of the sun, she is also a goddess of healing and was hailed as the patroness of physicians.

Originally the warrior goddess of Upper Egypt, Sekhmet was the protectress of the Pharaoh during times of war. Her name means "The Mighty One" and is derived from the word *sekhem*, which means "power."[109] The main center of her worship was in Memphis, where she formed the Memphis Triad with her husband, the creator god Ptah; and her son Nefertem, although there were many temples erected in her honor throughout Egypt. When the cult of Ra became prominent in Egypt, she became the sun god's daughter.

Sekhmet appears either in the form of a lioness or as a woman with the head of a lioness, with a sun disc crowning her head. Her other titles include *The Great One of Magic, The Lady of Action, The One Before Whom Evil Trembles, The Avenger of Wrongs,* and *The Lady of Slaughter.* Her breath created deserts, and it was believed that her body could radiate the brightness of the midday sun, giving her the title *Lady of Flame.* Her priests performed rituals to appease her wrath before a different statue of the goddess on each day of the year, which resulted in a large number of her statues being preserved.

Sekhmet's mythology is intrinsically linked with that of Hathor. Although they most likely began as two separate goddesses, their personalities eventually merged and came to represent two sides of the same goddess. While Hathor is the embodiment of joy, Sekhmet is the incarnation of rage and destruction. Where Hathor brings life, Sekhmet destroys it.

One of her most prominent myths details her attempt to destroy humanity. After creating all things, Ra lived on the earth, ruling over a great kingdom. Time passed, and Ra began to grow old and humans began to mock him, plotting to overthrow him after seeing

---

109. El-Shahawy, *The Egyptian Museum in Cairo,* 187.

how frail he had become. Hearing humanity's blasphemy, Ra grew angry. He sent his "eye," Hathor, to destroy humanity, as the other gods had counseled him that nothing could stand against the power of Hathor. But when Hathor went to fulfill Ra's command, she began to change, transforming into the lion-headed goddess Sekhmet. After much killing, she returned to Ra, who praised her for slaying his enemies. Feeling sorry for mankind, Ra told her that enough killing had been done, but the lion goddess had found the blood of the traitors too intoxicating; her fury could not be sated and she continued to kill people.

No longer wishing to punish humanity, Ra had seven thousand jars of beer mixed with red ochre and placed them before the enraged goddess. Thinking the beer was blood, Sekhmet drank and drank until she was drunk and happy. When she awoke the next morning, she was again the goddess Hathor, and humanity was spared. When she returned to Ra, he decreed that beer and wine would be consumed at her festivals to remember how close human beings came to destruction at the goddess's hands.

In some versions, Hathor becomes angry at Ra for tricking her. Feeling humiliated, she turns once again into a lioness and leaves Egypt to live in Nubia. Other versions say she quarreled with Ra because he replaced her with another "eye" while she was off slaughtering mankind for him. Without the goddess, Egypt became barren and all joy vanished from the land. Even more concerning, Ra was left without the protection of Sekhmet to guard him against his enemies. Finally, Ra sent the gods Shu and Thoth to find the goddess and bring her back to Egypt. Thoth, in the form of a monkey, was able to approach the lion goddess and through gentle persuasion, humor, and flattery convinced her to return home.

When they reached the Nile, the goddess bathed in the waters, and finally the last of the goddess's temper cooled. As she bathed, the waters turned red and Sekhmet once again transformed into the gentle Hathor. On the island of Philae there is a temple dedicated to Hathor, marking the spot where she bathed in the Nile's waters. During the first month of the year, just after the flooding of the Nile, a festival to the goddess was held in which Sekhmet/Hathor was honored with excessive amounts of drinking. After the first initial flooding of the Nile, its waters turn a reddish color from all the sediments that the flood water stirred up, mirroring the events in Sekhmet's mythology.

Sekhmet's journey to Nubia most likely symbolizes the sun's yearly cycle. During the barren winter, the sun goddess leaves for another land, and the earth's fertility is only restored when the goddess is coaxed back to her rightful place. Nubia most likely is named as the place Sekhmet departs to because it was situated south of Egypt, and during the short winter days the sun rises just south of due east and sets south of due west, with the winter solstice marking the sun's lowest point in the southern sky. Observing the sun's movements throughout the year, the Egyptians would have seen that the sun was moving farther to the south during winter. Their knowledge of the natural world then became integrated in their mythology. The idea that the sun hides or is angered and must be cajoled into returning to the world is a theme repeated in many of the solar goddesses we have already met. No matter what continent or culture we find her in, the story of the sun's disappearance and the efforts of the other gods to convince her to return is repeated again and again.

Just as Sekhmet protected the king of the gods, she was also a protector of the Pharaoh, a role she shares with Bast. She guarded him in battle, her rage contributing to his victory over his enemies. According to the *Pyramid Texts*, a collection of ancient Egyptian religious texts from the time of the Old Kingdom, she "conceived" the king, much like her alter ego Hathor gave birth to the divine king Ra. Her title of *Lady of the Bright Red Linen* or *Scarlet Lady* carried the meaning of her place of origin in the Delta, as well as represented the blood-soaked garments of conquered enemies. Festivals were held at the end of battle in order to stave off Sekhmet's bloodlust. As with Hathor, ritual inebriation became a sympathetic act in which the goddess's wildness could be soothed. During an annual festival held at the beginning of the year, the participants danced and played music to soothe the wildness of the goddess and drank great quantities of wine, ritually imitating the extreme drunkenness that stopped the wrath of the goddess.

In 2006 archaeologist Betsy Bryan uncovered the remains of a "porch of drunkenness" in the temple of Mut (another lioness goddess who absorbed many of Sekhmet's characteristics). Scenes depicting priestesses being served alcohol in excess with temple servants ministering to its adverse effects, in what must be the earliest depiction of a hangover, decorate the porch's walls. Ritual drunkenness also played a similar role in the worship of Hathor and Bast, as a vehicle to appease the sun and its goddess's wrath.

Although to today's practitioners it may seem odd that a goddess mainly concerned with battle and slaughter was considered the patroness of healing, in the Egyptian mind a deity who could bring about pestilence and harm also possessed the power to cure it. Just as Sekhmet could protect one in battle from harm, so too could she protect one's body against illness and disease. Her priests were considered physicians, and her temples became centers of healing. Many Egyptian statues show the goddess holding an ankh in one hand, symbol of life, demonstrating that despite her connection to death, she also held sway over life. Amenhotep III placed nearly six hundred statues of Sekhmet in the temple of Mut at Karnak, in an attempt to improve his failing health. Sekhmet's husband, the god Ptah, was also connected to healing along with craftsmanship. In the tomb of Petosiris, there is a reference to his herds being numerous thanks to the attention of the priests of Sekhmet, suggesting they were called on to heal both humans and animals.[110] Often, part of a patient's healing would involve going through ritual purification, along with spells and chants used to invoke the goddess's favor. There was even a formal ritual called "Appeasing Sekhmet," which was used to prevent diseases from spreading.

Working with Sekhmet

Sekhmet's nature is dualistic. On one hand she can be wrathful and bloodthirsty, yet she is also a goddess of healing and courage. While her nature appears vicious at first glance, her destruction makes room for growth and renewal. Like the fire she embodies, she can be both beneficial and destructive. While the *Book of the Dead* mentions her several times as both a destroyer and a force of creation, it is also emphasized that she is a protector of Ma'at. Ma'at was seen as the goddess of truth and harmony as well as a concept, representing the sacred balance of the universe that must be maintained in order for life to flourish. As a protector of Ma'at, Sekhmet's destructive nature is a catalyst for balance. Unlike the god Set, who represented chaotic destruction in Egyptian cosmology, Sekhmet's rage is necessary to bring harmony to the world. When she lets loose her destruction, it is not without cause. When she slaughters humanity, it is to destroy those who plot against Ra. When she defends the Pharaoh, it is as a mother defending her child. She does what is necessary, even if it requires her transformation from joyful Hathor to the raging lioness.

Rage, whether by a divine being or otherwise, is often seen as taboo when expressed by a female. We are suddenly labeled too aggressive or too masculine. Women are thought of as nurturers, which we are, but we cannot be gentle and nurturing all the time. Our nurturing, giving natures should not be, and are not, the limit to our personalities and identities as women. At times a little divine rage is necessary. Although we tend to think of anger and rage as negative

---

110. Nunn, *Ancient Egyptian Medicine*, 120.

traits, when channeled they can be powerful forces of healing and transformation. When you watch the news and see a story about a rape victim, an abused animal, or some other injustice, don't you get angry? When we are faced with injustice, when others try to trample us down or discredit our self-worth, divine rage can be a powerful tool. It is the fire within us that refuses to be smothered, the fire within us that inspires us to stand up for ourselves and what we believe in. When we embrace Sekhmet, when we let her rage, she breaks down the barriers and fears that we have allowed to paralyze us. She frees us and incites us to act, to move forward, rather than remain stagnant.

Sekhmet's connection to healing and to the joyful Hathor reminds us that she knows how to maintain a sacred balance. When the need arises, she shows her teeth and takes on whatever challenge lies before her, but afterward she transforms, returning once again to her tranquil state. The vehicle of Sekhmet's transformation into Hathor is important. Drunkenness, along with music and dance, was used in Egyptian ritual as a way to achieve a state of ecstasy and commune with the gods. It is not until Sekhmet becomes drunk, and symbolically communes with her divine nature, that she ends her rampage. She must enter this ecstatic state before coming into balance once again. One of Sekhmet's lessons is that by going through the process of transformation, and facing what we fear the most, we return to the center of our being and who we truly are. Her divine rage is purifying, allowing us to face what lies hidden within ourselves and come to terms with it.

SEKHMET INVOCATION
Sekhmet, mother of dread
Scarlet lady who devours the enemies of the gods
Beloved of Ptah, Eye of Ra
She-lion, scorching sun

I adore you, lady of the desert
Your fire burns within me
I drink in your divine spirit
Unconquerable Sekhmet,
Dwell within me

· ·
EYE OF RA INVOCATION
Hathor, Sekhmet, Bast
Joyful One, lioness, dawning light
Vengeful, Wrathful One,
Devourer who rends the enemies of light
Come now, O Goddess of the Sun
Illuminate every darkness
Fill us with your golden light

As Hathor you are the vibrant joyful mother,
Carrying the sun through the sky in your crescent horns
O Golden One, O Hathor, come!
Bring to us the light of joy!

As Sekhmet you are the Raging One
Your breath creates the deserts
As the regal lioness you avenge the gods
Your golden maw red with blood, you lay your enemies low
O Terrible One, O Sekhmet, come!
Bring to us the light of inner strength!

As Bast you are the wild desert cat, loving yet fierce
Nightly you slay darkness, that a new day may dawn
O Lady of the East, O Bast, come!
Bring to us the light of rebirth!
Hathor, Sekhmet, Bast

Illuminate every darkness
Fill us with your golden light

....
THE ARROWS OF SEKHMET SPELL

You Will Need:

7 red or gold small taper candles

Sekhmet incense (see page 173)

Sekhmet oil (see page 173)

Like Hathor, who appears at times as a seven-fold goddess, the number seven is also sacred to Sekhmet. The Seven Arrows of Sekhmet were a force of destruction when she attempted to destroy humanity. Although described as a weapon the goddess wields, this may be an indication that Sekhmet had multiple forms. The Seven Arrows of Sekhmet are the darker mirror image of the Seven Hathors. While the Seven Hathors guarded birth, Sekhmet's arrows destroyed the enemies of the gods. In one Egyptian spell, her arrows were called upon to guard against the Evil Eye.[111]

This spell can be used to protect oneself or to bring justice to a person or situation. Place the seven tapers (symbolizing Sekhmet's arrows) in a circle around the area where you will be working. On each candle draw a simple image of an arrow; a line with a "V" on one end for the point is just fine. Along the line that forms the arrow write what you wish to accomplish: e.g., "Protection." Hold each candle in your hands for a few minutes, filling it with your intention, then anoint it with Sekhmet oil or an oil that reminds you of the goddess. Light the incense and the candle. Invoke Sekhmet in whatever way you choose, whether that be chanting or simply visualizing her standing before you. When you feel her presence, say:

---

111. Pinch, *Magic in Ancient Egypt*, 39.

Scarlet Lady,
Maw bloody from battle
Mother of Kings
Defender of the land,
Your robes dyed red from the slaughter
Hear me, O Sekhmet,
You who impurity fears
Golden-skinned lioness
Lose your arrows
Let them fly

Visualize the candles glowing with Sekhmet's energy before they form into the shape of arrows and fly out into the universe.

SEKHMET OIL

For this oil, it is best to mix your essential oils with a carrier oil such as sweet almond oil or grapeseed oil (both of which have light scents and will not overpower the oils you add to it). Although you will be only adding a small amount of cinnamon oil, it has a tendency to irritate the skin if it is not diluted sufficiently with other oils.

3 teaspoons carrier oil
9 drops dragon's blood oil
6 drops cinnamon oil
7 drops dark beer

SEKHMET INCENSE

1 tablespoon frankincense
1 tablespoon benzoin
1 tablespoon dragon's blood resin
½ tablespoon ground cinnamon

7 cloves

¼ tablespoon myrrh

3 drops of dark beer

. . . .
SEKHMET CORRESPONDENCES
Animal: lioness

Symbols: eyes, arrows

Colors: red, yellow

Stones: amber, bloodstone, hematite

BAST

Take a deep breath. See yourself surrounded by white crystalline energy. As you take another deep breath, you find yourself standing on the bow of a long boat. As you look around, you realize the boat in sailing through a vast, shadowy expanse. You think through the dark you can almost see the faint glimmer of stars, but you are not sure if it is starlight or some other distant light. The boat is decorated lavishly, with gold covering much of it. Hieroglyphics are carved into the gold, and they glow and shimmer with a life of their own. Looking over the side of the boat, you see that there are oars attached to the hull every few feet that row and pull the boat through the air on their own accord.

On the far end of the ship there is a throne with a seated figure resting on it. The figure gives off a brilliant light that makes the thick darkness surrounding the boat fade to a gray twilight. You cannot see the figure's face clearly, and as you approach the throne you see that the person's face and body change every few moments. Like the rest of the ship, golden hieroglyphics decorate the chair—only these flow upward and float around the figure like little golden fireflies.

You take a step closer and bow reverently before the figure. At first it appears to be a man, with the head of a falcon, dressed in the robes of a pharaoh. Then it changes to a woman, the solar disc adorning a regal headdress, her brilliant eyes outlined in thick lines of charcoal. Then the figure changes yet again, and again. You watch mesmerized, knowing you must be on the Boat of a Million Years, the boat that carries the sun through the Duat, the underworld, to rise anew with the dawn. You would expect to find many gods on this voyage, but you realize all the many gods of the sun are here. The sun in all its many forms sits seated on the throne before you. It has many faces, but all sit enthroned on this sacred journey as one being.

Suddenly the smooth procession of the boat comes to an abrupt halt. You hear the sound of splintering wood as something crashes into the bow and pushes the boat of the sun off its course. The force sends you tumbling on the deck. When you look up, you see a serpentine shape coiling around the bow. The serpent is not quite solid. Instead it looks more like black, billowing smoke in the shape of a great snake.

The throned figure begins to change as it rises. No longer the being of many faces, the sun stands before you as a lithe woman, her skin a light, sun-kissed brown. A collar of gold and turquoise beads is draped around her neck. The tips of her fingers end in tiny claws like a cat's, and from the neck up she has the head of a feline. Slitted golden eyes regard you. She reaches out a clawed hand and helps you stand. "You were not expecting me, were you?" she purrs, her voice full of mischief, a feline smile crossing her lips. You admit you were not. The fierce lioness Sekhmet or the great warrior Horus would be the guises of the sun you would expect to appear in the midst of a battle. You tell her so, and she laughs. Holding out her hand, a great golden spear appears out of thin air, and the goddess takes it in her waiting hands. "I am

Bast, the lady of joy and exuberance, but even I am a warrior. Even I was once a lioness in times of old." Her face changes for a moment, becoming more fierce, then it turns back again to the mischievous-looking cat. "Do not all mothers become lions when their children are threatened? And I am mother to all."

With that, she leaps into battle. She moves faster than seems possible, darting this way, slashing the serpent. Finally she leaps onto the creature's back and plunges the spear deep into the shadowy flesh. With a shriek the serpent of chaos dissolves back into the darkness.

Bast returns to you, her form shimmering with golden light, a triumphant smile on her face. "Sometimes we must approach our battles with joy, with the love of all of life within us. If we do not keep this light close to our hearts, we lose sight of what it is we fight for." She cups your face in her hands and kisses your brow. "Be a force of light and joy in the world, and know that I will be with you in moments of joyfulness and in the darkest moments you face. My light cannot falter; my love endures through all time."

You feel the light of Bast fill you as the scene fades, and you know that the cat goddess will always be with you.

In our trio of Egyptian sun goddesses, Bast represents the gentle nature of the sun. She is a goddess of fertility, sexuality, music, the sun, abundance, and is a protectress of the pharaohs and the home.

Bast's name has several meanings. One translation is "Tearer" or "Devouring Lady," reflecting her origins as a goddess of protection and battle. In later periods, she was referred to as Bastet. This variation of her name included an additional female suffix, which may have been added to emphasize pronunciation. It has also been suggested that the additional suffix may have been used to emphasize her diminutive status in later periods. This would make her name "She of the Ointment Jar," a translation tied into the fact that her name was written with a hieroglyph that depicted a jar.[112] This may be why she eventually became associated with cosmetics and *bas jars*, a kind of heavy jar used to store perfumes. Her son the god Nefertem (also a solar deity) is the god of perfume and alchemy.

Each translation of her name casts Bast in a very different light. On the one hand she is the Devourer or Tearer, a fierce avenging goddess, while as She of the Ointment Jar, Bast is the goddess of pleasure and joy. The later addition of the suffix, and subsequently the new definition of her name, mirrors her changing role in the Egyptian pantheon, from a lion-headed goddess to a gentler goddess of motherhood and protection.

While Bast eventually evolved into the gentle cat goddess we are now familiar with, her origins are very similar to Sekhmet. The two goddesses share many similarities and, like Hathor and Sekhmet, their myths are often confused or combined. Both were called the Eye of Ra, and in some texts Bast is referred to as the mother of Nefertem and the fierce lion god Maahes, while in others Sekhmet is named as their mother. What is clear is that Bast was originally a lion-headed goddess like Sekhmet. In her earliest depictions she was shown as a woman with the head of a lion. She was sometimes paired with snake goddess Wadjet. As Wadjet-Bast she was always shown as a lion-headed woman with the solar disk and a cobra, which symbolized Wadjet. Other early depictions show her as a wild desert cat, and it is in this form that she is often portrayed slaying the serpent Apep.

In their earliest incarnations, Bast and Sekhmet were regional variations of one another. Sekhmet was the regional goddess of the sun and war for Upper Egypt and Bast the lioness of Lower Egypt. This explains Bast's connection with Wadjet, who was the patroness of Lower Egypt. As Wadjet-Bast she is the divine protector of Lower Egypt. When Lower and Upper Egypt became unified, the identities of these two goddesses began to merge, with Sekhmet's image eventually

---

112. Quirke, *Ancient Egyptian Religion*, 108.

becoming the more dominant one. Thus Bast became the cat goddess rather than the lioness, although even in her later depictions she is shown holding a lioness mask, hinting at her fierce beginnings.

While she lost some of her fiercer aspects, her protective nature remained. She was invoked in the *Pyramid Texts* as the "mother and nurse of the kings," and she was often depicted in cat form under the thrones of the Pharaoh, symbolically protecting the sovereign from his enemies.[113] Statues of Bast also show her holding an *aegis*, another symbol of divine protection. The aegis looked similar to a collar or cape that symbolized protection from a divine source. Bast's aegis was embellished with a lion's head. Ironically, in cat form, Bast holds a symbol showing her former lioness self.

Her names "Tearer" and "Devouring Lady" also suggest a fiercer, more warlike aspect similar to Sekhmet. Pharaoh Sety of the Eighteenth Dynasty referred to himself as "valiant in the very heart of the fray, a Bastet terrible in combat." [114] Yet in later texts from the temple of Philae, Hathor is described as "gracious or peaceful as Bastet and raging as Sekhmet," [115] emphasizing Bast's new role as the gentler side of the cat goddess and also drawing a parallel between the three solar goddesses.

Bast's solar attributes and her role as a divine protector are evident in her mythology. Just as Bast was the divine protector of the Pharaohs, so too did she protect her father, Ra, the sun god and King of the Gods. Every day, Bast traveled with Ra in his boat that pulled the sun through the sky. At night Ra traveled through the Duat, the Egyptian underworld, where he revitalized and brought light to the dead. Apep, a monstrous snake (in some versions he is crocodile) that represented chaos and disorder, waited just below the horizon every night to ambush Ra. The ever-watchful Bast battled the snake each night and defeated him, thus allowing the sun to rise again the

---

113. Capel and Markoe, *Mistress of the House, Mistress of Heaven*, 140.
114. Scott, "The Cat of Bastet," 6.
115. Junker, *Der Auszug der Hathor-Tefnut aus Nubien*, 32.

next day. Her nightly battle with Apep earned her the titles of Lady of the East and Goddess of the Rising Sun. Because of her nightly underworld journey, Bast is considered a protector of the dead, and mummified cats were buried with the dead to engender the goddess's protection in the afterlife.[116]

Ra and Bast's daily journey through both the sky and the underworld, as well as the titles given to her, clearly mark Bast as a solar goddess. She accompanies Ra in the solar boat that pulls the sun through the sky, and she defeats the serpent of chaos, Apep. Like most sun deities, Bast represents order, and Apep chaos. If she does not defeat the forces of chaos, the sun will remain in the underworld, and life and light will cease. By defeating Apep, she restores order to the world. The journey to the underworld is found in almost all the myths of the sun goddesses in one form or another. Sunna and Amaterasu make similar journeys to renew the sun's vital power. In the underworld, the sun becomes revitalized and renewed. Apep can be seen as the darkness within each of us; he dwells just under the horizon of our consciousness. He is our shadow self, the embodiment of our fears and negative emotions. To defeat him we need to embrace our inner light, the fire of Bast.

By the time of the Middle Kingdom, Bast had transformed from the lioness goddess to the benevolent cat goddess of music, dance, joy, and fertility. In this guise she represents the fertilizing heat of the sun. Like her totem animal, the cat, an animal known as a protective mother and for its large litters, she became connected to motherhood. She was often depicted with kittens, and women who wished to conceive would wear amulets showing the goddess surrounded by kittens. Her center of worship was Per-Bast (in Greek, Bubastis), also known as Tell Basta. When Herodotus visited the temple of Bast, he described it as one of the most beautiful temples in Egypt. He described it as

---

116. Werness, *The Continuum Encyclopedia of Animal Symbolism in Art*, 74.

being made from pink granite and surrounded by water on three sides, forming a type of sacred lake called an *isheru*.

These sacred lakes were also associated with other lioness goddesses such as the goddess Mut, whose temple was also surrounded by an isheru. The waters of the lake may have been seen as a way to appease the lioness goddess's wrath, since either drinking a certain liquid or being doused in water, as in Sekhmet's myths, had been known to cool the wrath of feline goddesses.[117] A grove of trees enclosed the shrine where a statue of Bast was kept. This garden enclosure within the temple walls seems to reflect Bast's fertile nature and the fertilizing rays of the sun, which allow vegetation and crops to grow and ripen.

Herodotus also described an annual festival honoring Bast in which worshipers sailed along the Nile playing musical instruments. When passing towns along the river, the women lifted their skirts, revealing their genitals. These women "sing the while, and make a clapping with their hands … while a certain number dance and some standing up uncover themselves. After proceeding in this way all along the river course, they reach Bubastis … More grape-wine is consumed at this festival than in all the rest of the year besides."[118]

The amount of alcohol consumed during this festival may indicate that Bast had a similar myth to Sekhmet's, where the goddess was appeased by consuming alcohol. Reenacting this myth by drinking wine would have been an act of sympathetic magick, to appease the goddess and cool her wrath. Like Hathor, who raised her skirts to entice Ra to return to the world, women during Bast's festival lifted their skirts and revealed themselves. Revealing the vulva symbolized fertility and Bast's ability to bring it into the world.

During the Ptolemaic Dynasty, when Egypt became part of the Greek Empire, Bast became equated with Artemis. The connection is presumably because of both goddesses' connection to childbirth,

---

117. Capel and Markoe, *Mistress of the House, Mistress of Heaven*, 135.
118. Herodotus, *The Histories*, 78.

and both were thought to protect pregnant women. Through her connection with Artemis, Bast became associated with the moon. Her connection to the moon is a late one, and one that arose from foreign influences. Similarly, Herodotus refers to Isis as a moon goddess, although she carries the sun atop her horned headdress and was never viewed as a moon goddess by the Egyptians.

At first glance, Bast seems to represent the gentler nature of the Egyptian sun goddesses, but her origins and her original function as a lioness goddess show Bast to be a goddess that encompasses the full spectrum of the divine feminine—from raging warrioress, devouring her enemies, to the loving mother who brings fertility and abundance to her people. Bast teaches us to enjoy life. She takes pleasure and joy in the present moment, knowing if need be she can transform from docile housecat to a fierce lioness, depending on the circumstances at hand.

Working with Bast

Bast exudes a joyful love of life. In modern worship, she is often viewed as a sort of "sex kitten," but this is far from true. Herodotus's description of her festival, where women lifted their skirts and revealed their genitals, led early historians to link her to sexual excess. While she is connected to fertility and pleasure, Bast could more accurately be called a guardian of life. She enjoys what life has to offer and finds the joy in every moment, but she also defends life when necessary. Like a midwife, she helps bring forth the light of the sun into the world each day. She nightly triumphs over darkness and chaos, so that life may continue. She is joyful and playful, yet fierce when the necessity arises. Bast reminds us to live in the moment and enjoy life. When life gets tough, she reminds us to take quick, decisive action. Bast doesn't sit and complain about life's problems; she attacks them head-on, knowing she will emerge triumphantly.

While Bast's more passive qualities are often emphasized, it is important to remember her origins as a lioness. Like Hathor and

Sekhmet, Bast has a dual nature. She is both the loving mother and the fierce desert wildcat. She can be a goddess of joy and pleasure or a warrioress ruthlessly destroying the enemies of light and order. She brings both creation and destruction. While Sekhmet and Hathor's dual personality manifests in two separate goddesses, in Bast we find all these qualities rolled up in one.

When I first started working with Bast, she appeared in my meditations as a wild desert cat, larger and wilder than a housecat but not quite as fierce as a lioness. She occupies a state in between the two. She is wild, yet gentle; fierce, yet motherly. Sometimes she may appear as a cat, but she has the heart of a lioness. As the protector of the Pharaoh, she is an excellent goddess to call upon for protection, especially when protecting animals or children. She also seems to be adept at finding her "lost" children. When our neighbor's cat went missing, I took one of the posters they had hung around the neighborhood and placed it under Bast's statue and spent a few minutes each day visualizing the cat retuning home safely. Three days later, my neighbor got a phone call from a good samaritan who had found the cat wandering near a busy road!

Like Hathor, Bast was celebrated with music, dance, and drunkenness. Honoring Bast can be as simple as listening to your favorite music and drinking a glass of red wine. As with Sekhmet, beer can be used in place of wine for rituals invoking Bast. The best way to honor Bast is by celebrating life. Sometimes we forget to really appreciate what we already have, to live in the moment and just enjoy being alive. We stress about work, what we are doing tomorrow, how much is in our bank accounts, or what we are going to make for dinner. We keep thinking about what happens next, what we are doing next, rather than what we are doing right now. Set some time aside each day to live in the moment. Stop whatever you are doing and take a deep breath, center yourself, and simply be.

Bast Invocation

Hail Bast!
Daughter of the Sun
Lady of the East
Eye of Ra
Lady of Flames
She who protects the two lands
As the wild desert cat you do stalk your prey
In the form of the raging lioness you do slay the enemies of light
It is you who guides the sun each day,
as the Boat of a Million Years dips below the horizon
And it is you who nightly battles Apep in the Duat
You are the destroyer of chaos,
The champion of light,
Protectress of kings and queens
The sunrise is your gift to us,
You who bears the light of the new day
Lady of light, of joy, and battle,
Fill me with your Golden Light!
Come to me, O Bast!

Eye of Ra Candle Spell

You Will Need:
1 red or gold candle
Bast, Sekhmet, or Hathor oil

This candle spell invokes the aid of all three Egyptian sun goddesses. On a red or gold candle inscribe what you wish to manifest. Hold the candle in your hands, visualizing what you wish to manifest. When the image is clear in your mind, anoint it with Bast, Hathor, or Sekhmet oil. If you are drawing something to you, anoint the candle from wick to base; if you are banishing something, anoint the candle from base to wick. Light the candle, saying:

> *Hathor, Sekhmet, Bast*
> *Eyes of Ra*
> *Burning fast*
> *Hathor, Sekhmet, Bast*
> *Rays of fire*
> *Noonday blast*
> *Hathor, Sekhmet, Bast*
> *Bring to me what I ask!*

....
BAST'S RITUAL TO BANISH INNER DARKNESS

You Will Need:

1 large bowl

Filtered or spring water

Bundle of fresh rosemary sprigs

String

Bast incense (see page 189)

For this ritual you will have to look up the exact time the sun rises in your area (you can find this information online or in your local newspaper). In this ritual you will be confronting your inner darkness, just as Bast confronts and defeats the serpent of chaos each night. This ritual can be performed to confront emotional scars from the past, to release the mental scars of an emotional relationship, or simply to release negative energy. This ritual can also be done as a devotional to Bast and to align with her energies as you will be symbolically acting out her part of her mythology. Ideally the ritual should be started just before dawn while it is still dark, and concluded as the sun rises. If this is not possible, the ritual should be performed during the morning hours.

Prior to the ritual, hold the rosemary sprigs tightly together. Take the string and wrap it several times around the base of the sprigs, to form a handle. The opposite end can remain loose, and will be dipped in water during the ritual. Fresh rosemary can be purchased in most grocery stores, but you could use another herb connected to purification (such as sage or catnip) in its place. If you cannot find fresh herbs, you can use your hands to sprinkle the water in place of the herbs.

It is not necessary to cast a circle, but you should cleanse the area you will be working in. You can do this by walking sun-wise around the area while shaking a sistrum (or rattle), while visualizing negative energies departing. Take a few deep breaths and center yourself. When you are ready, say:

Hail Bast,
You who nightly triumphs over chaos
Your light burns away all darkness
Your teeth rend and tear at the enemies of light
As you defeat darkness,
so too do I wish to dispel the darkness within myself

See Bast standing before you, while softly chanting her name as you do so. She appears as a tall woman with the head of a cat. As you look into her green eyes, you begin to merge, and you see your image and that of Bast become one and the same. Now take a few moments to become aware of the darkness around you—not just the darkness of pre-dawn but the darkness that weighs down your spirit. See before you all your personal demons, your fears. As Bast you begin to change shape, transforming into a fierce lioness. In this form you tear and rend at your inner darkness, until one by one each aspect of the darkness is destroyed. As you banish each fear, each personal shadow, you begin to glow brighter and brighter until you are a radiant sun filled with light.

As the first rays of light begin to shine over the horizon, hold the bowl up, if possible so that the morning light hits the water. Visualize the water being filled with the light of a new day, with the cleansing, healing energies of Bast. When you are ready, say:

> *As Bast defeats Apep, so too shall I defeat my inner darkness*
> *In Bast's name do I bless this water,*
> *That the light of Bast may wash away all that is dark within me*
> *… all that no longer serves my spirit*
> *… all that hinders my path*
> *… all fear*
> *… all rage*
> *… all sorrow*
> *… all pain*
> *That I may shine with the golden light of Bast!*

Dip the herb bundle in the water and run it along your body. If working with a group, one person can sprinkle the water on the other participants by dipping the herbal bundle in the water, then shaking it in front of the person being cleansed.

> *Beloved Bast*
> *Lady of the East*
> *Goddess of the rising sun,*
> *Who banishes all darkness*
> *I give you my love and thanks*
> *Hail and farewell!*

Visualize Bast departing, leaving you whole and cleansed. Take a few moments to enjoy the sunrise. When you are ready, pour the remaining water on the ground. Wine, beer, flowers, or food can be left as an offering to Bast.

....
Bast's Spell of Protection

You Will Need:

1 jar

½ cup salt

2 tablespoons pennyroyal

2 tablespoons dragon's blood resin

½ cup vinegar

Bast incense (see page 189)

Red wine (cranberry or another red juice can be substituted)

This spell calls upon Bast in her ancient form as the warrior lioness. Use it to bind a troublesome person, stop gossip, or to protect yourself or a loved one from harm.

If you wish, cast a circle. If you are binding a troublesome person or to stop someone from gossiping about you, write the person's name on a piece of paper. Imagine the person and the piece of paper becoming one and the same. Fold the paper and put it in the jar. In a bowl mix together the salt, dragon's blood, and pennyroyal. Fill the jar about halfway with the mixture, then add the vinegar, filling it to the top of the jar. When you are ready, say:

Devouring Lady
Bast, terrible in combat,
Tearing, rending the flesh from her enemies
Raging lioness when threatened
Gentle and peaceful mother when appeased
Lady of the East
Eye of flame and fury
Strike terror into the hearts of those who would harm me and mine
Spread your shield of protection over me (or person being protected)
Destroy the hateful words of those who speak against me
Let their words burn to ash and dust in their mouths
Let the hands of those who would act against me be bound

Let all those who would cause me harm
in thought, word, or deed feel the fiery wrath of Bast!

Envision Bast standing before you, with the body of a woman and the head of a lioness. She stands tall, proud, and strong, a shield in one hand and a sword in the other, ready to defend you. She begins to glow brighter, her light filling you with her strength and protection.

Bast stands before me, a protectress and guardian against all harm
Her arms hold me in her loving embrace
Her shield guards me from harm!

Thank Bast, and if you cast a circle, close the circle. Pour the wine outside as an offering to Bast.

TRIPLE EGYPTIAN SUN GODDESS INVOCATION
Golden Hathor
Raging Sekhmet
Joyous Bast
Eyes of Ra
Come now, O Goddesses of the Sun!
Joyful, wrathful, avenging ones
Heat of the desert
Heart of joy
Protectresses and mothers of your people
Come in the golden edge of flame
Come in the radiance of the dawning day
Come in the splendor of fire
Illuminate our hearts and minds
Fill us with the radiance of your spirit!
Hail Hathor!
Hail Sekhmet!
Hail Bast!

·················
Bast Incense
2 tablespoons myrrh

2 tablespoons sandalwood

1 tablespoon rose petals

························
Lioness Bast Incense
1½ tablespoons myrrh

1 tablespoon sandalwood

1 tablespoon dragon's blood resin

2 tablespoons rose petals

3 drops red wine

(Note: Use this incense to invoke Bast's warrior aspects.)

···········
Bast Oil
½ part catnip oil

1 part patchouli oil

1 part rose oil

2 parts sandalwood oil

························
Bast Correspondences
Animals: lioness, domestic cat

Symbols: sistrum, eyes, sun disc, aegis

Color: green

Stones: cat's eye, obsidian, jasper

CANAAN

Canaan roughly corresponds to the region encompassing modern-day Palestine, Israel, Lebanon, and parts of Syria. For a time Canaan was a province of Egypt, and many of the Canaanite gods also had temples in Egypt. One example would be Anat the warrior goddess, who had a temple in Memphis. The Canaanite gods also make appearances in the Bible, usually as demons. In 1929, clay tablets containing fragments of epic poetry concerning the myths of the Canaanite gods were unearthed in the ancient port city of Ugarit, near Latakia in Syria. The Canaanite pantheon, like that of nearly all Middle Eastern cultures, viewed the sun as female. In the *Epic of Baal*, the sun goddess pays a particularly important role, both as a mediator and in returning the god Baal to life. Like the Egyptians, the Canaanites viewed the sun as both a benevolent and destructive force. Given the arid climate, the sun was seen as a potent force in nature.

The Hittite sun goddess Arinniti's attendants carried "filled mirrors" as she traveled through the underworld. Author Janet McCrickard suggests these may refer to basins of water, which acted as mirrors or possibly as a tool used in scrying: "[One] holds a spindle; they [both] hold filled mirrors."[119]

---

119. McCrickard, *Eclipse of the Sun*, 149.

SHAPASH

You find yourself holding a torch as you walk through the dark. You see wispy figures floating around you. You realize these are the spirits of the dead. They float around you, seemingly unaware of your passage through their realm. Onward through this subterranean realm you go. On either side you see stone walls covered in vines, and you know you are deep within the earth.

Finally you come to a great chamber. In its center a woman crouches, looking at something on the ground. You walk over to her. She looks up and smiles. Her face is kind and warm and instantly makes you like her. She wears flowing red robes adorned with many gold beads so that she makes a jingling sound as she moves. She asks you for the torch, and thanks you for bringing it to her.

"This is exactly what I needed," she says. Torch in hand, she passes it over something on the stone floor before you. In the light you see that it is a set of white, bleached bones. As Shapash waves the torch over the bones, vines begin to sprout from the ground and wrap around the bones. Soon the vines form muscles and flesh. Slowly, a very living figure lies before you and takes breath. The man opens his eyes, and suddenly you find yourself with Shapash in the world above. Everything is dry and barren. The earth bakes in the heat of the sun. The man is gone, but all around you life begins to emerge. The shoots of plants appear from the ground, and soon the earth below you is covered in grass and greenery. Storm clouds appear, and fat raindrops begin to fall.

"Every year I travel to the realm of the dead," Shapash tells you. "And every year I must use my light to bring Baal back from the dead, so he may bring life to the world again. Without the god of life, my light burns and destroys all in its path. Unchecked,

*our passions run away from us, and the force that can heal and
inspire us can burn us."*

*You take in the scene around you. You feel the strength of
the earth and the power of life flowing through it, flowing up
through your feet and into the center of your being. Then, with
your hands upraised to the sun, you draw on the vital spark of
power that is Shapash, letting her light flow through you. You
feel a sacred balance forming within you. Earth and sky, fire and
water, blend and fill you, and you feel blessed and whole.*

Shapash (also called Shapshu, Shapsh, or Sapsu) is the Canaanite goddess of the sun, light, and divine judgment. She is a benevolent goddess, called upon not only to bring light to the world but also to act
as a judge in heavenly disputes, to bring health to the gods, and to
accomplish tasks that the other gods could not. In the conflict between
the gods Mot and Baal, she acts as a divine mediator, bringing peace
and avoiding the destruction of the earth. Like other sun goddesses,
Shapash's light is likened to a torch, and is called the "Torch of the
Gods." Another title is "Luminary of the Underworld," for she is also
given the task of shining her light in the underworld as well as guiding
the souls of the dead there. She acts as the herald or messenger of her
father, the supreme god El. In one text she is described as winging over
the heavens, bringing to mind the image of the winged solar disc, an
image that is prevalent among both the Canaanites and the Egyptians:
"The Gods' Torch Shapsh, Who wings over heaven's expanse."[120]

Much of what we know about Shapash comes from somewhat
fragmented poems inscribed on tablets recounting myths revolving
around the storm and fertility god Baal. Baal invited all the gods,
except the god of death, Mot, to a banquet at his palace atop Mount
Zephon. Unfortunately, Mot took offense at being excluded from the

---

120. Pritchard, *Ancient Near Eastern Texts Relating to the Old Testament*, 137.

guest list. Mot then invited Baal to his own feast in the underworld, but as soon as Baal entered the underworld, Mot killed him, swallowing him in his great maw. With Baal dead, the earth was plunged into a terrible drought. Crops withered, rivers dried up, and the earth slowly began to die in the absence of the fertile storm god. Baal's wife, the warrior goddess Anat, could not properly grieve for her husband without first finding his body. She enlisted Shapash's help, as the sun saw all that occurred on the earth below. Once Shapash found Baal's body, the two buried and mourned him. Anat cried rivers of tears, which Shapash drank up like wine. With the god of rain and storms dead, the sun's heat became oppressive, drying up all the earth's moisture. Drinking Anat's tears, or moisture, like wine indicates the beginning of the hot season, when the sun's rays bake and crack the earth.

Being a warrior goddess, Anat did not dwell in grief for long. In a rage Anat killed Mot, cleaving him into pieces with her sword. Then she used a millstone to grind his remains, finally scattering them in a field, like grain. Even with Mot dead, the earth still withered under the sun's extreme heat.

Shapash is never blamed for the drought, but is instead seen as out of balance. She requires the storm god to bring the rain and storms to balance out her vibrant rays. All seems lost until El, the supreme god, has a vision of Baal restored to life. With this news, Anat asks Shapash to search for Baal. It is implied that the mission is either too dangerous for the other gods or that they do not possess the necessary power to accomplish it.

Like other sun goddesses, Shapash is a divine "eye" in the sky. She witnesses all events on the earth below, her sight even extending to the land of the dead, where she finds Baal's spirit. Realizing she will have to embark on a dangerous journey through the underworld to find Baal, Shapash asks Anat to leave her offerings of wine and a garland of leaves: "Spill sparkling wine from thy vat; Bring a chaplet of leaves from thy native stock; And I will seek the victor Baal."[121]

Shapash then travels deep into the earth, bringing back Baal's spirit and restoring him to his body. El later praises her for completing her harrowing journey through the underworld, for drinking the wine of decay and eating the bread of corruption.[122] El also insinuates that her journey has given her dominion over the spirits of the dead: "O Shapash, over the shades shalt thou have dominion."[123] The theme of the sun traveling to the underworld during the night is an almost universal one, although in Shapash's story it is taken one step further, as she holds sway over the dead and shades of this realm, much like Hathor and Sekhmet in neighboring Egypt.

After seven years, Mot is also restored to life. Angered that he has been humiliated by Baal, both by being dismembered by Anat and being excluded from the feast, Mot challenges Baal, and the two engage in a fierce battle. Seeing this, Shapash intervenes. Mot agrees to remain in his underworld realm, and Baal keeps to the sky. Here Shapash acts as a judge and mediator, and restores a balance between life (Baal) and death (Mot). Her ability to subdue the two gods into peace shows the extent of Shapash's power. Mot is described as becoming frightened as the sun goddess speaks. Given Shapash's ability to restore the dead to life, Mot may have had reason to be afraid. The sun could both see into his realm and overcome death. Shapash's role as a dispenser of divine justice and her power over both gods and men is made clear. We are told that "Shapsh shall govern the gathered ones, Shapsh shall govern the divine ones.... gods ... mortals."[124] She is also said to have been a "judge" of heroes, perhaps judging their worthiness.[125]

121. Gibson, *Canaanite Myths and Legends*, 113.
122. Ibid., 19.
123. Ibid., 100.
124. Pritchard, *Ancient Near Eastern Texts Relating to the Old Testament*, 141.
125. Lewis, *Cult of the Dead in Ancient Israel and Ugarit*, 36.

Baal and Shapash's myth reflects a seasonal cycle. Baal's death co-incides with the summer months, when the sun's heat is at its height. During the dry season, the god of rain seems to have vanished, until he returns in the wet season. Unlike their neighbors the Egyptians, the Canaanites did not see the sun as the cause of the excessive heat. Rather, they saw an imbalance between the forces of life and death. To the Canaanites, who inhabited a dry and arid region, rain was the ultimate symbol of fertility. It allowed life to flourish and the crops to grow. Without Baal to bring balance to the sun's power, the earth begins to wither under the rays of the sun.

When Baal is killed by Mot, the heavens were said to have "stood still," grieving for Baal. Shapash is specifically mentioned here, insinu-ating that the sun appeared to stand still in the sky. This may refer to the summer solstice when the sun's heat is at its strongest (the heat and drought caused by Baal's absence). Beginning on the solstice, the sun appears to remain in the same spot for several days, before even-tually moving farther to the south. When Shapash retrieves Baal from the underworld, she restores the balance and prevents the destruction of the world.

Like Hathor, Shapash acts as a psychopomp, both in restoring Baal and in her nightly journey to bring her light to the underworld. She guides the spirits of the dead, and in the case of Baal leads the dead through the cycle of rebirth and to new life. She is mentioned in the funeral liturgy of King Niqmaddu III, one of the last kings of Ugarit, where she guides the king to the land of the dead and sits him upon an Otherworldly throne, so that he may rule in the afterlife as well.[126] While Mot embodied death and decay, it was Shapash who opened the doors to his realm, as well as returned the soul to the liv-ing world. The fact that Shapash was invoked to protect the spirit of the dead king also reflects her connection to kingship. Being the ruler

---

126. Shipp, *Of Dead Kings and Dirges*, 57–58.

of the sky, the sun becomes the divine protectorate of the mortal ruler as well.

Shapash's light was not always harmful. In the *Poems of the Gracious Gods*, El praises her for shining her light on his twin sons. In Shapash's presence, the young gods' limbs grow as flowers and vines in the light of the sun.[127]

To some extent, Shapash ruled over healing, possessing the ability to cure the victims of snake bites. Her daughter, Phlt, shared the same ability, and both were invoked in charms to cure snake bites: "She calls to Shapash, her mother: Shapash, mother ... My incantation (against) the bite of the serpent, (against) the venom ..."[128] In one myth, Phlt was bitten by a snake and required the aid of her suitor, the god Horon, to heal her. As her bride price, she requested snakes and reptiles. It seems odd for Phlt to ask for serpents as her dowry after having a close encounter with a venomous serpent, possibly suggesting she never actually needed Horon's help in curing the bite. Perhaps she simply wanted some attention from her suitor.

This story bears a resemblance to the myth of the Cherokee sun goddess Unelanuhi and her daughter, who was also bitten by a snake. When Unelanuhi's daughter (who is also a sun goddess herself) died from the bite, she unsuccessfully tried to rescue her daughter from the land of spirits. Similarly, Shapash's daughter is cured by Horon, who has some connection to the underworld, perhaps suggesting she has to be reborn in some way to be healed.

Phlt was called "the mare." It is unclear if this is simply a title or if Phlt could shapeshift into the animal. Phlt may be another form of Shapash, as they both share similar attributes. Whether she is another aspect of Shapash or simply her daughter, the connection between the sun and horse remains clear. Rather than having horses draw her chariot, Shapash gives birth to a divine mare. Professor Michael Astour

127. Gibson, *Canaanite Myths and Legends*, 22.
128. Eslinger, *Ascribe to the Lord: Biblical and Other Studies*, 59.

notes that "we must not be surprised by the sun-goddess being represented as the mother of a 'mare' and the grandmother of a 'stallion':
horses were traditionally consecrated to the sun."[129]

WORKING WITH SHAPASH

Shapash speaks to us of balance and transformation. Her light
shines brightly even in the land of the dead, and her loving rays can
bring health and cure illness. In Baal's seasonal battle with Mot, it
is Shapash who prevents the two gods from continuing their battle.
She prevents the destruction of the earth when she returns Baal to
life. When we feel off balance, when we need to bring order and harmony back into our life, we can call Shapash's light. Even though
it is the sun's heat that is parching the earth, it is the sun goddess
who brings her polar opposite, the god of storms and rain, back to
life. She realizes she needs Baal to balance her own energies. As with
the Celtic solar goddess, we see a connection between the sun—the
embodiment of fire—and water. In Shapash's myth, fire and water
work in harmony with one another, rather than being at odds. Like
Shapash, we need to recognize when we are out of balance, and work
to transform ourselves and our situation to restore harmony within
our lives.

In the *Epic of Baal*, Shapash asks Anat to leave her an offering of
wine and a garland of leaves, making these an appropriate offering to
her. In place of a garland, you can offer her flowers or herbs. Flowers
or any kind of greenery would be especially appropriate when calling
upon the sun's life-giving power. Gold is sacred to Shapash. A text
describing various palace rituals mentions shekels (a unit of weight
used before the advent of the coin) of gold being offered to the eternal sun goddess.[130] A piece of gold jewelry can be blessed and used
to call upon Shapash's energy outside of ritual work. Gold-colored

---

129. Astour, *Hellenosemitica*, 265.
130. Wyatt, "Religion in Ancient Ugarit," 35.

candles can also be used to honor Shapash and welcome her energies into your life.

························

SHAPASH INVOCATION
Torch of the Gods
Shapash, who wings over the heavens
Beloved mother sun
Messenger of El
Champion of Anat,
Whose eyes pierce through all the worlds
Come to me, Shapash,
You who entered the realm of Mot
And drank the wine of decay and ate the bread of corruption unscathed,
Who judges both gods and men and holds dominion over shades and spirits
Under your loving light we grow and prosper
Come to me, Shapash
Shine on me your loving gaze
Fill me with your eternal light!

··

SHAPASH'S RITUAL FOR TRANSFORMATION
You Will Need:
1 fireproof bowl
1 gold or yellow candle
Wine
Flowers or a garland
Pen and paper

In this ritual you will be asking Shapash to aid you in transforming an aspect of your life. You may wish to break a bad habit, bring about new opportunities, or seek inner transformation. Part of the ritual is a guided meditation, so make sure you are in a comfortable place when you perform the ritual. You do not necessarily need to cast a circle, but you may if you wish. You can just as easily sit in a comfy couch and set up your altar on a coffee table. Any rituals that involve a guided journey always work best if the practitioner is comfortable. If you are sitting in an awkward position or on a hard floor, you will be too concerned with your body's discomfort or a numb backside to enter an altered state of consciousness.

Just as the goddess Anat did in the *Epic of Baal*, you will be offering Shapash wine and a garland. In place of a garland you could use flowers or any kind of greenery from your backyard. Be as creative as you wish. You could pick flowers and weave them together or choose herbs that correspond to the type of transformation you seek and weave them together. Go with what feels right. Your intent when making an offering is more important than the actual offering itself.

Place the yellow or gold candle in the center of your altar to represent Shapash, with the fireproof bowl to the side. If you wish to cast a circle, do so. If you do not, you may wish to light some incense or smudge the room to cleanse it of negative or stagnant energies. When you are ready, call upon Shapash, saying:

O Golden One
Torch of the Gods
Herald of your father, El
Shapash, who wings over the heavens
Shapash, who holds dominion over spirits and men
Whose sight sees all
I call to you as Anat called to you
Guide and protect me when I walk in darkness
Let your light transform me, as it transformed Baal!

Sit quietly for a few minutes. See Shapash standing before you. Scatter the leaves or flowers around the candle you are using to represent Shapash. Next dip your fingers in the wine and lightly anoint the sides of the candle with it. Then light the candle, saying:

> *As Anat did, I offer you wine and greenery of the earth*
> *Shapash, guard my steps*
> *Guide me toward transformation*

See the candle being filled with Shapash's light. When you are ready, take the piece of paper and write on it what is holding you back from accomplishing your goal. Take as much time as you need. Honesty is essential here. Don't blame another person for preventing you from achieving your goals. You may wish to ask Shapash to transform your fears into courage or help you overcome an addiction, or transform sadness into a chance for new beginnings. When you are done, hold the paper in your hands and see the problem (or the emotion, depending on what it is you wish to transform) leaving you and filling the paper. When you are ready, say:

> *I enter the realm of Mot*
> *I seek transformation*
> *Beside me stands Shapash*
> *The Torch of the Gods lights my way*
> *Shapash, safely see me through the realm of death!*

Close your eyes, still holding the paper, and see yourself in front of a great cave. Long pillars of stone reach down from the top of the cave, resembling teeth. In your hands you hold a torch; its light pierces the dark as you walk deeper and deeper into the cave. After a while you come across a ghostly figure. Allow a moment to take in how the figure appears or what it says to you. The ghost represents all the things preventing you from achieving the transformation you seek.

Hold the torch in front of you. See Shapash's light filling you. As you do so, the torch burns brighter and brighter until the ghostly figure evaporates in the presence of Shapash's radiant light.

Take the piece of paper and light it in the candle's flame. Let it burn out in the fireproof bowl, while saying:

Shapash
Torch of the Gods
Your light illuminates every darkness
All that stands in my path is destroyed by Shapash's light
Shapash, transform me
Let me emerge from the dark reborn!

Close your eyes again. See yourself filled with Shapash's light. The dark cave is illuminated, and you shine so brightly. After a time you feel like you are moving upward, and ahead you can see the light of the sun piercing through an opening in the cave. You climb upward and emerge into the sunlight, cleansed and renewed.

I am filled with the light of Shapash,
The light of transformation and change
I am transformed in the light of a new day
In Shapash's name, so be it!

Thank Shapash and extinguish the candle. If you cast a circle, close the quarters and open the circle. Pour the remaining wine and greenery outside as an offering to Shapash.

Change and transformation can take time. I find it beneficial to continue connecting to Shapash's transformative light for a few days after the ritual. You can do this as long as you wish. It is especially helpful if you are trying to break bad habits or are going through a particularly difficult time in your life. Relight the candle for a few minutes over the next few days. When you do, say the following affirmation. You could also stand outside in the sunlight when you say it.

I am cleansed and reborn by the light of Shapash,
Just as Baal was reborn when Shapash sought him
from the realm of Mot
In Shapash's name I bring transformation into my life
Whenever I look up and gaze upon the sun
I know Shapash guides me still!

. . . .
SHAPASH'S SPELL FOR HARMONY

You Will Need:
1 large bowl
Spring water or filtered water

Shapash is often a mediator for the Canaanite gods. She brings the forces of life and death back into balance when Baal and Mot fight. As the herald of the supreme god El, her words hold weight, and even the god of death trembles when facing her. In this spell you will be calling upon Shapash in her capacity as a divine mediator and bringer of harmony. No one can be perfectly balanced all the time or eternally in a good mood. Life can get us down or we may argue with the ones we love. Our homes can retain the negative vibrations of arguments, negative people, and negative feelings. It is essential to cleanse our living space and our ritual spaces of these energies. You may want to do this spell after an argument with a loved one to clear the "air," or in this case to banish any negativity left behind. You may also want to do this spell every month or so to cleanse your ritual space.

At noon on a sunny day, fill the bowl with water and let it sit outside where the light of the sun can shine on it for at least an hour. If it is winter or you cannot leave it outside, place it near a sunny window. After the water has been charged by the sunlight, hold your hands over the water and say:

Light of Shapash, bring balance and harmony
Light of Shapash, chase away all that is dark
By the light of the mother sun who creates all life
And by the sacred waters, Baal, that sustain all life
Let it be so!

Sprinkle the water around your house or ritual area, moving in a clockwise direction around the room. The water can also be sprinkled on an altar to bless and cleanse it or to bless a ritual space during rituals involving Shapash. If you wish to store the water for later use, pour it into a dark-colored container. Add a few drops of alcohol as a preservative.

. . . .
Shapash Incense
2 parts myrrh
1 part frankincense
1 part cinnamon

. . . .
Shapash Correspondences
Animals: snake, mare
Symbol: torch
Colors: yellow, gold
Stones/Minerals: gold, pyrite

THE AMERICAS

Sometime during the last ice age, groups of people from Asia followed the animals they hunted across a land bridge that stretched between Siberia and Alaska. Over time they spread south, settling in North America and eventually making their way as far as South America either on foot or by following the coastline in primitive boats. This migration occurred in stages, with the ancestors of the Inuit most likely being descended from one of the later migrations.[131] With them, these people brought their myths and their ideas about the heavens. Keeping their origins in mind, it should come as no surprise that the stories and myths of many Native American cultures share many parallels with solar mythology throughout Asia and Europe.

The sun is a prevalent figure within the mythology of the Americas. In the indigenous cultures of both North America and South America, the sun was hailed as a divine being. At times the sun was male; other times it was seen as female; still other tribes saw it as a genderless force within the universe.

In most cases, the status of women in native cultures that worshiped the female sun differed from that of their cousins who viewed the sun as masculine. The Cherokee were a matrilineal society, tracing their ancestry through the woman's line. A family lived in the household of their

---

131. Garrett, *Native American Faith in America*, 25.

mother. If a couple divorced, the man left his wife's house and returned to his mother's house. Just as they held a high status in the household, women also held sway over tribal politics as well. Tunica women enjoyed a high status in their culture also, and in many cases gender roles among this tribe were reversed compared to those in surrounding areas. For example, Tunica men, not women, were in charge of agriculture. The majority of the tribes in what is now the southeastern United States viewed the sun as male, with the Tunica being an exception. Conversely, the role of women also differed in Tunica society.

In much of Native American lore, the sun plays a vital role in the creation of the world. It is usually not the first thing to be created, but rather the last. Often it has to be stolen or coaxed into existence. In several creation myths, the land, animals, and people are brought into existence only to dwell in darkness. Weary of living without light or warmth, they send someone to fetch the sun. According to the Haida people of the Pacific Northwest, Raven steals the sun; in Cherokee myth, Grandmother Spider Woman weaves a basket and carries the sun from the other side of the world to light the earth. In Maidu lore, the sun rises from the primordial waters only after her brother called to her; the heat of the Sun Woman created mountains and valleys as she rose from the depths. Another myth from the Maidu of Butte and Plumas counties in California says that the sun and moon were a brother and sister who lived in a stone house and refused to come outside to light the world.[132] Gopher dug a hole under the house and let loose a bag of fleas, so the brother and sister had no choice but to come out to escape the insects.

The Slavey people of northwestern Canada tell a different story. The sun existed in the world for a time, but one day it disappeared. For three years the world was plunged into a dark winter. Starving, the animals all gathered to see what could be done about the situation. Bear was the only animal who did not come to the council, and

132. Monaghan, *O Mother Sun!*, 142.

soon the other animals realized no one had seen any bears for the past three years. Convinced Bear had stolen the sun, the other animals traveled to the Upper World of the sky, where they came upon two bear cubs. Fox, Bobcat, and Mouse tricked the cubs into revealing that their mother had the sun hidden in a bag, and devised a way to steal back the sun. Bobcat disguised himself as a deer and lured the mother bear and her cubs away from the den; then Mouse snuck in and stole the bag. As soon as they returned to the world, they tore the bag open and the sun and its warmth rose back to its rightful place in the sky.

Although the stories differ, the themes surrounding the sun are surprisingly similar to those found in other parts of the world. Like Amaterasu, the sun must be drawn out of hiding, whether she is stolen, tricked, or lovingly called into the world. We find this same theme played out in the myths of other sun goddesses as well, such as Yhi and Sekhmet, who also have to be lured back to the world. The belief that the sun sank into the ocean to rest, as the Baltic goddess Saule does in her golden boat, is mirrored in the Maidu story of brother moon calling to his sister, the sun, to rise from the sea of creation.

The sun hiding in a cave or under the ground, another common theme in sun-goddess lore, is also present, here symbolized by the stone house the Maidu brother and sister refuse to leave, and the den of the bear mother. Although in Slavey lore the sun is genderless, the fact that the person who steals the sun, mother bear, is female is also significant. While the sun is not directly female, the energy surrounding the sun's abduction and concealment is given a feminine identity. She also mimics the sun's behavior, as bears disappear to hibernate in the winter, just as the sun in the subarctic home of the Slavey seems to disappear during the height of winter. When the sun returns with the spring, so do the bears, mirroring the sun's yearly cycle. Bear mother also plays a similar role to the Irish hag Cailleach, who steals the sun and hides it in a cave until someone rescues the maiden sun.

At times the sun begins as a deity; other times she begins as a mortal who transforms into a goddess. This transformation usually comes about as the means of escaping an unhappy sexual union. The Tunica of southeastern Arkansas and northeastern Louisiana recognized only nine deities, chief among them the sun.[133]

The Tunica believed the sun was once a beautiful girl who was seduced by Kingfisher. The bird came to her when it was dark and took her to his home. When she awoke in the morning, she found his house to be a nest in a hackberry tree. When she asked him for food, he brought her live minnows. Ashamed, either of her lover or that she had been tricked, she wished to leave but could not escape from Kingfisher's nest. Trapped, she began to sing. As she sang, she began to glow and her body gave off light, until she rose to the sky and became the sun.

The Inuit sun goddess Akycha was also a mortal. Like the Tunica sun goddess, Akycha also had a lover who visited her in the dark of night. Curious to know the man's identity, she marked his face with soot, only to discover it was her brother. Ashamed, she fled to the heavens, becoming the sun, while her brother who constantly pursues her became the moon. Like the story of Kingfisher and the sun goddess, the Inuit sun enters into a sexual union with a stranger whose identity is concealed. Once the truth comes to light, she is transformed into a supernatural force in order to escape her unwanted lover.

Despite the sun's unhappiness with her partners, there is a distinct connection between the sun, sexual maturity, and womanhood not only in native myth but also in cultural practices. A menstruation ritual among the Mescalero tribe reflects this connection. When a Mescalero girl began menstruating, a ritual was performed in which

133. Swanton, *Indian Tribes of the Lower Mississippi Valley*, 318.

the girl was painted with sun symbols on her forehead in red and white paint, after which she faced the rising sun.[134]

The sun also had a strong connection with order and time in several Native American myths. Unelanuhi, the Cherokee sun goddess, was called the "apportioner," a reference to the sun's ability to mark time, both through marking the day and her yearly cycles. In some creation myths, one of the animals' complaints, other than being cold and hungry, was that they could not tell day from night and thus never knew what day it was. In South America, the Toba people believed that their sun goddess Akewa aged throughout the year. In winter she was young and moved through the sky quickly, while as an old woman she shuffled slowly across the sky, accounting for the lengthening days of summer. Her constant aging and return to maidenhood marked the seasons and years. Without her yearly transformation, time would stand still.

UNELANUHI

You find yourself around a small campfire. Beside you others sit, trying to keep warm and talking to each other. As you squint to see better, you notice that the figures around you are not human but animals. And you realize that you sit among the First People, who could wear the shapes of men or animals as they pleased. Across the fire, Badger begins to complain it is too cold and there is no light to see. Everyone agrees, and there is much mumbling around the circle and complaining. Fox finally calls for everyone's attention: "I know where we can get light and warmth."

"Where?" everyone asks. Even you lean forward, curious. "Sun Woman lives on the other side of the world. I have seen here there on my travels. She lights the sky like a million campfires. There will be light and warmth for everyone if we catch her and bring her to live here!"

---

134. Kroeber, *Salt, Dogs, Tobacco*, 34.

All the animals agree and then begin asking who should go to bring this Sun Woman here. Badger thinks Fox should go, and Fox thinks Deer should be the one to go, and Deer thinks Sparrow is better suited to the task. Then finally Coyote looks to you and says, "I know who should go!" And he points at you.

Before you know it, you are on your way to the other side of the world, looking for Sun Woman. After a long time walking, you come to a valley. A light brighter than any you have seen glows from this place, and you creep closer, hiding behind some rocks to see what the source of the light is. At the center of the valley you see a woman; her skin shimmers, and light comes from her in waves. This must be Sun Woman. But now that you have found her, you are not sure how to get her to come with you.

Suddenly Coyote appears next to you. He looks up at you and says, "You can't catch Sun Woman looking like this!" He places a paw on you, and you begin to shrink and change. In a few moments you have become a spider. "Weave a basket and put Sun Woman in it, then bring her back to the rest of us!" he tells you.

After many hours of weaving, you finally have a large basket of silken threads. Again, Coyote appears. With a paw, he turns you back to yourself and together you creep up to Sun Woman. Quickly you scoop her up in the basket and carry her away.

Finally, back at the campfire, the other animals greet you with excitement. But unfortunately, when you empty your silken basket, the woman, arms crossed in anger, is just a woman. No light comes from her form. Confused, you look to Coyote, who shrugs and backs away as if to distance himself from the situation.

Suddenly you get an idea. You begin to dance. You scoop up Badger and waltz with him, then dance around the campfire, bringing all the animals into the merriment. Sun Woman watches your antics and soon begins to laugh. As her laughter builds, she begins to shine until finally the world is filled with her light.

The sun held a particularly important role to the Cherokee, a nation that never addressed their prayers to anyone but the sun.[135] The Cherokee sun goddess Unelanuhi was connected to both life and death. She was a goddess of creation, yet in other myths she is also responsible for bringing death into the world. Her name means "apportioner" or "allotting," since she divided day and night and the seasons with her movements through the sky.[136] She is also called *Aag hu Gu gu*, which means "Beautiful Woman." Her other, more ominous title is *Sutalidihi*, which means "Six Killer," referring to the number of times she tried to destroy the earth. Cherokee prayers frequently use the phrase "Sun, my creator," making her a primordial goddess of creation.[137]

In the beginning of time, Unelanuhi lived on the other side of the world and did not shine on the earth, leaving it dark and cold. The animals held a council in which Fox told them there was light at the other side of the world and they should send someone to retrieve it. The buzzard tried, but the light was so intense it burned off the feathers on his head and claw. When Possum tried, all the fur was burned off his tail. Finally Spider Woman succeeded in stealing the sun by placing it in a basket and pulling it back to the darkened earth along the strands of her web. Unfortunately, the sun's light was too intense, and people began dying from the heat. So the animals moved her up higher in the sky, until she was seven handspans high above the sky, where she remains to this day.[138]

Like the Japanese Amaterasu, Unelanuhi once hid from the earth and needed to be persuaded to return. Each day Unelanuhi traveled from her home on the other side of the sky to see her daughter, who made her home in the middle of the sky. Her daily visit explains why the sun travels daily to the height of the sky then descends again

---

135. Morrison, *Everyday Sun Magic*, 25.
136. Monaghan, *O Mother Sun!*, 168.
137. Mooney, *Myths of the Cherokee and Sacred Formulas of the Cherokees*, 440.
138. Monaghan, *Encyclopedia of Goddesses and Heroines*, 564.

to her home on the other side of the world. As Unelanuhi looked down on the earth along her travels, she noticed that the humans never looked at her directly, but squinted at her, making their faces look ugly. She became even angrier when she saw how lovingly they looked up at her brother, the moon. Finally she decided she would destroy her ungrateful children. Every day she prolonged her visit in the middle of the sky and sent down scorching rays that caused fevers and killed crops.

People died by the hundreds, until finally they went to the Little Men for help. These "Little Men" make appearances in other Cherokee myths as well, and appear to be the Native American version of the Faerie Folk. The Little Men told the people that the only way to save themselves was to kill the sun. The Little Men transformed two men into snakes, the spreading-adder and the copperhead, and told them to wait near the house of the sun's daughter and bite the sun when she came near. When the sun came by, the spreading-adder tried to attack but was blinded by her light; and after his companion's failed attempt, the copperhead slunk away without trying at all. So the Little Men tried again, this time turning one man into a rattlesnake and another into a great horned snake called the Uktena. Again the snakes waited for the sun goddess to pass by. When the sun's daughter walked by, the rattlesnake mistook her for the sun and accidently killed her. Consumed with grief, Unelanuhi shut herself in her house and refused to come out, leaving the world in a state of endless darkness.

Cold and unable to grow their crops, the people went back to the Little Men for help. This time the Little Men told them that if they wanted Unelanuhi to come out of her house, they would have to retrieve her daughter from the Dark Land of the West, where the spirits of the dead lived. There, the Little Men told them, they would find the spirits of the dead dancing in a circle. When the sun's daughter danced by, they were to hit her with rods and place her in a box.

Seven men were chosen, each given a rod of sourwood. It took them seven days to reach the land of spirits, and when they found the sun's daughter dancing with the other spirits, they each struck her with their rods until she fell to the ground, and then they put her in the box. As they made their way back home, the sun's daughter called to the men, telling them she was hungry and to open the box and give her food, but they ignored her. Then she called to the men, saying she was thirsty, and begged them to open the lid and give her water. Finally she told them she was suffocating, and asked them to open the lid a little to give her some air. Scared the girl would die again without enough air, they opened the lid, and the sun's daughter flew out of the box in the shape of a redbird. When the men returned empty-handed, Unelanuhi began to weep and flooded the world with her tears. Afraid everyone would drown, the most beautiful men and women of the tribe were sent to dance and sing for Unelanuhi. Their dancing made the sun goddess forget her grief, and she finally returned to the world.

In other versions, it is Unelanuhi who is killed by the rattlesnake, and her daughter then takes her place in the sky as the new sun goddess. The rattlesnake in this case is not a man, but a stick that the Little Men transformed into a snake by carving seven circles on it and throwing it into the path of the sun.

In yet another version of this story, Unelanuhi brings death into the world. In the beginning, men and women lived forever, but when the sun passed over the world, she saw that the world was not big enough for all the people and told them that it would be better if they died. Unfortunately, her own daughter was bitten by a rattlesnake and died. She then said that humans could live forever if they retrieved her daughter from the land of the dead. Again they were told to put the sun's daughter in a box and not to open the lid until they had returned from the land of the dead. Of course one of the men became curious and opened it, and that is why all human beings are fated to die.[139] In some versions of this myth, the sun is male.

Like Amaterasu and Hathor, Unelanuhi hides her face from the world after being angered. Like the shaman Uzume, whose comical dance brought Amaterasu out of her cave, Unelanuhi is also coaxed into returning through dancing. Like Hathor, she is no stranger to the land of the dead. Her home on the other side of the world can be seen as the underworld. To retrieve her daughter's spirit, the men must travel to the west, mirroring the sun's path as it sets, giving way to night. In the second version of the myth, she both brings death into the world and instructs the men how to retrieve her daughter's spirit from the land of the dead. Even her very first appearance in the world requires a trip to the underworld, when the animals travel to the other side of the world to retrieve her. As in the myths of other sun goddesses, the number seven is connected to her. The men must travel seven days to reach the land of the dead, and they hit her daughter seven times. When Unelanuhi herself is killed, it is with a stick carved with seven circles, circles again being another symbol connected to the sun.

Unelanuhi's story clearly illustrates the cycles of the seasons. At first she shines too brightly, indicating the heat of summer. When her daughter is killed, she retreats, bringing winter. When she is killed and her daughter takes her place, the seasonal shift between the bright sun of summer and the weaker, younger sun of winter is clear. Like Sunna, who gives birth to a daughter who will take her place in the sky before her death, Unelanuhi also births her replacement, who is ultimately herself in a younger guise. The very fact that in some versions it is Unelanuhi who is killed, and in others the daughter, indicates that they are one in the same goddess. The sun and her daughter simply represent different aspects of the sun's journey through the seasons.

---

139. Mooney, *Myths of the Cherokee and Sacred Formulas of the Cherokees*, 436.

In another story, Unelanuhi becomes a mediator in a marriage spat between the first man and woman. The man and woman had lived happily together, but soon they began to quarrel. Finally the woman left the man and began walking off to the east. Grieving the loss of his wife, the man followed behind her, but could not make her stop walking. Eventually, Unelanuhi saw this and took pity on the man. She asked him if he still loved the woman, and when he said yes, she decided to help the couple. Unelanuhi made the finest huckleberries spring from the ground, but the woman did not stop and continued to walk onward. Next, Unelanuhi placed blackberries in her path, but still the woman would not stop. Finally she tempted her with ripe strawberries, the first ever created. When the woman saw the strawberries, she stopped and began to eat them. As she ate the strawberries, she forgot her anger and began thinking of her husband (in some versions she becomes overcome with desire for him).[140] Since the woman had stopped to eat the strawberries, the man finally caught up with her and they returned home together. Today the Cherokee still keep strawberries in the home as a symbol of marital harmony.[141]

WORKING WITH UNELANUHI

Unelanuhi is both a creator and destroyer. Her light brings warmth and makes the crops grow, but she can also bring calamities and death. It is interesting to note that she sees the necessity in death. She sees there isn't enough room in the world for humanity if everyone is allowed to live forever and creates death to keep the living world in balance. This isn't a vengeful or spiteful act, simply a harsh necessity. For life to continue, there must also be death. Even the goddess cannot escape death, and she must grieve as mortals do when her daughter dies. She can also create harmony, as when she helped reunite the

---

140. Monaghan, *O Mother Sun!*, 108.
141. Neufeld, *A Popular History of Western North Carolina*, 25.

first man and woman and made the first woman forget her anger. In this aspect we can call upon Unelanuhi to soothe our own anger and jealousies. These emotions only create imbalance, just as Unelanuhi's jealousy over the admiring looks the moon received caused her to act against humanity, and eventually led to her daughter's death.

Unelanuhi can teach us to bring order to our lives, to make difficult decisions, and to learn how to recover from grief. Like us, Unelanuhi experiences loss; she loses her daughter and retreats from the world, consumed by grief. Like other sun goddesses, she leaves the world in darkness, but unlike other goddesses who leave due to being scared or hidden away by another, Unelanuhi is driven away by overwhelming sorrow. Losing a loved one can make us retreat within and can make us feel like the world and life has lost its light and appeal. Unelanuhi is not tricked like Amaterasu into returning; she brings her light back into the world when humanity sings and dances for her, showing the goddess that she is loved by her other children.

Call upon Unelanuhi to overcome grief, to bring balance into your life, or when facing a difficult situation.

UNELANUHI INVOCATION
Unelanuhi
Beautiful woman
You who divine time and the seasons,
Whose tears fill the seas,
And whose light makes the fields ripe and fruitful
Set your gaze upon this, your loving daughter/son
Unelanuhi, Apportioner
Unelanuhi, Mother Sun
Unelanuhi, fill me your with your sacred light!

GREETING THE MORNING SUN RITUAL

This is a simple ritual to help you draw upon the sun's energies. It is an excellent way to energize yourself in the morning and connect to the sun goddess. In the morning when you first wake up (or at dawn if possible), stand outside and take a few minutes to let the sun's rays warm your skin. If it is winter and too cold to go outside, stand by a sunny window. Hold your arms in an invoking position and visualize the golden light of the sun filling your body and energizing you. When you are ready, say:

> *Beautiful Mother*
> *Unelanuhi*
> *Jewel of the sky*
> *I greet you this morning, O Mother Sun*
> *As you rise out of darkness,*
> *Shine your loving gaze upon me this day*
> *Fill me with your light*
> *Hail Unelanuhi!*

GREETING THE EVENING SUN RITUAL

At sunset, go outside and face the setting sun. Raise your hands in an invoking position, then say:

> *Hail Unelanuhi!*
> *As your daily journey ends, you sink below the horizon*
> *Into the Ghost Country*
> *Into the realm of spirits*
> *Guide me through the darkness,*
> *As you tread the dark paths this night*
> *May the light of Unelanuhi fill me in my darkest hour!*

. . . .
UNELANUHI RITUAL TO OVERCOME GRIEF

You Will Need:

Fresh rosemary and sage

Red string

While the sun's retreat is usually a result of anger or a disagreement, Unelanuhi's is caused by grief. Anyone who has ever lost a loved one can understand the inward retreat one experiences during the mourning process. When dealing with grief and the death of a loved one, call upon Unelanuhi, who like ourselves is not immune to the loss of those she loves.

If possible, use sprigs of fresh rosemary and sage (you can find them in the grocery store). Bundle the rosemary and sage together and tie the base with the string to make a handle. Face the direction of the sun and take a moment to feel the warmth of the sun; it is the warmth of a mother's love. If you are indoors, stand near a sunny window or visualize the light of the sun shining on you.

Take the herbal bundle and run it over your body, starting with your head and shoulders and working downward. See Unelanuhi's light filling you, as the herbs absorb the grief and sorrow you feel. Do this as long as needed. When you are done, leave the herbs outside in a sunny spot. You can either break the leaves and stems apart and toss them to the wind or let the herbs dry outside for a few days, and then burn them and scatter their ashes.

. . . .
UNELANUHI MAY WINE

You Will Need:

1 bottle of white wine

1 bottle of pear juice

½ bottle of black cherry juice

½ bottle of strawberry banana juice (or just strawberry juice)
2 cups strawberries cut into fourths

In many regions, early May is when we begin to feel the sun's warmth again. Plants and flowers begin to bloom, and love is in the air. This is an excellent wine to use in Beltane celebration, as a libation to Unelanuhi, and in love spells.

Unelanuhi, bless this wine with your golden light
You who created the first strawberries,
To remind the first woman of her love
Unelanuhi, teach us to love ourselves and one another
Let us savor the sweetness of life!

. . . .
UNELANUHI CORRESPONDENCES
Animals: snake, spider, redbird
Symbol: solar wheel
Herb/Plant: strawberries
Colors: red, gold

AKYCHA

You are running through the sky. Your feet move so fast that sparks accompany every footfall. It is dark except for those occasional sparks from the speed of your passing. Every fiber in your being is consumed with the need to run, faster and faster. You know if you don't, the creature that is chasing you will catch up to you, and you cannot let that happen. Faster and faster you race across the sky, skipping over stars and occasionally looking down at the world below.

Soon you begin to tire. Even so, you refuse to look behind you. You hear your pursuer getting closer, closing in on you, but you are still too afraid to look back at him or her. It feels like you have been running forever when you finally falter. You can run no farther. Suspended in the darkened sky, you wait. Your body shakes. You have been running so long, but you have come to the point where you can run no more.

Something has changed within you. It is the tiniest of sparks, but the feeling is building. You think of all that you have left behind, all the things in life that you have set aside to put all of your energy into this flight. You have been running so long you aren't entirely certain who or what you have been running from. Something within you whispers, "Call forth the light within you, and you will have nothing to fear." A small spark of determination ignites at the words. A halo of light begins to give off a soft glow around you. Turning, you begin speeding toward your pursuer. As you do, the halo of light ignites into a brilliant flame. You light up the sky as you run, no longer fearful but filled with determination.

It is not long before you see who has been chasing you all this time. The form stops before you, and you are surprised to see yourself. Everything is a mirror image of yourself until you look into the eyes. They are haunted, and in them you see all the things that you fear and that weigh on your spirit. Looking at this haunted figure, you are unsure why you have been running this long. You look at your hands and the light that surrounds you. Then you reach out and embrace the figure before you. You wrap your arms around it and let the light that surrounds you fill the being before you. You watch as the figure dissolves and blows away in the wind. As it does, the light around you grows brighter and you know you are free.

Among the Inuit people who inhabit Alaska, Canada, and Greenland, the sun and moon are always brother and sister. They are known by various names—Akycha and Igaluk to the Inuits of Alaska, while those living in Greenland call the siblings Malina and Anningan. Regardless of their varying names, the stories the Inuit tell about the sun sister and moon brother are almost identical. Akycha and Igaluk's story is not a happy one, but its lessons remain relevant to us today.

Like most of the Inuit gods, Akycha and Igaluk were once mortals. The brother and sister lived happily together in their village far to the north until Akycha began to grow into a woman. Upon reaching menarche, she was old enough to take a lover and participate in the tribal copulation games. In winter all the young people gathered in the dancing hut, where they played the game of "snuffing out the light." The oil lamps would be extinguished, and in the darkness a sexual partner would be chosen at random. The idea of this practice was that neither partner would know the identity of the other and no fixed relationships would be formed.

It was taboo for siblings to be present during these games, but Igaluk, having been aroused by his sister's beauty, ignored the taboo and sought her out during the games. Each night he found Akycha and made love to her. Eventually Akycha became curious about her lover. One night she covered her fingers with soot from a seal-oil lamp and smeared it across her lover's face. When the lamps were relit, she found Igaluk's face marked with the soot. Her face burning hot with shame, she took a knife, cut off one of her breasts, and flung it at her brother, saying, "If you desire me so much, eat this!"

Then she ran from the hut, with her brother following close behind. Before she fled, Akycha lit a torch from a handful of moss dipped in blubber in order to light her way. Igaluk had also taken a torch, but during the chase he tripped and only a few embers remained lit, which is why the sun's light is brighter than the moon's. Eventually Akycha rose to the sky, becoming the sun in hopes of finally evading her brother, but he rose to the sky as well, transforming into the moon, where he chases her still.

As heavenly bodies, the story of Igaluk's pursuit of the sun plays out before our eyes each month. At the beginning of his chase, he is full and round with health, but as he doggedly pursues his sister through the sky he forgets to eat, and grows thin as the month goes by. Eventually he is nothing more than skin and bones, appearing as a sliver in the sky. Finally overcome with hunger, he leaves the sky for three days (the time of the new moon) to fill his belly and rest. Once he has recovered, he begins his chase once again.

Because of their eternal chase, each has bitter feelings toward the opposite gender. Parhelions (the illusion of white spots appearing alongside the sun, which are formed by ice crystals reflecting in the atmosphere) were thought to be the sun goddess decorating her hair in curls to celebrate a man's death. Seeing a parhelion before leaving on a hunt was believed to be an omen of one's death. Similarly, on solar eclipses, when the moon was believed to have caught up with the sun and attempts to resume their lovemaking, men stayed indoors, fearing the sun goddess in her anger would curse with illness any man she looked upon. During lunar eclipses, women remain indoors, fearing the moon would bring them illness and disease because of his bitter feelings toward his sister.

During the winter months in the Arctic, the sun retreats from the world, shutting herself into her house. In her absence the world is plunged into a time of cold and darkness. During these months her brother is charged with bringing her firewood to keep her warm, their feud forgotten for the time being. During this time the Inuit played string games—what we call cat's cradle today—in order to entice the sun's return. These games were accompanied by storytelling and special songs. The net pattern formed by the string was used as a kind of sympathetic magick to symbolically capture the sun and draw her back into the sky.[142] The net represented in the cat's cradle

---

142. Crowe, *A History of the Original Peoples of Northern Canada*, 33.

game is also reminiscent of other Native American myths in which Spider Woman catches the sun in her web.

During the summer the sun never goes inside her house, accounting for the days of continuous daylight during the Arctic summer. Although her reasons for staying hidden from the world are never mentioned, like the sun goddesses of other cultures, her habit of retreating from the world signals the seasonal cycles of summer and winter. Since her relationship and flight from her brother occur during winter, discovering the truth of her lover's identity may be the cause of her disappearance during this time of year.

The theme of incest between the sun and moon is not limited to Inuit mythology. We find the same story in Baltic mythology, where sun goddess Saule's daughter is either raped or willingly seduced by her father, the moon god. As in the Baltic tale, in some versions Akycha and Igaluk come together willingly, while in others the moon god initiates the encounter. Both brother and sister ignore the taboo of participating in the games while a sibling is present, making their coupling seem somewhat intentional.

The difference between the myths is that Saule's daughter represents a younger version of herself. When we consider that Saule and her daughter are the same being, the act of incest become symbolic of a seasonal shift. The moon's consort is the sun maiden during the winter months when the sun is "younger" and not as bright, while during the summer months he is consort to the more mature mother sun. But there does not seem to be any seasonal shift between a younger and older self at work in Akycha's myth. Her incest seems to be a warning against breaking taboos. The brother and sister tempt fate by breaking the rules. On some level the story is a commentary on human nature, with one party being remorseful for her actions while her brother seeks to continue breaking the rules. There will always be people who continue to do evil things, while others learn from their mistakes.

There is also a strong theme of transformation in Akycha's story. She doesn't begin her life as a goddess; instead she is mortal, and must suffer and make mistakes before she attains divinity. This transformation is preceded by a sacrifice, cutting off her breast. Similarly, another Inuit goddess, Sedna, who ruled over the ocean and all the animals who live in it, is also disfigured prior to transforming into a deity. In Sedna's case, she is thrown into the ocean by her father. As she clung to the boat, he chopped off her fingers, which sank into the water to become various sea creatures. Both goddesses are betrayed by those they love, and each sacrifices a piece of themselves (quite literally) to embark on a spiritual transformation, in this case transforming from mortal to goddess.

This kind of sacrifice is reminiscent of those made during traditional sun dances. Although the Native American peoples who participated in the Sun Dance, such as the Cheyenne and the Ute, viewed the sun as male, they felt it necessary to offer a sacrifice of flesh to the sun in order to gain spiritual blessings and insight. Participants would pierce their skin with hooks, which were ritualistically pulled out, taking a bit of flesh with them.

Transformation can be a difficult process. As was the case for Akycha, it sometimes requires us to face unpleasant truths. But for true transformation, we have to sacrifice our ignorance and the lies we let ourselves believe and see things for what they truly are. When we do this, we can transform ourselves and divinity shines through us, transforming us as it did Akycha.

Working with Akycha

One cannot help but feel sorry for Akycha. She blossoms into womanhood, and as she begins to grow into her role as a woman of the tribe and explore her sexuality, she is betrayed and taken advantage of by someone close to her. Her own feelings are turned against her. Feelings of love and trust turn bitter and shameful. Wishing to learn her lover's identity most likely indicates that she intended to form a more permanent relationship with her mysterious lover, but she instead has to face the harsh reality that she has been fooled by her brother. Igaluk's actions are intentional, but it is Akycha who unknowingly pays the price. Instead of facing her brother and holding him accountable for his actions, she runs from him and the shame she feels. She mutilates her own body, despite the fact that she is the victim and was not at fault.

In other myths involving the incestuous relationship between the sun and moon, the moon is punished, as when the Baltic Saule slashes the face of the moon or hacks him to pieces. But Akycha is eternally running from the moon, never able to escape her past. Because she never faces her brother, she leaves herself open for further attack, as when the moon was thought to overtake the sun during an eclipse. In running from her past, she allows her abuse to continue and never truly moves on with her life. Her unwillingness to face her past leads to her unhealthy hatred of men, whom she is thought to curse.

Many of us run, as Akycha does, from our emotions or from events in our past that are difficult for us to face. We think if we run fast enough we can escape them, or pretend they don't exist. But like Igaluk, they are never that far behind and are just waiting for the right moment to pounce and open up old wounds. When we run from our past, we can never face it and truly leave it behind us. Instead, running from our emotions only hurts ourselves; doing so disfigures us, as it did Akycha, scarring our future. In the end, all Akycha is left with is her pain, symbolized by her brother. When she flees, she leaves behind her family and friends and the life she could have lived. She never moves past her hurt, allowing it to eternally chase her.

Akycha's lesson to us is to face the emotions and events that have scarred us. She knows that if we don't, we'll be running from them forever. For those who have faced any kind of physical or emotional abuse, she is an excellent goddess to work with to overcome any kind of emotional roadblocks.

Winter, when Akycha shuts herself into her house, is a good time to invoke Akycha and ask her to help you overcome the past. During these months, take time to look within. What holds you back? What events or emotions do you need to move past? Ask Akycha to help you leave these things behind so you may move forward.

A torch or an oil lamp can be used to represent Akycha during rituals or on an altar dedicated to her. Balls made from seal skin and filled with either seeds or sand have been found at many Inuit archeological sites. These balls were used to represent the sun or other solar imagery and were decorated with circular bands that were dyed red. These balls, sometimes referred to as "Inuit balls," were used in ceremonial games somewhat akin to modern hacky sack to mark the new year. The sounds of the seeds inside the ball were thought to repel bad luck and evil spirits.

Circles and spheres are common symbols used to represent the sun in many cultures. You could construct your own version of an Inuit ball to represent the sun's energy on an altar to Akycha, or you could use a crystal ball or another spherical object to represent the sun goddess. When working with Akycha, I use a small crystal ball made from citrine (a stone connected to the sun's energies) in place of a statue to represent her.

AKYCHA INVOCATION

Akycha, you who have suffered,
Who has been betrayed by those you loved
I suffer as you have suffered
Hear my cries, sister sun
Warm my heart and heal the wounds of my spirit
Akycha, bring brighter days

....
Akycha Incense
1 part moss
1 part pine needles

....
Tears of the Sun Ritual

What You Will Need:

1 large glass bowl

3 rosemary sprigs

1 large bottle of spring or filtered water

1 white or gold candle to represent Akycha

This ritual can be used to confront emotions and traumatic events from the past. Often we don't acknowledge our feelings. We bury them and let them continue to influence us and wound our spirits. When we ignore our emotions, we fail to really look at our feelings and understand why we feel a certain way. If we don't take time to examine our emotions, we can never move past them.

Pour the water into the bowl and leave it in a place where the sun can shine on it for at least an hour. (If you cannot leave the bowl out in the sun or if it is overcast, hold your hands over the bowl and visualize the rays of the sun infusing the water with a brilliant golden light.) Bring the bowl of water back inside. You could perform the ritual in your sacred space or in your bathroom (as you will be washing the water over your body).

Light the candle, saying:

Akycha, beloved sun
Guide me through the dark

Sit in a comfortable position. Ground and center. See the light of the sun shining above your head. The sun's light fills your body, moving from the crown of your head to the soles of your feet. Spend some extra time sending that golden light to your heart chakra, the center of your emotional being.

Take a deep breath and simply allow yourself to feel. Allow your emotions to come to the surface. Dip your hands into the water and lightly wash the water over your face and arms (or the rest of your body if you wish). See the light of the sun washing away the emotions and energy you wish to release. Continue to allow all the emotions you wish to shed to come to the surface. Recognize and acknowledge them, then allow them to dissolve and flow away with the blessed water. If you wish, you may say an affirmation as you do this, such as "I release you" or whatever feels right to you.

When you are ready, pour the rest of the water on the ground outside and thank Akycha.

REVEAL THE TRUTH SPELL

You Will Need:
1 white candle or oil lamp
Pen and paper

On a piece of paper write the situation or problem you wish Akycha to help you with. Underneath what you have written, write "Truth Revealed." Hold the candle or lamp in your hands while chanting Akycha's name. Visualize her light entering the candle. The candle glows with the light of the sun, a light so bright it reveals all truth and dispels lies and deceit. See Akycha's light shining on the situation at hand to give you clarity and reveal hidden motives or the deceit of others.

When you are ready, say:

What was hidden I bring now into the light
Akycha, burn bright
Reveal the truth to me day or night

Let the candle burn out, or burn it for a few minutes each day until the candle is spent.

. . . .

AKYCHA CORRESPONDENCES
Symbols: oil lamp, torch, ball, or sphere
Herb/Plant: moss
Colors: red, yellow

AUSTRALIA

The myths and lore of the Aboriginal sun goddesses are many and varied. As there were many Aboriginal peoples, we find several similar sun goddesses on the Australian continent, many of whom fill the same function and may be regional and tribal variations of the same solar goddess. Yhi's story is perhaps the most vivid and complete, but she is by no means the only solar goddess honored by the Aboriginal people. Other Aboriginal sun goddesses include Walo, Gnowee, Wuriupranili, Bila, Pukwi, and Alinga.

Gnowee lived on the earth before there was a sun. Everyone carried torches to see in the dark, and one day when Gnowee was out gathering yams, her baby son wandered off. Each day, carrying a large torch, Gnowee climbs into the sky, illuminating the earth below as she searches for her lost son. The sun goddess of the Tiwi people is Pukwi. She created the earth in the Dreamtime. Each day she travels across the sky, stopping at midday to make a fire to cook her lunch, which is why it is hottest during that time of day.

As Bila, the sun was a cannibal woman who lit the world with the light of her cooking fire, over which she cooked men and women. Kudnu the Lizard Man and Muda the Gecko Man decided to stop her from eating all of the world's people and attacked her with a boomerang. Scared, Bila turned into a great ball of light and vanished below the horizon. Kudnu threw his boomerang in each direction until he captured the sun goddess, setting her in motion across the sky.

The goddess Wuriupranili carries a torch, the sun, across the sky each day. At night she extinguishes the torch in the ocean and uses the embers to guide her way beneath the earth to the east so she can begin her journey again with the new day. The Narrinyeri say the sun is a beautiful woman who goes underground each night to visit the dead. The sun at one time had a mortal lover, and even after death she could not part with him and spent the night in his arms in the land of the dead. In the morning she rises, clothed in a red kangaroo skin that tints the dawn a reddish color, a gift from her lover.

YHI

You find yourself sitting by a campfire. The night air is dry but fragrant, and all around you red and brown rock formations rise up toward the stars. You take a moment to gaze up at the stars. They are brilliant in the clear night sky. You look down into the flames again and silently ask the universe to see a wonder. You think of the stars again, and all the beauty around you, and wonder how it all came to be.

Soon your eyes close. You can still feel the warmth of the fire and hear the wood pop as it is consumed, but in your mind's eye you are in a much different place. You walk across a barren landscape. Everything is cloaked in a misty twilight. Above, no stars twinkle in the sky. Everything is silent, as if all of life is asleep.

You walk for a time until you come the base of a great mountain. The earth here is jagged and dotted with many caves. The emptiness of this place saddens you, and all you wish to do is find somewhere where there is the faintest bit of life.

As if answering your thoughts, you hear a faint sound. It seems to be coming from one of the caves. You listen for a minute, trying to discern the source of the sound. You approach the largest cave and step inside. The sound becomes clearer and you realize it is singing. The cave is large enough that you can stand comfortably, and so with one hand on the cave wall to guide you, you creep deeper into the dark toward the singing. Slowly it grows louder. There are no words to it, but it makes you think of a star-filled sky, summer days, and every beautiful thing you can think of. It is as if the song contains all of life. The closer you get, the more rich the sound, and the more images it stirs within you. One part makes you think of the waves of the ocean crashing on the shore; another makes you feel as if you can smell the rich scent of a pine forest.

Finally you come to a large cavern deep within the mountain. There is a woman curled up asleep in the center of the chamber. A faint glow emanates from her nut-brown skin. She is singing in her sleep. As you come closer, you see her tossing and turning. Not in a fitful way, but as if whatever she is dreaming is too great to allow her to keep still. As she moves, a lock of dark hair falls over her eyes, and, not thinking, you reach out and brush it away. The woman stills, the singing stops, and she opens her eyes. You only see her eyes for a moment. The most brilliant light emanates from them and fills the chamber, and you cry out and shield your eyes with your arms. Those eyes lack pupil or iris; all you could see was the blinding light, as if you had been looking at the sun too long.

The cavern begins to shake. You feel things brush by you and move around the cavern, but you don't dare take your hands away from your ruined eyes to try to see what moves past. A pair of hands reaches out and gently grasps your own. Keeping your eyes firmly shut, you allow Sun Woman to move your arms down. She kisses each eye in turn. Gingerly you flutter your eyelids. Your eyes no longer hurt, and when you open them fully, the brilliant light that washes off the woman in waves of yellow and red fire is no longer blinding.

You look into her eyes again, and you are mesmerized by the golden fires that burn there. She smiles at you and beckons for you to stand. When you do, you see that the cavern is teeming with life. All kinds of animals spring into existence from the corona of flames the surrounds Sun Woman. They leap out of the flames and make their way into the world through the passageway you entered.

The goddess takes your hands, and together you walk back to the world outside. As her feet fall on the earth, grass and flowers blossom and begin to spread out to cover the world. Trees spring into existence. As she reaches down to touch the dust of a great valley, it fills with water, and soon you see schools of fish and other marine life flitting through the waves. Everywhere she looks, everywhere she steps, life is awakened.

Finally, when everything around you is full of life, the goddess turns to you. "I am Yhi the dreamer, the bringer of life and light. All that I have dreamed in my long slumber I have brought into existence." She bends down and whispers in your ear conspiratorially, "But we are all dreamers. We dream and dream and forget that we can also bring those dreams into reality. I see dreams swinging in you, filling your mind and heart. Remember the dreamer must wake eventually. Bring the light within you into the world."

You feel the light of Yhi begin to fill you. It flows into every pore of your body; it shines through every cell. You breathe in the fire that surrounds the sun goddess, and feel all the potential within you stir.

As you watch, the light around Yhi grows brighter. Soon you cannot see the woman at all, only a magnificent sphere of light. Yhi shoots up into the sky, and you see her dancing among the clouds, reveling in all the beauty of creation that lies before her.

Yhi (pronounced *y-EH*, like "yeah") is a goddess of light, the sun, and creation. According to the indigenous people of southwestern

Australia, it was Yhi who brought light into the world when she opened her eyes and created all the plants and animals as she walked across the earth. Like her sister sun goddesses in other cultures, she also travels to the underworld, bringing with her the transformative power of creation, and through her daily travels across the sky brings order and harmony to the world.

Yhi lay sleeping in the Dreamtime before the world's creation, when a loud whistle woke her up. Yhi opened her eyes, flooding the world with light. The earth warmed under her rays, and wherever Yhi's feet touched the ground, the earth stirred and plants sprang from the once barren ground. Yhi walked to the north, south, east, and west until she had stepped on every inch of land, making the earth beautiful and green.

For a while Yhi rested and looked out upon all the new plants and vegetation. Although they were beautiful, they were rooted in the earth and could not move, and Yhi wished to see something that could move and dance as she could.[143] Yhi then descended deep beneath the ground, plunging the earth into darkness, seeking something that could move and dance as she could. In the dark, cold caves of the earth she found evil spirits. These spirits tried to sing Yhi to death, but her light was too strong and she melted the darkness away. Her warm rays melted the ice in the caves, and out of the water appeared butterflies, bees, and every sort of insect. Next, Yhi traveled to the frozen mountaintops. Her light melted the ice, and water ran down the mountains to form the rivers and oceans. Out of the water sprang fish and turtles and all the world's water creatures. Then Yhi shined her light in the mountain caves, waking up the spirits of the land and air. Soon the world was dancing with new life.

Pleased with her creations, Yhi told them she must return to her own world and turned into a great ball of light and sank below the horizon. Through Yhi's movements across the sky, she gifted her

---

143. Monaghan, *Encyclopedia of Goddesses and Heroines*, 276.

creations with the seasons and the division between day and night. Although Yhi left the world, as the sun she watches over her creations in her daily journey across the sky. She also placed the morning star in the sky so that the animals would not be without light when she was away. So the morning star would not be lonely, she created Bahloo, the moon man. The stars in the night sky were said to be the children of the morning star and the moon man.

The Karraur people tell a story in which Yhi fell in love with the moon man Bahloo. Bahloo refused her marriage offer, stating that the sun goddess had taken too many previous lovers. This angered Yhi, and she threatened the sky spirits that she would not shine her light on the world if they did not guard Bahloo and keep him in the sky. Unhappy with this forced union, Bahloo often attempts to escape the sky realm. Every twenty-eight days, during the new moon, he escapes from the sky, making it appear as if the moon has disappeared, only to be chased back into the sky by the sky spirits. This is why the sun is said to chase the moon, and why the moon disappears once a month.

For a long time, all the animals lived happily, but eventually they grew discontented. So Yhi returned to the earth to find out why the animals were no longer happy. The lizards wanted legs; the bats wanted wings; the kangaroos wanted to jump; and the seals wanted to be able to swim. Yhi, ever the loving mother, gave them all what they asked.[144]

Yhi is also credited with creating the first man and woman. She created the first man, but after seeing that he was lonely, she decided to create the first woman to keep him company. She shined her light on a flower, and it changed into the first woman.[145]

Like most sun goddesses, Yhi's light is connected to the eye. When she opens her eyes after being woken up, her light radiates into the world. Like the Celts, the Egyptians, and the Balts, the Aboriginal

---

144. Monaghan, *Encyclopedia of Goddesses and Heroines*, 276.
145. O'Hara, *Sun Lore*, 101.

people saw the sun as a divine "eye" in the sky. Like Saule, who was believed to walk among the fields to make them grow, wherever Yhi walks, plants and vegetation spring from the ground.

As the primal mother, she creates all life and is the cosmic mother of all. The way in which Yhi creates life is interesting. Like other sun goddesses, Yhi travels to a cave, but her journey is not to escape the world; rather, it is to bring new life out of the darkness of the under-world. She banishes the darkness within the earth and melts away the ice of the caves, thereby defeating the evil spirits she encounters there. It seems more like she is transforming the spirits with her light rather than destroying them. Cleansed and purified by her light, the evil spirits transform into the animals of the earth. Her light not only purifies the darkness but also brings that which is ethereal, symbol-ized here by the spirits, into the material realm, represented by the manifestation of the animals in physical bodies. Like the Cherokee goddess Unelanuhi, she brings order into chaos by creating the sea-sons and the division between day and night.

Working with Yhi

Yhi teaches us how to transform our inner darkness and how to usher new and better things into our lives. Yhi's confrontation with the evil spirits of the earth, which she transforms into the earth's animals, can be seen as a symbolic confrontation with the shadow self. When Yhi shines her light on this inner darkness, it transforms, becoming something new and vibrant. When we face our inner de-mons, Yhi can help us transform our darkness into inner light and strength. Yhi reminds us that creation and destruction are linked. Conquering our inner darkness is only half of the process; creating something new and beneficial from our inner fears and illusions is what truly leads us toward rebirth.

As a goddess of vegetation and plant life, Yhi is an excellent god-dess to call upon when working with herbs or to help your garden prosper. Flowers, which she used to create the first woman, are especially sacred to her.

Call upon Yhi to confront your inner darkness, for inner illumination, for herbal magick, and to bring new beginnings.

. . . .

YHI INVOCATION

Yhi, Great Mother
Lady of the Sun
Bringer of light, mistress of creation
Awake, awake!
Yhi, open your eyes
Shine your light upon your child
Fill me with inner light
Chase away the darkness
Yhi, singing the song of creation,
The earth stirring at your touch,
Flowers blooming where you walk
Bring to me your sacred light!
Yhi, awake, awake!

. . . .

YHI CONFRONTING THE SHADOW-SELF RITUAL

You Will Need:
Drum or a CD of drum music
Flowers as an offering to Yhi
1 white candle
1 bowl of water

The following ritual can be used to confront your shadow-self or come to terms with your inner fears or traumatic events from the past. Yhi's light transforms all she shines upon. When she confronts the evil spirits of the earth, she does not destroy them; she purifies them, and changes them into new beings. Confronting the shadow-self is a similar experience. Our shadow-selves are not something that can be banished; they must be acknowledged and the issues and feelings they represent confronted and transformed in order for us to become whole. We each have a shadow-self. This being is the sum of all our darker emotions, our fears, our ego, the traumas we try to bury in the subconscious and forget. The shadow-self is not evil. Most of the time it simply wants to be acknowledged. When we face our inner darkness, we can transform it. When we learn to acknowledge our true feelings, the shadow-self can be an ally.

It is not necessary to cast a circle for this ritual, but you may if you wish. Turn off all the lights in the room. Just as Yhi traveled into the dark earth, so too should your ritual begin in darkness.

In your sacred space, take a few deep breaths, and ground and center. Say:

> *In the Dreaming Yhi slept*
> *And when she slept the earth was dark and barren*
> *There was no light, no warmth, no time*
> *I travel within, to confront my inner darkness,*
> *As Yhi traveled deep within the hollows of the land,*
> *To the ice-filled caves of the inner earth*
> *To confront the darkness that lurked there*

Take the drum and begin playing a slow, steady beat. You do not have to be a musician to do this. A steady rhythm will suffice. If you do not have a drum, you can use a CD with drum music. Something simple with a steady beat would be ideal, as this will help you maintain an altered state of consciousness. Say:

> *Yhi, guide me as I travel*
> *Yhi, guide me as I travel*
> *Deep, deep down*

Down to my inner darkness
Down to the shadow realm/land
Yhi, guide me as I travel
Deep, deep down

Close your eyes and continue drumming. See yourself traveling down into the depths of the earth. You walk through earthen passageways, descending deeper and deeper. As you travel, the earth around you becomes cold and ice covers the walls. Finally you come to a large cavern deep in the heart of the earth. You can travel no farther, and as you look around, you see shadows moving in the darkness. It may be one shadow, or many. Call to the shadow, tell it to reveal itself.

Take as much time as you need. How does your shadow-self look? How does it make you feel? What does it say when you speak with it? If there is more than one, acknowledge each one as it comes up to you; see it for what it really is. The shadow is a part of you; it is the feelings, emotions, and experiences you wish to bury, to deny and keep hidden, but they are a part of you. Although the shadow can be painful, the lessons it represents have helped shape your life, and confronting them now will further help you to grow past them and go on to new and better things.

Soon the cave begins to brighten. Yhi appears beside you, her form glowing with an inner radiance. She places her hands on your shoulder, filling you with her sacred light. Filled with Yhi's radiant light, you turn and embrace your shadow-self. It is not something evil; it is you with all your flaws and fears. See the shadow-self become filled with the light of Yhi. Acknowledge the lessons you have learned from the shadow. As you do so, you see the shadow begin to disappear, transformed in the light of Yhi.

Open your eyes. Light the candle, saying:

With Yhi's light I banish the darkness within
I am transformed within Yhi's light!

Take a few minutes to think on Yhi's light and its transformative powers. Know you are filled with her light. When you are ready, hold your hands over the bowl of water. See Yhi's light filling and blessing the water, and say:

> *As Yhi brought new life from the sacred water,*
> *So too do I create new light and beginnings in my life*

Preform a self-blessing by dipping your fingers into the water and anointing your chakras, feet, and hands with the water, while saying:

> *The light of Yhi shines within*
> *Lady, banish every darkness!*

When you are ready to close the ritual, thank Yhi and extinguish the candle. If you cast a circle, close the circle. Leave the flowers on the altar or outside after the ritual, as an offering. Pour the water outside on the ground.

. . . .
YHI INCENSE
1 part jasmine
1 part dried strawberries
1 part hibiscus
1 pinch cinnamon

. . . .
YHI CORRESPONDENCES
Symbols: eye, cave
Colors: gold, yellow, green
Herbs/Plants: flowers

PART THREE
MODERN SUN WORSHIP

The magnificence of the sun, and the vast importance to mankind of its light and heat, would undoubtedly point it out in the earliest ages as an object worthy of admiration and reverence. It is certain that ... its worship was almost universal, assuming various shapes and representing various principles.

—The National Encyclopedia:
A Dictionary of Universal Knowledge

For me, the realization that the sun goddess is not an anomaly was a revelation. She represents a side of the Goddess I felt was missing in my practices. I found her myths fascinating, but despite this I didn't quite know what to do with what I had learned. Knowing the sun goddess exists was great, but how did I call on her power? We are so used to seeing the moon as the be-all-and-end-all symbol of the Goddess that it can be hard to change our mindsets. How did I connect with her and work with the energies unique to the solar orb? When were her sacred times? What were her rituals? At the time I had no immediate answers to those questions, and for a long time I simply saw the sun goddess as an interesting concept, but one I had no clue how to apply to my spirituality.

Eventually, as I continued to encounter the solar goddess in mythology and worked with goddesses who embodied the sun, she began to make her way into my practices. One summer solstice I wrote a ritual honoring the sun goddess, instead of the sun god. At first the very idea sounded like blasphemy to the group I was working with, but we all found the ritual to be so moving, the Goddess's presence so strong, that it quickly became a tradition to call on the sun goddess each Litha. During a healing ritual, I invoked Brighid as the sun. To bless a home I had just moved into, I sprinkled water I had blessed by letting the sun's rays shine on it. When I felt rundown and stressed, I meditated on the sun and drew her power within me. Slowly the sun goddess emerged in my rituals and daily practices in a way I had never imagined possible.

Choosing to honor the sun goddess in your spiritual practices doesn't mean you have to throw away all your moon magick books or tear out all the moon rituals from your Book of Shadows. It simply requires us to recognize that the Goddess is present in all things, and to celebrate and honor her many faces, whether they be solar, lunar, or otherwise. Whether we whisper a silent prayer to the morning sun or call upon her in more dramatic ways on the solstices and equinoxes, when we celebrate the sun we are participating in a practice as ancient as the human race.

In this section we will be exploring modern sun worship and how to integrate the sun, and its power, into a modern spiritual practice. You will not only find rituals and seasonal celebrations invoking the sun goddess, but you will also discover practical ways to draw the sun's energy into your daily life and spiritual practices. All the exercises in this part of the book are ones I have personally used. Feel free to use them as is or rework them to suit your own needs. Think of them as a guide to help you create your own solar rituals and practices. Whether we choose to use these techniques once in a while or on a regular basis to incorporate the sun more fully into our worship, the sun goddess can be a radiant and powerful force within our spirituality. All we need do is welcome her power into our lives.

CONNECTING WITH THE
SOLAR FEMININE

Everything on earth comes from the sun,
and like souls reaching for the Goddess,
all things seek the light and energy of this nearest star.
—Clea Danann, *Sacred Land*

The feminine sun, and for that matter working with sun energy in our magick or ritual practices, is a foreign idea to most Pagans. It is one thing to recognize that at times the sun can be an expression of the Goddess's power, and it is another to actively incorporate this knowledge into our spiritual practices. So where to be begin? How do we connect to the power of the sun?

One of the most important practices, one that is the cornerstone to all the rest, is building a daily spiritual practice. Forming a daily spiritual practice sounds easy, but at times it can be quite difficult. It's amazing how hard it can be to set aside ten minutes of our busy day. By the time we are done with work, running errands, taking care of the kids, the pets (or both!), we are mentally frazzled and physically exhausted. The last thing we want to do is add one more item to our to-do list. But when we take the time to connect with divinity each day, the result can be life-altering. A daily spiritual practice gives our other spiritual practices and pursuits a foundation. It helps us center our energy and thoughts. It makes the sacred an active part of our everyday lives instead of something we work with occasionally, and allows us to work through life's roadblocks.

At times we even avoid this simple practice out of fear. In her book *Crafting a Daily Practice*, T. Thorn Coyle tells us that "we often avoid daily practice not out of laziness, or lack of discipline, but because we know that profound changes will occur in our lives and we are not sure we are up to shouldering what feels like the burden of the unknown. Something inside of us fears the loss of normalcy and the familiar."

As part of my own daily spiritual practice, I set aside ten minutes each day to connect with the divine. Most often this comes in the form of meditation. I ground and center, and open myself to the sacred. If I have a chance, I may choose to do this outdoors, whether on my deck or while hiking on the Appalachian Trail during the summer months. One week I may center my work on connection with, and learning the mysteries of, the Morrigan or Sekhmet, or reconnecting to the element of air or fire. Other days I may simply wish to recharge my energy after an exhausting day. Regardless of what you do as your daily spiritual practice, what is important is that you actually take the time to do it.

The easiest way to foster a relationship with a deity and learn their mysteries is to incorporate them into your daily spiritual practice. All the exercises in this chapter can be used to build a closer connection to the sun. They can be practiced as frequently as you like, but I encourage you to incorporate them into your daily practices for a set period of time. Perhaps you choose to work with the energy of the sun for a week, a month, or a season. Whatever you choose, the more you connect with the sun, the more her energy will play a role in your life.

Exercise 1: Creating a Sun Altar

Whether I am working with a deity, element, or concept of any sort, one of the very first things I do is create an altar. For me it is a fundamental step to entering into a relationship with a given deity or energy. By creating an altar, you are mentally opening yourself to working with a deity, as well as sending your intent out into the universe. It is also a place where you can sit and meditate, make offerings, and do spiritual work revolving around that deity.

Creating an altar to honor the solar feminine (and the solar masculine too if you like) is a wonderful way to welcome the sun's energy and power into your life, and can create an excellent sacred space to practice sun magick, or simply take some time to sit and meditate.

. . . .
Solar Altar Blessing

You Will Need:
Incense of your choice
1 candle or tea light

Preferably place your altar in a place where the sun can shine upon it, such as near a window.

Once you have the objects you wish to place on your altar, burn incense of your choice, perhaps one that reminds you of the particular solar deity you are planning on working with. Waft the incense over the altar. Light the candle, saying:

> *Hail the immortal sun*
> *Lady of light, radiance, and healing,*
> *I draw to this place your sacred fire*
> *As it burns upon this altar,*
> *Let it also burn within me*
> *So mote it be!*

Exercise 2: Daily Devotions

In many cultures we find daily practices used to honor and connect with the sun. In Tibet, monks greeted the sun each dawn. The Cherokee bowed to the sun in the morning and evening. Daily devotions are simple ways to honor the sun and to draw her energies to you on a daily basis. Below are a few simple practices that will only take a few minutes of your day and will help align yourself with the sun. You could do your daily devotion in front of your altar or in front of the bathroom mirror each day. Where you do it is not as important as taking the time to align yourself with divinity.

Morning Sun Devotion

Take a moment to visualize the sun shining above you. See its golden energy pour down and fill you from head to toe. Hold your arms outstretched, palms up, and say:

Mother sun, lend me your strength
Fill me this day with your grace

Afternoon Sun Devotion

Sun in glory, Lady of Life
I drink in your radiance
May your vibrance shine through me this day

Evening Sun Devotion

Sun sinking in the west
The shadowy halls of the underworld you walk
Hidden sun, light in the dark,
Guide me through the night

Exercise 3: Sun Meditations

Drawing in Sun Energy Meditation

If possible, sit outside in a sunny spot where you will not be disturbed or, if it is cold out, stand by a window where the sun's light can shine on you. Sit in a comfortable position. Close your eyes. Feel the warmth of the sun on your skin. Take three deep breaths in and out and allow your body to relax. Raise your hands, palms up, above your head (as if you were reaching up to lift something off a high shelf). See the sun's energy streaming toward you, and then draw it between your outstretched hands until you hold a fiery, golden orb of light. Slowly lower your hands. As you do, see the sun's energy filling your body. See the sun's energy filling your crown, then lower your hands to your chest and see it filling your heart and the core of your being. Lower your hands again and see the sun's energy fill the lower part of your body, going down to the soles of your feet. Repeat this as many times as you wish.

You could also use this technique to send sun energy into another person, as it is especially effective for healing. Visualize the sun within your hands, then move your hands with your palms facing the person, then move your hands slowly from the person's crown to their feet.

This can be done right before any kind of sun magick or working with sun gods. It is also a easy way to recharge your personal energies. If you are tired and need an energy boost during the day, use this exercise to recharge your energy levels. It is also an excellent way to raise energy for any type of healing work.

A Grounding Sun Meditation

Sit comfortably. Hold your hands palms up. See a ray of golden light shining on you. Concentrate on the light. What color is it? How does it make you feel? Imagine it's warmth on your skin. Take a deep breath, and as you do, see the sunlight filling you. Take two more deep breaths, until you feel filled with sunlight. Now place your hands palms down on the ground to either side of you. Imagine reaching down through the earth—down, down to the fiery core of the planet. Take a deep breath in, pulling up the fires that are at the heart of the earth. Take two more deep breaths until you are filled with the fires of the earth. Place your palms over your heart. See the golden sunlight and the fires of the core of the earth mix and blend as they fill and circulate through your being. Say:

Fires above, fires below,
Within, without I am whole

Sun Magick

*It is vitally important for women to access their Sun energies within,
rather than projecting them onto the men in their lives,
just as it is equally important for men to access their Moon
energies within, rather than projecting them onto women.*
—Maria Kay Simms, *A Time for Magick*

Take a moment to think back to the last spell or ritual work you performed. Most likely, one of the first things you did was check what phase the moon was currently in. Or perhaps you waited to cast your spell until the moon was in the particular phase that aligned with the goal you had in mind. Just as the moon and the goddess have become intrinsically linked in modern Paganism, so too have the moon and magick. We draw upon the energies of the moon and cast our spells in tandem to her monthly cycles.

As the sun is the counterpart of the moon, you would assume we would spend as much time working with the magick of the sun as we do its lunar sibling, but we tend to only practice solar magick on the solar Sabbats, where the emphasis is often on the seasonal shift connected to the holiday, rather than working directly with the sun's energy. Most likely, our reticence toward sun magick comes from our unfamiliarity with it. Whether we see the sun as male or female, the sun can be a potent force within our magick. While we will be discussing how to work primarily with the feminine sun, the techniques in this chapter can be used to work with the energies of the male sun as well.

Whether you wait for a particular hour or a time when a heavenly body is in the right place or phase, or simply for that gut reaction that tells you "now" is the right time to work your spell, timing is essential in magick. Like the moon, the sun moves through several phases, both daily and seasonal, each with their own particular energies and uses in spellwork and ritual.

While the seasons and the sign of the zodiac the sun is currently in are both factors in sun magick, the easiest phase of the sun to use is the one it cycles through each day. Each day we witness the sun's transformation as she rises and travels across the sky before finally setting in the west.

At first I didn't really think of the sun as having phases like the moon. But as I spent time drawing on the energy of the sun during different times of the day, I realized that each day we witness one of the sun's most basic cycles as it rises, climbs the sky, and finally sets. When I worked with sun energy at dawn, it felt different from the energy I drew upon at midday or sunset.

On one occasion I had been planning to cast a spell to bring new beginnings into my life. I had planned to cast the spell earlier in the day but had stayed late at work. By the time I came home, the sun was setting, and as I stood outside watching the sun set behind the hills, it just didn't feel like the right time to cast the spell. The energy of the setting sun made me think of endings, of journeys through the underworld, and I ended up waiting until the morning to do my spellwork. It struck me then how different the energies of the rising and setting sun felt to me, just as the energy of the full moon had a completely different feel from that of the new moon.

The easiest cycle of the sun to use in your magick is the one we witness each day. The daily rising and setting of the sun is excellent for spellwork that needs to be done immediately, and it does not require you to wait until the sun is in a certain sign.

When working with sun magick, it is also very helpful to know exactly when sunrise and sunset occur, as of course these times change slightly on a daily basis. You can find this information in your local newspaper or in an almanac. There are also several applications you can download to your cell phone that will give you the times for sunrise and sunset, as well as the dates for solar eclipses.

If you cannot cast a spell exactly at dawn, for example, performing your magick in the morning hours will be just as effective. The same is true for midday and sunset. In general, as the sun is connected to the element of fire, spells involving sun magick tend to manifest quickly. Fire is an element of fast action, and you may find the desired results of your spells unfolding sooner than you expect, and in bold ways.

DAILY SUN PHASES

Sunrise: Sunrise is a time of new beginnings, purification, and change. It is an excellent time to do spellwork to break bad habits, start a new venture or a new phase in life, or call upon healing energy. Sunrise is also sacred to sun goddesses connected to creation, such as Yhi and Amaterasu.

Noon: At noon the sun reaches the highest point in the sky and is at the zenith of its power. The heat of the sun is so strong that in countries close to the equator it is common to stop all work and spent time indoors or in the shade to escape the afternoon heat. This is an excellent time to add extra energy to a spell, especially for spellwork for success, prosperity, physical vitality, and quick action. The energy of the noonday sun is similar to that of the full moon. It is a time for manifestation and bringing your desires into existence and reality. Noon is also the time to work with goddesses such as Sekhmet and Unelanuhi, who represent the heat and the destructive aspects of the sun. Call upon these warrior goddesses for courage and strength.

Sunset: Sunset is a time for banishing, transformation, honoring the dead, releasing painful emotions, and breaking addictions. Sunset may seem like a strange time to work with goddesses connected to light, but it is an excellent time to call upon the energies of the sun goddess as she travels through the underworld. Sunset is especially sacred to Hathor, who greeted the spirits of the dead far in the west as they transitioned from life to death, and to Bast, who protected Ra as they traveled through the underworld. This is a time to call on the sun goddess to bring about transformation, purification, and illumination, and to honor the light within.

Seasonal Sun Phases

As the sun moves through the seasons, her energy continues to change. As the summer sun, she is the radiant goddess of abundance and growth. During the winter, she is a goddess of inner light and new beginnings.

Spring: In early spring we celebrate Imbolc and draw the light and heat of the sun back into the world. It is a time of beginnings. Winter is not quite gone, but in many places the lengthening days and the sun's warmth bring the first hints of green life back to the earth. Draw upon the spring sun for new ventures, new beginnings, and fresh starts. This is also a good time of year to draw upon and strengthen your own inner light.

Summer: During the summer months, the sun stays within the sky the longest. Its light brings forth the bounty of nature. Crops grow and ripen. We spend more time outside enjoying nature. The summer months are a time to draw on the sun's abundance. It is the perfect time to cast spells relating to health, vigor, abundance, and fertility.

Fall: Fall is a time of transitions. It can feel as though summer is not quite over, while winter has not yet begun. The sun's time in the sky begins to shorten. Work with the energies of the autumn sun for help moving through times of transitions. The fall equinox is also an excellent time to draw upon the sun for spells involving balance and harmony.

Winter: During winter the sun's time in the sky is shortest. This is a time to contemplate the sun's journey through the underworld and to draw her light within us so she may guide us through the dark months. Draw upon the winter sun to battle depression and doubt, and for new beginnings.

SUN SPELLS AND RITUALS

The following are a few simple spells and rituals you can use to draw upon the power of the sun in your magickal practices.

. . . .
A SUN CATCHER PROTECTION SPELL

You Will Need:
A sun catcher
Incense of your choice

If possible, sit outside on a sunny day or near a sunny window. Light the incense and pass the sun catcher through the smoke. Hold the sun catcher up in the sunlight. See it being infused with the sun's power. When you are ready, say:

> *Lady of the immortal sun,*
> *Guide and guard me till the day is done*
> *Protect this house and those within*

Place the sun catcher in a window in your house. If possible, place it by the front door or in a place where people enter the house.

SOLAR SPELL TO FIND LOST OBJECTS

Sit comfortably. Close your eyes, ground and center. See a ray of sunlight shining before you. See the object you wish to find in the ray of light. See it in as much detail as possible. When you have the image in your mind's eye, say:

> *Hail to my mother on high*
> *Blazing, fierce*
> *Immortal eye*
> *Help me to find what's lost,*
> *and return it to me*

SUN SPELL FOR CREATIVITY

You Will Need:
1 white candle
Pen and paper

On the piece of paper, write what you wish to accomplish. This can be as simple as the word "Inspiration" or ideas for whatever project you are working on, whether this is something artistic or writing a term paper. Then take the candle in your hand for a few moments. See the light and vibrant power of the sun filling the candle. Place the paper with your goal under the candle.

The following chant is based on the Hindu Gayatri mantra, which calls on the sun's power. Light the candle, saying:

> *O, splendid and playful sun,*
> *I offer this prayer to thee*
> *Enlighten this craving mind*
> *Light the spark of creativity*
> *May your radiance guide me*
> *I salute your magnificence and praise the eternal sun!*

Let the candle burn for a few minutes. Relight it for a few minutes each day or when you are working on your creative endeavor.

. . . .
DRAWING DOWN THE SUN RITUAL

Stand with your feet slightly apart. Hold your arms slightly away from your body with your palms facing down toward the earth. Take three deep, cleansing breaths. Imagine your feet becoming roots, sinking deep into the earth. Down and down they go until they reach the very heart of the planet, and the burning molten core at its heart. Draw that fire up into your being with three deep breaths. On the third breath, bring your hands slowly up, drawing that fiery energy with it, and place your palms over your heart. Next see the sun burning bright in a clear sky. Hold your arms up, palms facing the sky. See the brilliant light of the sun flowing down into the core of your being. Say:

> *I call upon the radiance of the sun*
> *I call upon the fire that burns at the heart of the earth,*
> *And the radiance within myself*
> *May I burn with inspiration*
> *May my passions bring life to my work*
> *May I ever know that to create is to destroy,*
> *That from the ashes we rise again and again*

Before you, see a figure of light and flame begin to form. She steps forward, passing right through you, becoming one with you. Feel the energy of the goddess of the sun fill every cell of your being. When you are ready, say:

> *I am the spark that engulfs; I am the light of a new day, the traveler of shadowed lands, and the sun in her glory. I am Sekhmet, Sunna, Saule, Amaterasu, Sulis, Yhi, and many more.*

I am the mother of all things, the light that calls the seed from beneath the dark soil, and the cleansing fire that burns away the old. I am the bringer of swift justice and the bright flame of inspiration. I ask only that you see the radiance that burns within you. That you sing, feast, and dance in my exaltation, knowing that like myself you shall rise and rise again from the ashes of the old.

If you have any spellwork or ritual work planned, do it. When you are ready, thank the sun goddess. To release any excess energy, place your hands on the ground and see the energy flowing into the earth.

. . . .
Basic Sun Ritual

You Will Need:
Solar incense of your choice
Candle to represent the sun
Solar oil of your choice

This is a basic ritual to call upon the goddess of the sun for spellwork or devotional work. Cast the circle in whatever manner you wish, then stand in the center of your ritual space with your feet slightly apart. Ground and center. Say:

Hail O Mother Sun!
Light within me and without me
Help my inner light to burn with the radiance of the sun
In the underworld your golden rays bring warmth to the dead
Shine upon me in my darkest hour
Midnight sun, instill in me your wisdom
Fill me with your healing
Let me shine with your resplendent light

Anoint your forehead, saying:

> *Hail to the dawning sun,*
> *Sun maiden of new life and healing!*

Anoint your heart, saying:

> *Hail to the noonday sun,*
> *Mother of all life*
> *All-seeing immortal eye*

Anoint your feet, saying:

> *Hail to the setting sun,*
> *Lady who journeys through the realm of shades and spirits*
> *You who overcome every darkness,*
> *Radiant goddess of rebirth*

Stand in the East. In your mind see the sun as it rises with the dawn:

> *From the East I call upon the Sun Maiden and the powers of Air*
> *Goddess of dawn, who breaks the dark*
> *Lady of new beginnings, you are the breath of the new day*

Stand in the South. See the sun high in the sky, its light and warmth filling you. Say:

> *From the South I call upon the noonday sun and the powers of Fire*
> *Flame-enshrouded warrioress,*
> *Dispensing divine justice*
> *You fan the flame of courage and perseverance*

Stand in the West. See the sun setting below the horizon, and say:

From the West I call upon the setting sun and the powers of Water
Mother of all, who sails upon the ocean
in your golden boat at each day's end
You are the lady of the West, of harvest, rest, and fulfillment

Stand in the North. Imagine how the sun passes through the under-world, making its way to the new day. Say:

From the North I call upon the midnight sun and the powers of Earth
You who greet the dead
Sun of the underworld
Nightly you battle the forces of chaos
You are the light in the darkness, bringing us rebirth

Do any planned spellwork or pathworking. When you are ready, close the quarters.

East:

Hail and farewell, powers of air and dawning light

South:

Hail and farewell, powers of fire and blazing light

West:

Hail and farewell, powers of water and the sinking sun

North:

Hail and farewell, power of earth and the light within

Close the circle.

. . . .
INVOKING THE GODDESSES OF THE SUN RITUAL
You Will Need:
Solar incense of your choice
Candle to represent goddess

This ritual calls upon the many faces of the sun goddess. I have included the names of goddesses from several pantheons, but if you wish to work with deities from a single pantheon, you can replace the name with those you wish to work with. You could include male sun deities as well. As with all the rituals in this book, feel free to incorporate your own ritual style, or use this one as inspiration to write your own solar ritual.

Cast the circle, saying:

A circle of fire, bright as the sun
A circle of protection
This rite has begun!

Stand in th East. In your mind see the sun as it rises with the dawn:

Hail to the East
The powers of the dawning sun
You are Yhi, who opened her eyes at the first dawn
and created the world

You are Aine, who inspires the soul with sweet melody
Hail to you, mother of light and new beginnings!

Stand in the South. See the sun high in the sky, its light and warmth filling you. Say:

Hail to the South
The powers of the noonday sun
You are Sekhmet, lady of fire and scorching heat
You are Brighid of the mantle,
Healing our hearts and inspiring our deeds
You are Saule, mother of ripe fields and the summer sky
Hail to you, mother sun, lady of ferocity and fertility!

Stand in the West. See the sun setting below the horizon, and say:

Hail to the West
The powers of the setting sun
You are Sulis of the healing waters and all-seeing eye
You are Hathor, whose light greets the dead
You are Shapash, who walks the pathways
of the underworld, torch in hand
Hail, lady of the dwindling light, goddess of the passing day!

Stand in the North. Imagine how the sun passes through the underworld; maybe it is drawn in the Egyptian Boat of a Million Years through the Duat, or it is Saule in her boat drawn by swans. Say:

Hail to the North
The powers of the midnight sun
You are Bast, who rises triumphant from the night to herald a new
day

You are Amaterasu, who hides her radiance in the sacred cave
Hail to the light within, hail the light that is reborn each day!

At this point you could invoke a particular sun goddess with whom you wish to work or simply the solar feminine in general. Return to the center of the circle. Light the candle representing the sun goddess. Say:

Mother sun, who journeys through the dark each night
To rise again in glory
Ignite in me your vital spark
Illuminate my mind and heart

Perform any planned spellwork or pathworking. When you are ready, thank the sun goddess, saying:

O, mother sun
Wrap me in your light
Lend me your strength and might
Be with me this day and through the dark night

Close the quarters, saying:

Hail and farewell to the power of the
dawning/noonday/evening/sun of the underworld
May your light always be within me

Open the circle.

Conclusion
Dancing with the Sun

For many of us, myself included, part of the appeal of Paganism is to reclaim a part of the divine that has been lacking in our spirituality. For those of us who grew up learning that God was male, we have reclaimed the power and image of the Great Goddess. But as I walk my path I find I am constantly reclaiming the Goddess again and again. She constantly challenges me to see and experience her in new ways. When I look at the sun each day, I see Sunna, Bast, and Sulis, yet I also see Apollo, Lugh, and Ra. On a full-moon night I look up at the beauty of Diana or the face of Mani or Thoth. I am reminded that all things dwell within us. Male and female, Goddess and God. I remember that the Goddess can be a force of strength and action. She is a warrior, yet also a loving mother. She is the fire that fuels my passions and teaches me to bring them into manifestation. She is the unwavering fire that drives us onward. And I am reminded to challenge how I define femininity.

Recognizing the sun goddess is about bringing balance to both the Goddess and her worship. Just as we honor the masculine and feminine in the divine, we must also explore the depth of what femininity, and masculinity for that matter, truly means. The radiant, ever-renewing goddess of the sun is not a new concept. She was an aspect of womanhood that our ancestors knew well. When we worship the sun, we are treading an ancient path, one we must now learn to reclaim, and in doing so return the sun goddess, in all her many guises, to her rightful place. We must learn to dance in the light of the sun, and tread in the light of the moon, and find a sacred balance within each.

Appendix I
Solar Stones and Gems

Amber: In Baltic myth, this resin was thought to be the tears of the goddess Saule. It was one of the first stones or substances to be used by early humans in Asia, Africa, and Europe for amulets and decoration. Amber can be used to transform negative energy and emotions and is associated with luck.

Brass: This metal is connected to protection, wealth, and banishing negativity. Use it in spells to banish negative thoughts and emotions. Charge a brass ring or piece of jewelry with the energy of the sun to draw wealth into your life.

Citrine: Named for the French word for lemon, *citron*, as many citrines have a juicy lemon color. Citrine has been used against overindulgence, to ward against treachery, and to dispel evil thoughts.

Garnet: Garnet is a stone commonly associated with Brighid and can be charged with her energy for healing and inspiration. Garnet is said to grant loyalty and affection, although folklore claims that if the stone loses its luster, the owner should take it a sign of treachery.

Gold: The metal known as gold has symbolized power and wealth since the beginning of recorded time. Even today, many governments endeavor to have the gold equivalent of their paper currency in their state reserves. Use gold to strengthen self-confidence and spellwork for prosperity.

Sunstone: There are several stones given this name, among them a form of feldspar and quartz with an orange hue known as Oregon sunstone. This stone became popular in Renaissance jewelry. Use sunstone in protective and healing spells. It is also a good stone to use to boost your energy levels. If you feel as though you are dragging, carry sunstone with you. It is also useful for bringing positive energy into a room.

Tiger's eye: The various "eye" stones have always been considered strong talismans. It was believed that a person possessing one could see everything, even behind closed doors. Egyptians carved it into god figurines, to represent divine vision. Tiger's eye is a fine stone for promoting wealth and money.

Turquoise: The Navajo associated the color blue and turquoise with the sun and the south. Turquoise is a protective stone. Some native peoples in what are now the United States and Mexico used turquoise in tombs to protect the dead; others used them as offerings to the gods or for protection on shamanic journeys.

Appendix II
Solar Herbs

Angelica: Use for protection, healing, and visions, and in all protection and exorcism incenses. Angelica creates a barrier against negative energy and fills you with radiant energy. It removes curses, hexes, or spells that have been cast against you. In folklore it was said to give a joyful outlook on life.

Bay: Use bay in any clairvoyance endeavors. Place bay leaves under your pillow for prophetic dreams. Burn bay leaves to cause visions.

Cedar: Cedar, especially in Native American traditions, is connected to protection and banishing negative spirits. Burn it to banish unwanted spirits and energy and in protection spells.

Eyebright: Mental powers, psychic powers

Ginseng: Love, wishes, healing, beauty, protection, lust

Goldenseal: Healing, money

Rowan: Rowan is connected to both fire and protection, especially from faeries. Use rowan for spells of protection and to break spells.

Sandalwood: Burned to exorcise spirits, conjure beneficial spirits, and promote spiritual awareness, sandalwood incense is also used for protection, astral projection, healing rituals, and in wish-magick.

Sunflower: Sunflowers have long been connected to the sun, as the plant reaches high over those around it to get to the sun's light. Use sunflower petals or seed in spells for prosperity and wealth.

Witch hazel: Use for protection and love spells.

CREATING SUN WATER AND SUN TEA

Sun water and sun tea can be used in healing and during rituals and spells. To create sun water, fill a glass bowl with filtered water and place it in a sunny spot where the light of the sun can shine on it. If it is winter, you can place the bowl near a sunny window. Hold your hands over the water and visualize the light and energy of the sun filling the water until it shines with a golden light. Allow the water to remain in the light of the sun until you feel it is fully charged with the sun's energy. You can use this water to sprinkle around an area to cleanse it, to wash ritual items, or to make healing teas and infusions.

Creating sun tea is very similar to making sun water, with the addition of soaking herbs in the water. Like sun water, you can use sun tea to bless a particular area or for spell and ritual work. You could also follow the same process to bless and steep a cup of tea with the sun's healing energy. Choose herbs connected to the work you are planning on doing. Place the herbs in a large bowl, then pour in six cups of water (you may choose to add more or less water as needed). Place the bowl in a sunny window or outside in direct sunlight and allow it to steep for thirty minutes to an hour. If you choose to make your tea outside, place plastic wrap over it so nothing blows into the bowl.

Healing Sun Tea

1 part orange peel

2 part echinacea

½ part cloves

Prosperity Sun Tea

2 parts ginseng
1 part orange peel
½ part cinnamon

Relaxation Sun Tea

7 whole cloves
2 tablespoons chamomile

Bibliography

Andrews, Tamra. *A Dictionary of Nature Myths*. New York: Oxford University Press, 2000.

Astour, Michael. *Hellenosemitica: An Ethnic and Cultural Study in West Semitic Impact on Mycenaean Greece*. Leiden, the Netherlands: E. J. Brill, 1967.

Balys, Lietuviu. *Treasure Chest of Lithuanian Folklore*. Publisher unknown: 1951.

Barry, Phillips. *The Bridge of Sunbeams*. New York: American Folklore Society, 1914.

Benjamins, Eso. *Dearest Goddess: Translations from Latvian Folk Poetry*. Arlington, VA: Current Nine Publishing, 1985.

Bleeker, Claas. *Hathor and Thoth: Two Key Figures of the Ancient Egyptian Religion*. Leiden, the Netherlands: Brill, 1973.

Budge, E. A. *The Papyrus of Ani*. Mt. Shasta, CA : Star Rising Publishers, 2000.

Capel, Anne, and Glenn Markoe. *Mistress of the House, Mistress of Heaven*. New York: Hudson Hills Press in association with Cincinnati Art Museum, 1996.

Chadwick, Henry. *Early Christian Thought and the Classical Tradition*. New York: Oxford University Press, 1966.

Coyle, T. Thorn. *Crafting a Daily Practice: A Simple Course in Self-Commitment*. Berkeley, CA: Sunna Press, 2012.

Crawford, John. *The Kalevala: The Epic Poem of Finland*. New York: J. B. Alden, 1888.

Crowe, Keith. *A History of the Original Peoples of Northern Canada*. Montreal, QC: McGill-Queen's University Press, 1991.

Dixon, Rowland. *Maidu Myths*. New York: The Knickerbocker Press, 1902.

Dorson, Richard. *Peasant Customs and Savage Myths, Volume 1*. Chicago: University of Chicago Press, 1968.

Ebersole, Gary. *Ritual Poetry and the Politics of Death in Early Japan*. Princeton, NJ: Princeton University Press, 1989.

Eidelberg, Joseph. *The Biblical Hebrew Origin of the Japanese People*. Lynbrook, NY: Gefen Publishing House, 2005.

El-Shahawy, Abeer. *The Egyptian Museum in Cairo: A Walk Through the Alleys of Ancient Egypt*. Cairo: Farid Atiya Press 2005.

Ellis, Jeanette. *Forbidden Rites: Your Complete Guide to Traditional Witchcraft*. Ropley, UK: O Books, 2009.

Eslinger, Lyle. *Ascribe to the Lord: Biblical and Other Studies*. Sheffield, UK: Sheffield Academic Press, 1988.

Feldman, Burton. *The Rise of Modern Mythology, 1680–1860*. Bloomington: Indiana University Press, 1972.

Friberg, Eino. *The Kalevala: Epic of the Finnish People*. Turku, Finland: Finnish North American Literature Society, 1988.

Garrett, Michael. *Native American Faith in America*. New York: Facts On File, 2003.

Gibson, John. *Canaanite Myths and Legends*. New York: T & T Clark International, 2004.

Gimbutas, Marija. *Ancient Symbolism in Lithuanian Folk Art*. Philadelphia, PA: American Folklore Society, 1958.

Graves-Brown, Carolyn. *Dancing for Hathor: Women in Ancient Egypt*. New York: Continuum, 2010.

Green, Miranda. *Animals in Celtic Life and Myth*. New York: Routledge, 1992.

———. *Celtic Myths*. Austin: University of Texas Press, 1993.

———. *Symbol and Image in Celtic Religious Art*. New York: Routledge, 1989.

Gregory, Lady Augusta. *A Book of Saints and Wonders*. New York: Oxford University Press, 1971.

Grimm, Jacob. *Teutonic Mythology: Volume II*. Mineola, NY: Dover Publications, 2004.

Guest, Charlotte, trans. *The Mabinogion: From the Welsh of the Llyfr coch o Hergest (The Red Book of Hergest)*. London: Quaritch, 1877.

Gurney, Oliver. *The Hittites*. New York: Penguin Books, 1990.

Gwynn, Edward, trans. *The Metrical Dindshenchas*. Dublin, Ireland: Royal Irish Academy, 1903.

Haley, James. *Apaches: A History and Culture Portrait*. Norman: University of Oklahoma Press, 1997.

Harpur, Patrick. *The Philosophers' Secret Fire*. Chicago: Ivan R. Dee, 2003.

Harva, Uno. *Finno-Ugric and Siberian Mythology*. Boston: Marshall Jones Company, 1978.

Heinze, Ruth-Inge. *Proceedings of the Tenth International Conference on the Study of Shamanism and Alternate Modes of Healing*. Berkeley, CA: Independent Scholars of Asia, 1993.

Herodotus. *The Histories*. Digireads.com Publishing, 2009.

Hollander, Lee. *The Poetic Edda: Volume 1*. New York: Columbia University Press, 1936.

Ireland, Stanley. *Roman Britain: A Sourcebook*. New York: Routledge, 2008.

Jacobson, Esther. *The Deer Goddess of Ancient Siberia: A Study in the Ecology of Belief.* New York: E. J. Brill, 1993.

Jung, Carl. *Mysterium Coniunctionis.* Princeton, NJ: Princeton University Press, 1970.

Junker, Hermann. *Der Auszug der Hathor-Tefnut aus Nubien.* Berlin, Germany: G. Reimer, 1911.

K, Amber, and Azreal Arynn K. *Candlemas: Feast of Flames.* St. Paul, MN: Llewellyn Publications, 2001.

Kinsley, David. *The Goddesses' Mirror: Vision of the Divine from East to West.* Albany: State University of New York Press, 1988.

Kirby, W. F. *Kalevala: The Land of the Heroes.* Dover, NH: Athlone Press, 1985.

Kramer, Samuel. *Mythologies of the Ancient World.* New York: Anchor Books, 1989.

Kroeber, Alfred. *Salt, Dogs, Tobacco.* Los Angeles: University of California Press, 1941.

Latham, Robert. *The English Language.* London: Walton and Maberly, 1850.

Latimer, Hugh. *Sermons: Volume 2.* New York: E. P. Dutton & Co, 1926.

Leeming, David, and Jake Page. *Goddess: Myths of the Female Divine.* New York: Oxford University Press, 1994.

Lehmann, Johannes. *The Hittite: People of a Thousands Gods.* New York: Collins, 1977.

Lerner, Gerda. *The Creation of Patriarchy.* New York: Oxford University Press, 1986.

Lewis, Theodore. *Cult of the Dead in Ancient Israel and Ugarit.* New York: Scholars Press, 1989

Lönnrot, Elias. *The Kalevala: An Epic Poem After Oral Tradition.* New York: Oxford University Press, 2008.

Markale, Jean. *Women of the Celts.* Rochester, VT: Inner Traditions International, 1972.

Matsumae, Takeshi. "The Heavenly Rock-Grotto Myth and the Chinkon Ceremony." *Asian Folklore Studies*, vol. 39, no. 2 (1980).

Matthews, Caitlin. *Voices of the Goddess: A Chorus of Sibyls*. London: Thorsons Publishing, 1990.

McCrickard, Janet. *Eclipse of the Sun: An Investigation into Sun and Moon Myths*. Somerset, UK: Gothic Image, 1990.

McGrath, Sheena. *The Sun Goddess: Myth, Legend and History*. New York: Sterling, 1997.

Meehan, Bridget Mary. *Praying with Visionary Women*. Lanham, MD: Rowman & Littlefield, 1999.

Milisauskas, Sarunas. *European Prehistory*. New York: Academic Press, 1978.

Mitchell, John. *Following the Sun: A Bicycle Pilgrimage from Andalusia to the Hebrides*. New York: Counterpoint, 2002.

Monaghan, Patricia. *Encyclopedia of Goddesses and Heroines*. Santa Barbara, CA: Greenwood, 2010.

———. *The Goddess Path: Myths, Invocations, and Rituals*. St. Paul, MN: Llewellyn Publications, 1999.

———. *The New Book of Goddesses and Heroines*. St. Paul, MN: Llewellyn Publications, 2002.

———. *O Mother Sun!: A New View of the Cosmic Feminine*. Freedom, CA: Crossing Press, 1994.

Mooney, James. *Myths of the Cherokee and Sacred Formulas of the Cherokees*. Asheville, NC: Historical Images, 1992.

Morrison, Dorothy. *Everyday Sun Magic: Spells & Rituals for Radiant Living*. St. Paul, MN: Llewellyn Publications, 2005.

Müller, Max. *Introduction to the Science of Religion*. New York: Arno Press, 1978.

———. *Lectures on the Science of Language*. London: Green and Co., 1873.

Natan, Yoel. *Moon-o-theism: Religion of a War and Moon God Prophet*. London: Lulu, 2006.

Neufeld, Rob. *A Popular History of Western North Carolina: Mountains, Heroes & Hootnoggers*. Charleston, SC: History Press, 2007.

Nunn, John Francis. *Ancient Egyptian Medicine*. Norman: University of Oklahoma Press, 1996.

O'Hanlon, John Canon. *Life of St. Brigid Virgin: First Abbess of Kildare, Special Patroness of Kildare Diocese, and General Patroness of Ireland*. Dublin, Ireland: Joseph Dollard Publication, 1877.

———. *Lives of the Irish Saints*. New York: The Catholic Publishing Society, 1907.

O'Hara, Gwydion. *Sun Lore: Myths and Folklore from Around the World*. St. Paul, MN: Llewellyn Publications, 1997.

Olcott, William Tyler. *Sun Lore of All Ages: A Collection of Myths and Legends Concerning the Sun and Its Worship*. New York: G. P. Putnam's Sons, 1914.

Olson, Harvey. *Olson's Orient Guide*. New York: Lippincott, 1962.

Paxson, Diana L. "One of Ten Thousand: Rhiannon—The Mare Mother." *SageWoman Magazine*, issue 73 (2007).

Pinch, Geraldine. *Magic in Ancient Egypt*. Austin: University of Texas Press, 2009.

Pritchard, James. *Ancient Near Eastern Texts Relating to the Old Testament*. Princeton, NJ: Princeton University Press, 1950.

Quirke, Stephen. *Ancient Egyptian Religion*. New York: Dover Publications, 2003.

Remler, Pat. *Egyptian Mythology A to Z*. New York: Chelsea House, 2010.

Sand, Elin. *Woman Ruler: Woman Rule*. San Jose, CA: iUniverse, 2001.

Scott, Nora E. "The Cat of Bastet." *Metropolitan Museum of Art Bulletin*, new series, vol. 17, no. 1 (Summer 1958).

Shipp, Mark. *Of Dead Kings and Dirges*. Boston: Brill, 2002.

Simms, Maria Kay. *A Time for Magick*. St. Paul, MN: Llewellyn Publications, 2001.

Skinner, John, trans. *Confession of Saint Patrick and Letter to Coroticus*. New York: Image, 1998.

Snow, Justine. *The Spider's Web: Goddesses of Light and Loom*. Philadelphia: University of Pennsylvania, 2002.

Stokes, Whitley, ed. *Sanas Chormaic: Cormac's Glossary Codex. Translated and Annotated by the Late John O'Donovan. Edited, with Notes and Indices, by Whitely Stokes*. Calcutta, India: O .T. Cuter, 1868.

Sunquist, Melvin. *Wild Cats of the World*. Chicago: University of Chicago Press, 2002.

Swanton, John. *Indian Tribes of the Lower Mississippi Valley*. Mineola, NY: Dover Publications, 1998.

Turner, Frank. *The Greek Heritage in Victorian Britain*. New Haven, CT: Yale University Press, 1981.

Varner, Gary. *The Mythic Forest: The Green Man and the Spirit of Nature*. New York: Algora, 2006.

Vogel, Carole. *Weather Legends: Native American Lore and the Science of Weather*. Brookfield, CT: Millbrook Press, 2001.

Volker, T. *The Animal in Far Eastern Art*. Leiden: Brill, the Netherlands, 1975.

Waddell, Lawrence. *The Buddhism of Tibet*. London: Luzac & Co., 1899.

Weber, A, ed. *Nineteenth Century Science*. New York: Broadview Press, 2000.

Werness, Hope B. *The Continuum Encyclopedia of Animal Symbolism in Art*. New York: Continuum, 2004.

Williams, Frederick. *Callimachus: Hymn to Apollo*. New York: Oxford University Press, 1978.

Winn, Christopher. *I Never Knew That About Ireland*. New York: Thomas Dunne Books/St. Martin's Press, 2007.

Wyatt, Nicolas. "Religion in Ancient Ugarit," in Hinnells, John R., ed. *A Handbook of Ancient Religions*. New York: Cambridge University Press, 2007.

Yang, Lihui, and Deming An. *Handbook of Chinese Mythology.* Santa Barbara, CA: ABC-CLIO, 2005.

Zair, Nicholas. *Reflexes of the Proto-Indo-European Laryngeals in Celtic.* Boston: Brill, 2012.

INDEX

GET MORE AT LLEWELLYN.COM

Visit us online to browse hundreds of our books and decks, plus sign up to receive our e-newsletters and exclusive online offers.

- **Free tarot readings** • **Spell-a-Day** • **Moon phases**
- **Recipes, spells, and tips** • **Blogs** • **Encyclopedia**
- **Author interviews, articles, and upcoming events**

GET SOCIAL WITH LLEWELLYN

Find us on Facebook
www.Facebook.com/LlewellynBooks

Follow us on

www.Twitter.com/Llewellynbooks

GET BOOKS AT LLEWELLYN

LLEWELLYN ORDERING INFORMATION

 Order online: Visit our website at www.llewellyn.com to select your books and place an order on our secure server.

 Order by phone:
- Call toll free within the U.S. at 1-877-NEW-WRLD (1-877-639-9753)
- Call toll free within Canada at 1-866-NEW-WRLD (1-866-639-9753)
- We accept VISA, MasterCard, and American Express

Order by mail:
Send the full price of your order (MN residents add 6.875% sales tax) in U.S. funds, plus postage and handling to: Llewellyn Worldwide, 2143 Wooddale Drive Woodbury, MN 55125-2989

POSTAGE AND HANDLING:
STANDARD: (U.S. & Canada)
(Please allow 12 business days)
$25.00 and under, add $4.00.
$25.01 and over, FREE SHIPPING.

INTERNATIONAL ORDERS (airmail only):
$16.00 for one book, plus $3.00 for each additional book.

Visit us online for more shipping options. Prices subject to change.

FREE CATALOG!

To order, call
1-877-NEW-WRLD
ext. 8236
or visit our website

Celtic Lore
& Spellcraft
of the
Dark
Goddess

INVOKING
THE
MORRIGAN

Celtic Lore & Spellcraft of the Dark Goddess
Invoking the Morrigan
STEPHANIE WOODFIELD

Experience the life-transforming beauty of Celtic Witchcraft by calling upon the Morrigan—the Celtic embodiment of the victory, strength, and power of the divine feminine.

In this comprehensive and hands-on guide, Stephanie Woodfield invites you to explore the Morrigan's history and origins, mythology, and magic. Discover the hidden lessons and spiritual mysteries of the Dark Goddess as you perform guided pathworkings, rituals, and spells. Draw on the unique energies of her many expressions—her three main aspects of Macha, Anu, and Badb; the legendary Morgan Le Fay; and her other powerful guises.

From shapeshifting and faery magic to summoning a lover and creating an Ogham oracle, the dynamic and multifaceted Dark Goddess will bring empowering wisdom and enchantment to your life and spiritual practice.

978-0-7387-2767-7, 432 pp., 7½ x 9⅛   **$19.95**

Everyday Sun Magic
Spells & Rituals for Radiant Living
DOROTHY MORRISON

The sun impacts our lives like no other force in the universe. In addition to sustaining life on Earth, the potent energy of this mighty star can lend a powerful spark to daily magic.

Taking readers on a magical exploration of the sun, Dorothy Morrison teaches how the sun can be used as a viable magical tool. She gives in-depth information on the sun's cultural and religious history, its phases and energies (rainbows, solar eclipses, sun storms, and so on) as they apply to magic, and astrological implications. *Everyday Sun Magic* is also packed with over 140 spells, chants, affirmations, and rituals spanning 89 categories, such as health, employment, friendship, romance, weather, gardening, prosperity, marriage, legal matters, travel, addiction, and dieting.

978-0-7387-0468-5, 336 pp., 5³⁄₁₆ x 8   **$12.95**

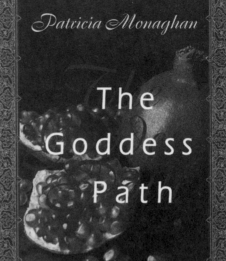

Patricia Monaghan

The
Goddess
Path

Myths, Invocations & Rituals

The Goddess Path
Myths, Invocations, and Rituals
PATRICIA MONAGHAN

Now you can find more meaning and joy in your life, journey inward, find the divine, and become transformed when you read *The Goddess Path* by Patricia Monaghan.

The Goddess Path can be your guide to speed you on your spiritual quest. Think of this book as a signpost on your spiritual travels, designed to help you nurture your own connection to the goddess and share in her boundless wisdom. Call her into your life with beautiful and ancient invocations. Create your own rituals to honor the lessons she has to teach. As you ponder life-changing questions and venture on brave new experiments, you fan the divine spark into flame—and, in that fire, you are transformed.

978-1-56718-467-9, 288 pp., 7½ x 9⅛   **$18.95**

Candlemas
Feast of Flames
AMBER K AND AZRAEL ARYNN K

Beyond the darkness of winter, there is an oasis of light and warmth on the journey from solstice to spring. Known as Candlemas, Imbolg, Brigantia, or Lupercus, it is a hope-filled celebration held in early February to welcome the returning light and the promise of spring. *Candlemas* sheds light on the origins, lore, and customs of this ancient holy day with:

- Myths and stories: Brigit the Goddess, Brigid the Saint, and her meaning today
- Candlemas magick and divination: flame scrying, hearthside divination, candle magick, and protection magick
- Late winter goodies and feasts: Brede's braid bread, Guinness stew, bubble and squeak, mulled cider or wine
- February festivals and traditions: rituals for purification, blessings, and renewal from the Irish, English, Scottish, Welsh, Norwegian, Greek, Roman, and Chinese traditions
- Seasonal crafts and games: Brigid's crosses or sun wheels, "Begging for Biddy," and a Brigit corn dolly

978-0-7387-0079-3, 264 pp., 7½ x 9⅛   **$17.95**
